FILM REGULATION IN A CULTURAL CONTEXT

Traditions in World Cinema

General Editors
Linda Badley (Middle Tennessee State University)
R. Barton Palmer (Clemson University)

Founding Editor
Steven Jay Schneider (New York University)

Titles in the series include:

Traditions in World Cinema
Linda Badley, R. Barton Palmer and Steven Jay Schneider (eds)

Post-beur Cinema: North African Émigré and Maghrebi-French Filmmaking in France since 2000
Will Higbee

New Taiwanese Cinema in Focus: Moving Within and Beyond the Frame
Flannery Wilson

International Noir
Homer B. Pettey and R. Barton Palmer (eds)

Films on Ice: Cinemas of the Arctic
Scott MacKenzie and Anna Westerståhl Stenport (eds)

Nordic Genre Film: Small Nation Film Cultures in the Global Marketplace
Tommy Gustafsson and Pietari Kääpä (eds)

Contemporary Japanese Cinema Since Hana-Bi
Adam Bingham

Chinese Martial Arts Cinema: The Wuxia Tradition (2nd edition)
Stephen Teo

Slow Cinema
Tiago de Luca and Nuno Barradas Jorge

Expressionism in the Cinema
Olaf Brill and Gary D. Rhodes (eds)

French-language Road Cinema: Borders, Diasporas, Migration and 'New Europe'
Michael Gott

Transnational Film Remakes
Iain Robert Smith and Constantine Verevis

Coming-of-Age Cinema in New Zealand
Alistair Fox

New Transnationalisms in Contemporary Latin American Cinemas
Dolores Tierney

Celluloid Singapore: Cinema, Performance and the National
Edna Lim

Short Films from a Small Nation: Danish Informational Cinema 1935–1965
C. Claire Thomson

B-Movie Gothic: International Perspectives
Justin D. Edwards and Johan Höglund (eds)

Francophone Belgian Cinema
Jamie Steele

The New Romanian Cinema
Christina Stojanova (ed.) with the participation of Dana Duma

French Blockbusters: Cultural Politics of a Transnational Cinema
Charlie Michael

Nordic Film Cultures and Cinemas of Elsewhere
Anna Westerståhl Stenport and Arne Lunde (eds)

New Realism: Contemporary British Cinema
David Forrest

Contemporary Balkan Cinema: Transnational Exchanges and Global Circuits
Lydia Papadimitriou and Ana Grgić (eds)

Mapping the Rockumentary: Images of Sound and Fury
Gunnar Iversen and Scott MacKenzie (eds)

Images of Apartheid: Filmmaking on the Fringe in the Old South Africa
Calum Waddell

Greek Film Noir
Anna Poupou, Nikitas Fessas, and Maria Chalkou (eds)

Norwegian Nightmares: The Horror Cinema of a Nordic Country
Christer Bakke Andresen

Late-colonial French Cinema: Filming the Algerian War of Independence
Mani Sharpe

Australian International Pictures (1946–75)
Adrian Danks and Constantine Verevis

Film Regulation in a Cultural Context
Daniel Sacco

Please see our website for a complete list of titles in the series
www.edinburghuniversitypress.com/series/TIWC

FILM REGULATION IN A CULTURAL CONTEXT

Daniel Sacco

EDINBURGH
University Press

Edinburgh University Press is one of the leading university presses in the UK. We publish academic books and journals in our selected subject areas across the humanities and social sciences, combining cutting-edge scholarship with high editorial and production values to produce academic works of lasting importance. For more information visit our website: edinburghuniversitypress.com

© Daniel Sacco, 2023, 2025

Edinburgh University Press Ltd
13 Infirmary Street
Edinburgh EH1 1LT

First published in hardback by Edinburgh University Press 2023

Typeset in 10/12.5 pt Sabon
by IDSUK (DataConnection) Ltd

A CIP record for this book is available from the British Library

ISBN 978 1 4744 8238 7 (hardback)
ISBN 978 1 4744 8239 4 (paperback)
ISBN 978 1 4744 8240 0 (webready PDF)
ISBN 978 1 4744 8241 7 (epub)

The right of Daniel Sacco to be identified as the author of this work has been asserted in accordance with the Copyright, Designs and Patents Act 1988, and the Copyright and Related Rights Regulations 2003 (SI No. 2498).

CONTENTS

List of Figures   vii
Acknowledgements   viii
Preface   ix
Traditions in World Cinema   xiii

Introduction   1

PART I

1   The Road to Classification   21
2   The New French Extremity Emerges   44

PART II

3   The Banning of *Fat Girl* in Ontario   63
4   Protecting Australians from *Ken Park*   81
5   *Irréversible* and the Case for Violence   98

PART III

6   Critical Censure and *The Brown Bunny*   117
7   *Wolf Creek*'s Hostile Audience   140

8 Censorship, Distribution, and Control	164
Afterword	179
Works Cited and Consulted	184
Index	194

FIGURES

3.1	Anaïs Reboux and Roxane Mesquida in Catherine Breillat's *Fat Girl*	69
3.2	Anaïs peeking at her sister's sex in *Fat Girl*	71
3.3	Anaïs returning her attacker's gaze in *Fat Girl*	75
4.1	James Bullard and Maeve Quinlan in Larry Clark and Edward Lachman's *Ken Park*	87
4.2	Julio Oscar Mechoso and Tiffany Limos in *Ken Park*	89
4.3	James Ransone in *Ken Park*.	90
5.1	Albert Dupontel and Michel Gondoin in Gaspar Noé's *Irréversible*	106
5.2	Jo Prestia and Monica Belucci in *Irréversible*	107
5.3	Alex reading in the park in *Irréversible*	110
6.1	A characteristic shot from *The Brown Bunny*	125
6.2	Vincent Gallo as Bud Clay in *The Brown Bunny*	126
6.3	Daisy (Chloë Sevigny) fellating Bud in *The Brown Bunny*	129
7.1	Greg McLean's *Wolf Creek*	158
7.2	Mick (John Jarratt) stares disdainfully in *Wolf Creek*	160
7.3	Mick loads his rifle in *Wolf Creek*	161
8.1	Gérard Depardieu in Abel Ferrara's *Welcome To New York*	171
8.2	Devereaux exiting the shower in *Welcome To New York*	172
8.3	Pamela Afesi in *Welcome To New York*	174

ACKNOWLEDGEMENTS

I would like to acknowledge the extraordinary support of Murray Pomerance. The completion of this manuscript was made possible by his tremendous encouragement, assistance, and guidance over the past several years. I would also like to thank the editors of this series, Linda R. Badley and R. Barton Palmer, for their generous contribution of time, ideas, and expertise to this project. Special thanks are owed to Thomas Doherty, Heather Rollwagen, Steven Bailey, Stephen Muzzatti, Gillian Leslie, William Allinson, Max Boer, Kire Paputts, Lisa French, Mark Poole, Philip Brown, Brian MacLachlan, Alanna McKnight, and Irina Lyubchenko. I also wish to acknowledge the constant support of my family, Vincent and Tiia Sacco, as well as Katherin, Sal, Sofia, and Belle Cutillo. Finally, I would like to express my most heartfelt gratitude to Aidan Moir, whose unwavering patience, kind-heartedness, and encouragement made this undertaking possible.

PREFACE

During my graduate studies, I became interested in what critics were calling the "New French Extremity," a strand of auteur filmmaking (and critical scholarship) highlighting a fascinating intersection in French filmmaking: aesthetic traditions of form and content that characterized mid-to-late twentieth-century European art cinema, and elements of the (primarily American and Italian) exploitation genre films that had, for many years at that time, figured centrally in my recreational film viewing and participation in cult cinema fan culture. As I began to investigate the existing scholarship surrounding the New French Extremity (or NFE), I was impressed to find most of it had successfully transcended what is commonly known as the "media effects model" of cinematic violence and "deviant" sexuality in film. There was a definite sense in much of this NFE scholarship that ideas about causal or even correlative relationships between violence in (and outside of) films were outdated, lacking empirical validity, and obstructive to the kinds of deeper critical analysis these texts invite though their innovative styles and dynamic presentation. At the same time, the divided reactions and sensational controversies that linked these films as much as any aesthetic commonality were part of what drew me toward them as objects of cultural study. I saw in the films of the New French Extremity a unique critical opportunity. I spent a portion of my prior studies in scholarly defense of the merits and cultural significance of contemporary horror films. Despite serious engagement from certain prestigious scholars and critics (Robin Wood, Alan Jones, Mark Kermode), the popular horror film has been a favorite target for derision not only in academic circles, but in popular discourse more broadly (with a swift dismissal usually reserved for pornography).

Fat Girl, Irréversible, Trouble Every Day, Twentynine Palms; these films planted a theoretical seed. These were cinematic artworks that possessed the impact of horror films—not just in psychological (and physiological) impact on the spectator—but in their potential cultural impact as well. The visceral affective quality of these films drew the sort of high-profile controversies that so often act as flashpoints for larger cultural debates. The films were shocking and abrasive—but defensible as serious films, by serious filmmakers clearly pursuing more than box office (or as is more commonly the case with horror, straight-to-video distribution) revenue.

My graduate training until that point, though rewarding, had not necessarily equipped me with sufficient training in the philosophy of art to precisely articulate why these films had artistic merit, while an ocean of similarly violent and sexually explicit "schlock" titles did not. However, reading the seminal sociologist Howard Becker shifted my thinking. For Becker, the categories we use to make sense of the social, and by extension, cultural world are not fixed objective realities. They are thoroughly relative and rooted in the social and moral definitions of whoever is espousing them. More importantly—Becker stresses that individuals will *act* towards things according to how they define and label them. Cinema is no exception. If a film is claimed to be obscene, reprehensible, dangerous, exploitative, or harmful, it has an effect. If that claim is made by a politician, journalist, critic, or censor, that effect intensifies. Again, my thinking shifted. Rather than a philosophical aesthetic question (are these films "art?"), I could interrogate the practical interest of the filmmakers in determining what it is they must do to be *considered* art. What fundamentally separates a film that *some* call art from a film that *no one* calls art is, ultimately, this very process of labeling itself.

I soon learned that Catherine Breillat's *Fat Girl*, a film as worthy of being labelled art as any in my view, had been banned in my home province of Ontario, Canada from 2001 until 2003. I suddenly felt an intangible (but no less powerful) personal connection to the material I had been studying. My knowledge of film censorship, a particularly pronounced and dramatic form of cultural control, had been couched in overtly historical contexts. I had no prior cause to consider it as a contemporary phenomenon. In discussing my research with colleagues, I found Ontarians generally surprised to learn that our governmental ratings system had veered into overt censorship recently enough as to fall within the twenty-first century. For millennials growing up in the file-sharing culture of the Internet, film censorship was not so much anathema as obsolete. However, I was not yet ready to concede this point—given the systemic nature of social control. The absence of an individual, easily identifiable "censor" does not necessarily imply the absence of censorship—or other proscriptive forms of cultural regulation.

It is not my intention with the latter half of this book to dilute the meaning of the term "censorship" beyond the point of usefulness by forcing too wide a range of social, cultural, political, and market phenomena under a single conceptual umbrella. Nevertheless, the film censorship case studies I examine here suggest an increased *limiting* of governmental film censorship's reach, in some sense the end of a century-or-so historical process. I feel that expanding the scope of definitions and research regarding film *regulation* (a more inclusive term) is the best way to guarantee this research can retain relevance in the present and future media landscape. I think a primary strength of this manuscript is the parallels it draws between the rhetorical practices of censors, and those of the other players—critics, distributors, audiences—that have seemed to assume the social control of film culture. In some of the cases involving governmental censorship—for instance *Fat Girl* or *Irréversible*—the rights of filmmakers and audiences prevailed. It strikes me that the latter cases—*The Brown Bunny* or *Welcome to New York*—are stories of artistic battles lost. One must then carefully consider whether censorial imperatives, made less threatening by an absence of governmental enforcement, cannot in fact be more formidable obstacles for adventurous films and filmmakers. This is no doubt a contentious claim for many reasons, some of which I hope to have meaningfully addressed in this research.

A few important notes:

1) The idea of "merit" is ultimately a problematic one. To argue for a film's protection from censorship based on merit, no matter how qualified the arguer, is a concession to censorial logic. To argue some films should not be censored is of course to tacitly concede that others should. Despite my reluctance to embrace free speech "absolutism," I do feel some fundamental separation should exist between issues surrounding a film's content, and those surrounding the right of viewers to access it.
2) There is always an argument to be made that, historically, censorship considerations often forced filmmakers to be *more* creative in their addressing of sensitive subjects. Classic dialogue such as "we'll always have Paris," or scenes like Cary Grant and Ingrid Bergman's protracted succession of three-second kisses in Hitchcock's *Notorious* owe some (partial and indirect) debt to censors and their aversion to explicitness. If it had not been necessary for Rod Serling to cloak his scathing social critiques in fantasy and allegory, we would not have *The Twilight Zone*.
3) In the same vein, I certainly would not claim that the films examined in this study contain no problematic content. While I subscribed to auteurism, I do not believe the filmmaker has the final say on the meaning or impact of his or her work, and I have tried to approach the claims of

critics, CEOs, advocacy groups, and censors themselves as coming from a place of sincerity (difficult as that may at times be). I believe there are limits of good taste, and that it is certainly possible for a filmmaker to employ shock in irresponsible ways. That said, there is a meaningful difference between saying something to be provocative and being provocative to say something.

Lastly, this is not a work of prescriptive policy study. I believe the films examined here, which I have gone to some lengths and devoted much of the text to analyzing, are in themselves a form of solution to the problems raised in this study. While labeling (or more accurately "classification") processes were, at times, detrimental to the cultural status of these films, it might be equally productive to look at this dynamic through a reversed lens. That is, labels can obstruct films, but just as significantly, films can obstruct labels. In their various transgressions (particularly of genre categories), these films force a kind of sensitivity from the labeler. If, for example, it is declared that pornography may be censored but art may not, what does the censor do if faced with a film that is seemingly both? As evidenced in certain outcomes of cases explored in this study, perhaps they re-evaluate their criteria. The solution to the rigid categorization of films is, in some important sense, more films that resist and defy its systems.

TRADITIONS IN WORLD CINEMA

General editors: **Linda Badley and R. Barton Palmer**
Founding editor: **Steven Jay Schneider**

Traditions in World Cinema is a series of textbooks and monographs devoted to the analysis of currently popular and previously underexamined or undervalued film movements from around the globe. Also intended for general interest readers, the textbooks in this series offer undergraduate- and graduate-level film students accessible and comprehensive introductions to diverse traditions in world cinema. The monographs open up for advanced academic study more specialised groups of films, including those that require theoretically-oriented approaches. Both textbooks and monographs provide thorough examinations of the industrial, cultural and socio-historical conditions of production and reception.

The flagship textbook for the series includes chapters by noted scholars on traditions of acknowledged importance (the French New Wave, German Expressionism), recent and emergent traditions (New Iranian, post-Cinema Novo) and those whose rightful claim to recognition has yet to be established (the Israeli persecution film, global found footage cinema). Other volumes concentrate on individual national, regional or global cinema traditions. As the introductory chapter to each volume makes clear, the films under discussion form a coherent group on the basis of substantive and relatively transparent, if not always obvious, commonalities. These commonalities may be formal, stylistic or thematic, and the groupings may, although they need not, be popularly identified as genres, cycles or movements (Japanese horror, Chinese martial arts cinema, Italian Neo-realism). Indeed, in cases in which a group of films is not already commonly identified as a tradition, one purpose of the volume is to establish its claim to importance and make it visible (East Central European Magical Realist cinema, Palestinian cinema).

Textbooks and monographs include:

- an introduction that clarifies the rationale for the grouping of films under examination
- a concise history of the regional, national or transnational cinema in question
- a summary of previous published work on the tradition
- contextual analysis of industrial, cultural and socio-historical conditions of production and reception
- textual analysis of specific and notable films, with clear and judicious application of relevant film theoretical approaches
- bibliograph(ies)/filmograph(ies).

Monographs may additionally include:

- discussion of the dynamics of cross-cultural exchange in light of current research and thinking about cultural imperialism and globalisation, as well as issues of regional/national cinema or political/aesthetic movements (such as new waves, postmodernism or identity politics)
- interview(s) with key filmmakers working within the tradition.

INTRODUCTION

By the beginning of the twenty-first century in the West, the notion of government-appointed bodies mandated for censoring cinematic content had fallen considerably out of fashion as institutional censorship was largely curtailed. The necessity of shielding potentially vulnerable viewers from offensive, and in some cases socially "dangerous" content, had become secondary to the priority of protecting the rights of adult viewers to freely seek out whatever entertainment they wished, so long as it did not constitute criminal activity. Many government institutions previously charged with suppressing morally or legally challenging films or stripping them of problematic content, such as the British Board of Classification (BBFC), Office of Film and Literature Classification (OFLC) in Australia, and the Ontario Film Review Board (OFRB) in Canada, accordingly shifted the emphasis of their activity from censorship—the regulation and expunging of film content deemed obscene—to "classification," a method of merely informing consumers as to the content of films they were about to see. Several high-profile cases from the early twenty-first century reveal the particulars of this shift. In some instances, controversies surrounding the treatment of films by classification institutions generated significant media and political backlash, ultimately spurring key changes in film regulation and exhibition practices in the countries concerned.

The "liberalization" of classification policies that marks the shift away from overtly moral censorship practices, and the effects of which are most apparent in the period between 1997 and 2004, seemed to promise a utopian ideal for ground-breaking, envelope-pushing cinematic artistry. No longer would the political conservatism of the censor's taste be a hurdle that filmmakers, exhibitors, and distributors would have to overcome. Barring widely shared concerns regarding the exposure of underage children to material deemed inappropriate, classification boards have acted themselves to limit the extent to which they can prohibit images from entering the public market. Many filmgoers think that since the growth of the Internet, this move has been insufficient. New technologies have emerged—consider the ease with which online file-sharing platforms provide access to wide-ranging and sometimes provocative forms of entertainment culture, and how such ready access suggests that even if censorial institutions continued in their previous modes of operation, enforcement of their policies would now be largely impossible to implement. The circulation of visual material has become too vast and too expansive to police with any efficiency.

Can we then assume that the censorship of cinematic works is effectively a thing of the past? If so, what has become of the impetus to regulate and police film content? Has it disappeared, too, or has it continued silently to exist?

Perhaps, while no longer practiced routinely and explicitly by various arms of government and state proxies, film censorship continues to operate in less obvious ways. The strongest scholarship about film censorship constantly re-enforces the notion that the specific activities of censorship institutions offer too limited a view of their broader social function, thus blocking a valid and practical understanding of how film censorship operates. Early scholarly research tended to approach the phenomenon of film censorship from a policy perspective—examining formal laws and state-imposed sanctions as the defining features of interactional relationships between censors and censored materials. However, as post-structuralism and cultural studies emerged as popular theoretical approaches, research into film censorship practices has become decidedly more complex. Scholars such as Annette Kuhn and Sue Curry Jansen have called for a broader understanding of the various complex social processes and discursive practices that result in marginalization or prohibition of certain artistic voices. In the work of these theorists, instances of censorial bodies attempting to regulate film content and availability are framed as only one part of a much further-reaching social "apparatus." Michel Foucault famously used the concept of "apparatus" to describe:

> A thoroughly heterogeneous ensemble consisting of discourses, institutions, architectural forms, regulatory decisions, laws, administrative measures, scientific statements, philosophical, moral, and philanthropic propositions—in short, the said as much as the unsaid. Such are the elements of the apparatus. The apparatus itself is the system of relations that can be established between these elements. (194)

In her ground-breaking work *Cinema, Censorship and Sexuality*, Annette Kuhn applied this concept to the censorship of early cinema in Great Britain. She challenged previous scholarly attempts at theorizing screen censorship as a pre-defined object. Rather than operating in isolation, she saw censorship as something that emerges from the interactions of certain practices and processes, the interrelations between which are always in a state of fluidity (6). Kuhn's work emphasizes that the notion of censors, operating independently of the weave of social institutions to effect policies of containment, proves too simple a rendering of the situation. In Kuhn's understanding, "censorship" is no less than the varied set of complex relations that can be established between heterogeneous webs of discourse, law, administrative measure, and philosophical or moral proposition involving the regulation of cinematic content.

If the activities of government censor boards comprise only one part of the regulation process, others of which include news media outlets, film and video industry interests, religious institutions, media watchdog and pressure groups, perceptions of public opinion, and the wider ideological climate, how could the liberalization of government censorship practices alone herald censorship's end? Is film censorship "gone," then? Or does it continue to operate in subtle, perhaps insidious ways?

These complex questions require an equally complex method of response. While scholars of film reception and censorship, such as Julien Petley and Daniel Hicklin, working in the intellectual tradition of Kuhn and Jansen, have made strides in analyzing the processes by which, for example, the BBFC has re-evaluated and reformed its role in the regulation of film content, such writing tends to focus primarily on the discourses of sex, violence, and censorship surrounding the release of certain films, and the relationship of classification institutions and their policies to broader understandings of the role of art and culture, as well as government regulation more generally, in society. While such an approach is certainly instructive from a reception and policy studies point of view, one goal of this project is to expand this area of study to provide greater consideration of the textual properties of the relevant films themselves, in hopes of determining what precisely about these works so confounds common understandings of social acceptability with regards to cinematic content.

It is my contention that a number of transgressive post-millennial art films, such as Catherine Breillat's *Fat Girl* (2001), Larry Clark and Edward Lachman's *Ken Park* (2002), and Gaspar Noé's *Irréversible* (2002), highlighted the need for reform in the policies of classification boards by making plainly evident, through their complex and sophisticated narrative, thematic and stylistic treatment of explicit sex and violence, the inherent cultural value in cinematic risk-taking, and the untenable rigidity of classification criteria employed by such institutions. As films with clearly arguable artistic merits—merits that became contentious themselves—these cinematic works clashed with conventional understandings of acceptable art. This study seeks to examine why these films specifically came to be deemed "obscene" by some, and how or why censorship practices were or were not implemented to rectify this situation.

It would be erroneous to suggest that these "problematic" films were solely responsible for the censorship controversies they ignited. In addition to their unusual cinematic properties, they contributed to the loosening of film content restrictions by provoking (perhaps deliberately) the foremost opponents of such reform, namely, moral entrepreneurs for whom sexually explicit films pose a threat to conservative values and traditional standards of decency and tastefulness. A comprehensive understanding of these controversies involves a rhetorical analysis of the claims put forth against the films that sparked them, claims advanced by way of obscenity guidelines that, far from being objective realities, are already products of the assertion of their own moral definitions by a range of groups. For a complete understanding of the rhetorical activities that precede the implementation of censorship practices, it is imperative to ask who and what institutions gain from targeting obscene content?

In each case explored in this study, various political, administrative, or economic interests and motivations shaped the ways in which cinematic content was characterized and how characterization invoked values or rationality. Indeed, these interests went beyond addressing obscenity itself, in being facilitated by various strategies including using (supposed) evidence (typically with reference to earlier successful censorship) as a means of defining obscenity for others; presenting this evidence in a fashion that eschewed nuanced portrayals and instead focussed on the worst aspects of a film as though they were representative; and attracting public attention by stimulating outrage. Before the content of the films themselves can be fully and usefully addressed, it is crucial to outline some key features of this rhetorical claims making process.

Censorial Claims Making as Rhetorical Activity

The influential sociologists Malcolm Spector and John Kitsuse labeled it the purview of the sociologist to study social problems, not as objective conditions but as results of the processes by which they come to be defined as such. Their goal in *Constructing Social Problems* was to analyze "how categories of social problems and deviance are produced, and how methods of social control and treatment are institutionally established" (72). This notion of judgemental categories as "produced" led them to focus on ways that institutional controls were directly preceded by the "claims-making activities" of groups putting forward their own definitions of deviance—that is, ways of pointing to "problematic" individuals and activity that would serve to benefit the pointers. What links moral claims, whether they take the form of verbal, visual, or behavioural statements, are the rhetorical strategies aimed at encouraging audiences to think and feel in particular ways. If the interest of interactionist sociologists of the 1970s was not in the "truth" of claims, but rather in the question of which claims end up being believed as "true," then an understanding of successful censorship claims must consider not only those who make them, but also the audiences who ultimately hold the power to evaluate such claims as true or false.

The most vocal advocates of film censorship tend to approach cinematic obscenity fundamentally as a social problem. If film content is deemed obscene, it is most often because censorial claims makers have successfully construed this content as, in various ways, socially dangerous or harmful. Such claims of harmfulness are often presented as rooted in the objective reality of scientific fact. However, Joseph Gusfield has emphasized the need for rhetorical analysis of truth claims in every field, arguing, "the discovery of public facts is a process of social organization [. . .] Public facts must be picked, polished, shaped and packaged" (qtd. in Conrad and Schneider 27). In other words, claims about the putatively threatening quality of obscene film content must not be approached as though based in objective evidence, but considered primarily in terms of the rhetorical decisions of claims makers: as they choose from available arguments, as they place their selected argument in a dramatic sequence, and as they choose which arguments to give particular emphasis. The groups of claims makers that comprise the "social problems industry" (Loseke 29), including government officials, media spokespersons, organizational sponsors, and educators all rely on rhetorical strategies when asserting their definitions of harm and indecency.

Sociologist Joel Best has highlighted several ways in which social problems claims display an acute awareness of audiences' needs and interests, that is, "play" to audiences in an engaging fashion. Persuasive rhetoric forms the basis of what Best calls the "warrants" of claimants: "statements that justify drawing conclusions from the grounds" of an argument (31). Warrants play a key role in claims making, by authorizing the solutions prescribed by a particular argument. The success of various claims is highly dependent on the warrants that rhetorically frame them. While strategies for packaging claims often result in over-simplification or generalization, they are employed specifically for their power to compel audiences. Obscenity, like any other social problem, is dependent on persuasive rhetoric if censorship is to gain justification as a valid response. Obscenity must be constructed and sold as problematic.

Researching the formulation of links between problematic social conditions and individual lifestyle practices, Gusfield concluded that scientific presentations of research do not simply "happen to" compel concurrence. Rather, the selection and presentation of reported material is meticulously calculated to induce belief. This is perhaps even truer now than at the time of Gusfield's writing. It is imperative to ask who and what institution gains by rectifying a condition deemed problematic, and how responsibility for provoking action is awarded. His analysis suggests a certain hierarchy of designation in the claims making process. For example, not all claims makers share an equal ability to exert ownership over social problems. Some individuals or groups possess greater power, influence, and authority to shape the public perception of a problem. Furthermore, the charging of specific (heroic) individuals with the task of providing and implementing solutions is less politically significant as a means of controlling actual problems than as a symbolic and ceremonial process, inviting contemplation and affecting the social or political status of those who support or reject the values of a particular lifestyle. Gusfield's conclusions are relevant to discussions of obscenity and censorship in their highlighting of the extent to which claims that underlie censorial efforts—i.e., that certain filmed images pose a threat to the moral well-being of audiences—utilize definitions of obscenity that become, by virtue of their adoption, highly politicized.

Some of the most revealing research into the activities of claims makers can be located within the literature on the various moral panics of the 1980s and 1990s, such as those characterizing Ronald Reagan's "War on Drugs" or the much-scrutinized Satanic daycare panic (see Victor, De Young). These cases are particularly valuable in understanding the nature of claims making as carried out by radio and television news media. Moral-panic literature shows how media institutions dramatize social problems as part of profit maximization procedures. In such cases, the perceived immediacy of a threat may result in decreased likelihood of claims being verified by investigation or substantiated by credible evidence, or in the more pointed vilification of scapegoats. Such cases illustrate how claims makers use popular modes of dissemination, and the qualities particular to these media, to stir sentiment and propose solutions to the specific pressures of a particular cultural context.

Claims-makers use (supposed) evidence as a means of defining the reality of a social problem for others; they typically present this evidence in a rhetorical fashion, eschewing nuanced portrayals and focussing on the worst aspects of a condition as though they were representative. Further, their success is highly contingent on attracting attention, stimulating outrage, and generating resources for a cause. And finally, they often have political, administrative, or economic interests and motivations, which go beyond simply addressing a problem for its own sake. In the case of moral panic, the media is typically found to engage in the "routinization of character" (Reinarman 80), attracting audience attention by rhetorically crafting atrocity tales as though they were typical. Such scholarship contributes to a more complete understanding of the claims making activities that precede the implementation of censorship responses. Politicians, lobbyists, journalists, pundits, teachers, researchers, and social activists may differ widely in the sort of claims they make and the channels through which they make them, yet all these players can be conceptually linked by their use of rhetorical persuasion in the attempt to define the reality of certain social conditions.

Lastly, audiences are afforded far less attention than claims makers in most constructionist censorship research. Perhaps this is unsurprising, given that accurately assessing what audiences are thinking and feeling provides the analyst with its own set of unique challenges. Most constructionist research attempting to do so has focussed on the ways in which individuals or groups react to media stories, and the dramatic extent to which popular wisdom, the cultural repertoire of "truisms" about social problems that individuals develop, influences the receptivity of audiences (Lowney 333). Audiences weigh claims about cinematic content through a cultural filter, paying closer attention to those that seem logical or meaningful based on popular wisdom. Accordingly, claims that do not respect or correspond to cultural messages become far easier for audiences to dismiss. Any common characteristics of successful claims are fundamentally linked by the appeal they hold for audience members; or their usefulness as tools in making sense of practical social experience. This is to say, censorial and censorious claims about film content do not emerge from a vacuum. It is the cultural propensities of audiences that ultimately shape the content of these claims: the desire to see social problems as rooted in individual causes; the desire for simple solutions; the inclination to see only certain groups as victims or perpetrators, et cetera.

Any study of cinema's regulation in the contemporary age cannot afford to overlook the vital role played by audiences themselves in censorial (or censorious) discourses. Studies in censorship have historically interrogated the subject as a question of official bodies deliberating the harm that may be caused to a potential (hypothetical) viewer. That scope must be expanded to include—among various complex economic, legal, commercial, and critical phenomena—normative definitions of appropriate textual relations and responses that are internalized and monitored by the individual. As Theresa Cronin argues, "contemporary regulation of film for an adult audience depends on the process of subjectification and [. . .] represents a form of governmentality that depends increasingly on the inculcation of norms of spectatorial engagement and audience behavior" (Cronin 19). In other words, audiences now police themselves.

Post-Classification Censorship

In *Censorship: The Knot that Binds Knowledge and Power*, Sue Curry Jansen calls for an understanding of censorship that moves beyond its overt, "regulative" forms (rules put into place by a state body with the explicit remit to censor) toward a conceptualization of "constituent censorships," meaning those "encompassed within a broader definition of the term including diffuse as well as overt forms" ("Censorship" 12). While my analysis of the cases of *Fat Girl*, *Ken Park*, and *Irréversible* focus primarily on the former, on the policies of regulatory bodies and institutions acting upon these bodies, it also attempts to suggest that liberalization of such policies prompted a significant reduction in both the demand and deployment of "regulative" film censorship during this period. In certain respects, film classification in Great Britain, Australia, and Canada remains a process of state regulation, in which government institutions shape and control consumer access to cinematic material. However, such control need not originate with the state to fall within Jansen's alternative definition of censorship as "all socially structured proscriptions or prescriptions that inhibit or prohibit dissemination of ideas, information, images and other messages through a society's channels of communication" (221).

Jansen's broad understanding of censorship connects the marginalization of certain artistic voices to a wide range of social and market phenomena, such as the internalization of mores and taboos by consumers and the use of manufacturing resources to shape consumer demand. Three notable examples studied here are particularly useful in suggesting models of "post-classification censorship" in the American system: the critical, and subsequently public rejection of Vincent Gallo's *The Brown Bunny* (2003) following its première at the Cannes Film Festival; the "F" rating of Greg McLean's *Wolf Creek* (2005) by research firm Cinemascore's audience polling data, and the dramatic re-cutting of Abel Ferrara's *Welcome to New York* (2014) by Wild Bunch Films.

This study adopts a particularly fluid definition of "film regulation" as a process of control invariably resulting in interference with production, exhibition, and distribution of cinematic content, while operating in varied, diverse contexts of governmental, economic, and discursive regulation, and potentially including political motivation, industry initiatives, and voluntary acts of self-censorship. As Guy Phelps has argued, "Censorship is a complex topic where fact and theory, law and morality, art and science meet headlong in a thicket of confusion. Anyone seeking to construct a liberal censorship has to confront the inherent contradiction in the term." (61) Therefore, any reference in the following chapters to the "liberalization" of censorship practices is not necessarily intended to imply a step toward unbridled freedom of artistic expression. Instead, "liberalization" merely suggests that *how* film content is regulated has shifted its vocabulary, its instruments, or its means of self-presentation, the apparent aims and goals of which are not always realized in the results.

As Jansen's writing suggests, even the freest of free markets contains diverse mechanisms of control, where censorship is not an explicit practice but an inevitable process of market systems. Censorship is not a mere matter of government interference. As famed Polish filmmaker Andrzej Wajda once noted, "Real censorship is motivated by fear about going beyond the prevailing ideas of decency, taste, and even social and moral prejudices" (107). While Breillat, Clark and Lachman, and Noé were forced to contend with overt practices of censorial intervention or prohibition, Gallo, McLean, and Ferrara faced forms of regulative censure that, despite their relative covertness, still arise from various processes embodied by complex and contradictory relations of power.

The Importance of Cultural Context

While this study focusses primarily on Western commercial markets, risking an overly occidental perspective, there are two primary motivations and concerns that lead the analysis in this direction. First, barriers of language make it difficult to examine the critical and commercial discourses of foreign-language markets in detail, there being little practical need for English translations of film reviews or advertisements. Secondly, censorship takes place in a variety of national contexts, which are often products of complex political and historical processes too varied and nuanced to receive sufficient attention here. Studies on the development of film censorship in, for example, Asian and European countries that were governed, at some point, by totalitarian regimes, including Germany, the Soviet Union, China, and Turkey, demonstrate how significant variations in political or inherently ideological climates see censorial practices adopted for subtly different purposes.

For just one example, in the case of Turkish cinema, various censorship commissions existed throughout the twentieth century to protect public morality and uphold law and order, not unlike mechanisms of the BBFC, or the American Catholic Legion of Decency. However, the official standards of cinematic acceptability in Turkey were much more closely defined in relation to national identity and the legitimacy of the state (Mutlu 143). The most heavily censored images were those reflecting or promoting the diverse social and cultural fabric of the country (144). In other words, amidst a history of military interventions and divisions along ethnic and religious lines, cinematic censorship was used to specifically promote a nationalist discourse that constructed Turkish society as a single and homogenous body.

In nations where intervention of authoritarian military regimes in the production of cultural meaning is frequent and routine, the screen representations deemed most potentially harmful are often those portraying the nation itself. In most cases, such as that of Turkey's Film Control Commission Board, the involvement of the state is limited to the prohibition of dissenting voices. However, governments such as China's are actively involved, like the 1930s American Catholic Church, in the promotion of certain agendas within the industries of cultural production (Xiao 126). As in Turkey, film censorship in China has a strong nationalistic dimension, but also functions as a protection against American cultural imperialism and economic domination by Hollywood (127). Such variance highlights the extent to which processes and practices of censorship are culturally and historically specific.

This study argues with particularity that as overt film censorship became unfashionable specifically in Western liberal democracies, the institutions previously charged with its deployment engaged in a process of goal displacement, prioritizing categorization, and arguing for its necessity if vulnerable age groups were to be protected from inappropriate material as audiences had been in the past. This case is made with reference to a sampling of cinematic works that provoked censorial and censorious impulses throughout the shift away from overt Western censorship in the 2000s.

Chapter 1 broadly traces the various historical trajectories leading to the shift away from censorship and toward classification-oriented models of film regulation in the late modern West. It argues that the turn of the millennium marked the end of a gradual shift in cultural attitudes, in which the necessity of shielding potentially vulnerable viewers from offensive, and in some cases socially "dangerous" content, became secondary to the priority of protecting the rights of adult viewers to freely seek out whatever entertainment they wished. The chapter examines key factors underlying the motivations of British, Canadian, and Australian censorship boards to engage in a process rebranding: of loosening their restrictive regulatory policies and emphasizing the productive aspects of their role as institutional protectors of artistic freedoms (protectors of the very same freedoms they had hitherto blithely curtailed as leading moral entrepreneurs). This chapter is meant to provide the necessary and culturally specific historical contexts for the case studies to follow. This also involves a detailed comparative analysis of the American ratings system, a voluntary and industry-initiated commercial model, along with the more overtly censorial model of government policy in Great Britain, and the Australian and Canadian systems, which now bear its influence. This chapter includes brief examinations of historical cases in diverse cultural contexts, in which innovations in the stylistic presentation of onscreen sex or violence significantly coincided with changes in film content restriction policies, offering comparative analyses of the relevant similarities and differences, including: the BBFC's censorship of Sam Peckinpah's *Straw Dogs* (1971), the British "video nasty" scandal surrounding titles such as Abel Ferrara's *The Driller Killer* (1979); and the BBFC's defense of David Cronenberg's *Crash* (1997).

Chapter 2 examines four films that exemplify the connection between self-reflexive aesthetic strategies, violent sexuality, and polarized reception, with which the "New French Extremity" is most frequently associated. Classifying films of the NFE proved problematic in Britain, Canada, and Australia, with strict policies toward onscreen sexual violence representing a key point of convergence between the regulatory policies in all three countries. Censored or censured with varying degrees of severity, all four films contain numerous dramatic transgressions against social sensitivities and cultural tastes. Reception of these films invoked the looming spectre of "violent pornography," a

INTRODUCTION

designation that cross-culturally piques the worst fears of moral crusaders for whom cinema retains potential to threaten what they celebrate as traditional standards of decency. Expanding the scope of the New French Extremity's influence beyond formal censorship boards, this chapter also examines "scandal" that accompanied these films on the international film festival circuit. In several cases, the language of censorious film reviewers suggested an uncommonly personal mode of critical engagement. Critics focussed on the apparent lack of a "redeeming" contextual framework for graphic violence, as well as highlighting personal stances toward their own experience of viewing the films. As exercises in genre transgression, NFE films draw upon iconography from "exploitation cinema" and reinterpret the language of mainstream genre convention through a new discursive lens. A major precipitating factor in negative criticism was a failure of the films to adhere to classical standards of categorization, which drew scrutiny from critics reluctant to re-evaluate their own criteria for typification.

Chapter 3 examines the controversy surrounding the release of Catherine Breillat's *Fat Girl* (2001) in Ontario, Canada. After refusing classification to this critically lauded film on the grounds that it constituted "child pornography" (underage *characters* were shown engaged in sexual activity), the Ontario Film Review Board came under fire from the Canadian press, as well as several lawyers, filmmakers, and politicians who condemned the apparent lack of discretion in downgrading sophisticated artistic expression to the level of rough pornography. The lenient treatment of the film elsewhere, internationally as well as in neighbouring Canadian provinces (the film was rated 16+ in the French-speaking province of Quebec), exacerbated the perception of the board as outmoded in its reasoning. As an evidently direct result, the OFRB eventually overturned its decision and amended its policies to limit its own ability to regulate mainstream narrative cinema. I argue the scenes that the board initially sought to excise were those most vitally bound to Breillat's confrontational feminist politics, and that the board's ill-advised proclamation that it could excise *Fat Girl*'s "potentially harmful" elements, and simultaneously preserve the power of Breillat's intended message, and uphold the importance of freedom of artistic expression, proved disastrous in a fashion that demonstrates why the defence of government censorship in the context of Western liberal democracies inevitably becomes a practical impossibility.

Chapter 4 emphasizes the consistent centrality of viewer (and actor/character) age distinctions in the film classification practices of Australia, but also Britain, Canada, and America, noting the parallel propensities toward moral panic that has been fostered historically in each distinctive national-cultural milieu. It examines the reception of Larry Clark and Edward Lachman's *Ken Park* (2002) in Australia, with specific focus on its unconditional (and still active) banning by the Office of Film and Literature Classification (OFLC), as well as the subsequent police raiding of an illegal protest screening that took place in Sydney in July of 2003. An analysis of the OFLC's rationale for refusing classification to Ken Park highlights issue taken with the film's "too realistic" depiction of "psychological abuse" of children, exemplified in a handful of its key sequences. While Clark's previous cinematic study of troubled adolescence, *Kids* (1995), received widespread mainstream critical and commercial celebration for its confrontational realism, *Ken Park* was condemned on the same grounds. The film's banning in Australia is contrasted with its equally notable failure to find a distributor in America and Britain. I argue that the discourse of censorship surrounding *Ken Park* has symbolic significance, in that the protection of children—precious in the eyes of would-be censors as symbols of innocence and uncorrupted moral virtue—has become the last surviving rationale for film censorship in a culture largely prepared for its retirement. Classification remains a popular process of regulation precisely because children are perceived as vulnerable to "psychologically damaging" (previously "morally corrupting") material, as children have not developed a full armature of expression, thus cannot, themselves, credibly claim invulnerability to disturbance from filmed images.

Chapter 5 examines Gaspar Noé's *Irréversible* (2002), a transformative benchmark in the artistic use of cinematic violence. The film's aggressive presentation of brutality drew both the attention and scrutiny of the global film community. While channelling the themes and motifs of Sam Peckinpah's 1971 rape-revenge drama *Straw Dogs*, *Irréversible*'s structural complexity brings the ethical act of watching cinematic violence to the forefront of its textual concerns. Its compositions, shot lengths, editing, soundtrack, and narrative are organized into patterns that directly relate to issues of perception and prompt the spectator to reflect on the experience of viewing the film. I argue that this self-reflexive approach to onscreen violence allowed Noé to circumvent aggressive censorial impulses, chiefly those aimed by and toward the British Board of Film Classification. After much deliberation by the BBFC, the uncut release of *Irréversible* in Britain (as well as Canada and Australia) was timely evidence of significant progress in the shift away from censorship, and more particularly, of the desire of classification boards to publicly abandon the process of asserting the moral view of classification examiners onto others, a process that fails when faced with the wholly self-aware sex and violence of Noé's filmmaking. As part of a concerted effort to distance classification from moral judgement, the BBFC found itself defending *Irréversible*, signifying a victory for artistically serious and socially responsible cinematic representations of (even particularly brutal) violence over those who have feared and warned against the capacity of such representations to inflict moral harm.

Chapter 6 suggests that the ideological climate of a "post-censorship" media landscape necessitates the formation of a conceptual link between film classifiers and mainstream commercial film critics, who are likewise engaged in processes of labeling that steer audiences toward some films and away from others. While critics lack the power to explicitly censor, they frequently engage in displays of *censure*, by way of public performances of personal taste that disapprove of certain narrative and aesthetic strategies. Along with classification examiners, the subjective opinions of film critics can provide a key stage in the social processes by which certain kinds of filmed content are designated as problematic. As a particularly dramatic example, this chapter examines the tumultuous Cannes premiere of Vincent Gallo's *The Brown Bunny* (2003), and the subsequent ad hominem lambasting of the film by mainstream critics. Gallo's perceptions of his film's reception as wholly negative has since prompted him to engage in self-censorship, refusing to publicly release any of his subsequent films. While the analyses in this book tend to focus on those scenes most relevant from a censorship standpoint, I provide a more thorough textual reading of *The Brown Bunny* for two reasons. First, few serious critical examinations of the film exist. Second, I argue that the censorious reaction to the film was not solely the product of its sexually explicit climax, but rather the relationship of this sequence to the film's broader organizational structure, as well as what critics perceived as Gallo's "narcissism," a mislabeling of his performative "outsider" status.

Chapter 7 examines the practice of cinemagoer polling, and its utilization in gathering what film studios view as actionable future intelligence. It focusses on Australian director Greg McLean's horror film *Wolf Creek* (2005) and its audience score of "F," as calculated by the market research firm Cinemascore. Using pollster teams across the United States in twenty-five cities at any one time, Cinemascore collects ballots from audiences attending opening night screenings. *Wolf Creek*, a distinctly Australian and violent (though artistically rendered) genre exercise, joined the list of only eighteen other films that have received this failing score since the company's founding in 1979. The chapter argues that the firm's grades, given by audiences who had a desire to see the movie on opening night (meaning they had a substantial level of anticipation), become de-facto reflections of how closely a film conformed to established expectations—further evidenced by the fact that films tending to score highest are often part of already successful franchises. This chapter illustrates how box office reporting, once confined to industry journals, had become a vital part of discourses surrounding Hollywood film by 2005. The displacement of serious film criticism by this and other research firms, along with review aggregator websites, in the years since has accelerated the process by which Hollywood cinema comes more and more to resemble other kinds of mass manufactured content—reflecting a limiting of original design and a reluctance of studios to gamble on filmmakers outside of the American cultural mainstream.

A final chapter tracks the trajectory of classification practices during the global boom of the digital marketplace in the fifteen years since the end of the main period in question. It examines how these practices, while explicitly informing viewers as to the content of films, also provide economic incentives for individual filmmakers who self-censor, as well as for distributors who demand that products adhere to content regulations that are arbitrary and restrictive at times. I argue that the routine economic censorship, which the financial structure of a global digital market necessitates, remains vastly preferable to previous modes of formal government censorship practice. Moreover, changes in distribution platforms have rendered previous functions of classification boards utterly obsolete. However, this chapter examines how voices of self-proclaimed moral authority interact with these changes to continue shaping standards of cinematic "acceptability" in new and significant ways. I broadly consider the looming presence of monopolistic screening platforms, the influence of social media spectator feedback, and select examples of notable overlaps between censorious moral and economic processes. One such case is the controversy surrounding Abel Ferrara's *Welcome to New York* (2014)—a film clearly referencing sexual allegations made against French politician Dominique Strauss-Kahn—which was heavily recut (without Ferrara's consent) for its distribution in America by IFC Films to obtain a more commercially friendly 'R' rating. Although the uncut film was released internationally, most of its US audience saw a substantially (and problematically) altered version. This serves as an illustrative example of market disciplines placing external constraints upon film content, thereby distorting the moral implications of the representations contained therein.

The Films as Texts

The filmmakers examined in this study can be conceptually linked by their provocative use of sex and violence, but also by their experimental formal treatment of such subjects. These filmmakers have gained notoriety for presenting challenging cinematic content within new and radical modes of aesthetic understanding and, in so doing, have frequently drawn scrutiny and censorship for transgressing boundaries of cinematic acceptability. As such, their work is extremely useful not only in forming theoretical approaches to certain kinds of phenomena related to cinematic spectatorship, but also in interrogating how notions of artistic transgression are determined largely by cultural contexts of reception. In each case, the films employ aesthetic and narrative strategies that question how viewers are involved, implicated, and engaged in the experience of viewing. They can perhaps be thought of constructively as part of what Horeck and Kendall call a "new cinematic extremism," artful films that feature the staples of genres such as horror and pornography but present these through self-reflexive techniques that viscerally engage the spectator by way of sensory involvement.

Conventional approaches to theorizing cinematic experience do not necessarily apply to these films, as they tend to reject the traditional role of the passive film viewer and do not necessarily constitute entertainment in the traditional sense. Rather, they demand a certain amount of visceral engagement from spectators and in this way require some radically new conceptions of spectatorship theory that go beyond typical narrative or semiotic readings. At the same time, the controversies that surround the films I have included here are central to a full understanding of their cultural impact. This study combines critical analyses of these texts, in relation to understandings of narrative and aesthetic strategies, with an examination of their broader place in film culture.

I hope to frame these films both within new conceptions of the cinematic text-spectator relationship as well as in relation to broader social responses to artistic transgression. Unpacking the question of what constitutes cinematic "transgression" in the contemporary media landscape raises numerous important questions. Is this designation simply a product of interactional relationships between cultural contexts of production and reception? Can more formal and aesthetic connections be drawn between separate and distinct modes and strategies of cinematic provocation? To what extent is cinematic "shock" dependent upon the intersection of a range of cultural and textual factors? How is censorship culturally and historically specific?

Several scholars have attempted to theorize the complex relationship between recent transgressive cinematic works and their spectators. Asbjørn Grønstad has suggested that such films are essential to considering the ethical life of images in contemporary culture (7). Tim Palmer has examined the process by which the international scrutiny provoked by such films has tended to overshadow the experimental stylistic treatment which makes them so affecting (59). Tanya Horeck and Tina Kendall have identified the primary hallmarks of extreme cinema as, firstly; a disregard for genre boundaries and secondly; a tendency to combine the aesthetics of art cinema with tactics associated with exploitation or pornography (8). Daniel Hicklin's work has formed an analytic connection between changes in film regulation policy and changes in artistic criticism, systematizing the interactional relationship between these processes as being subject to a wide range of influencing institutions, including those representing government, industry, and media organizations (118). Martin Barker has surveyed audience responses to challenging films, interrogating predictive claims built from theorizations of how film might affect audiences and reframing processes of film regulation and censorship as camouflaging moral judgements ("Watching" 114).

This project attempts to expand upon these previous studies by interrogating the interactional relationship between the aesthetic properties of challenging cinema and the discursive processes involving sex, violence, and censorship surrounding its reception. Textual analysis of these films allows their formal properties to be considered beyond their "shocking" nature and located within broader aesthetic and semiotic strategies, and offers a counterinterpretation to opposing claims of sensationalism. Simultaneously examining the discourses of sex, violence, and censorship surrounding these films reveals how changes in social attitudes and cultural trends correspond with the emergence of challenging new models of spectatorship. In this sense, journalistic criticism, audience response, and censorial regulation are taken to reflect broader cultural attitudes towards issues of artistic acceptability in contemporary culture. This exploration aids in the formulation of analytical connections between the "shocking" elements of a cinematic text and the social and historical conditions of its reception. Only when viewed in tandem can they be seen to form a complete picture of the intersections between critical, academic, regulatory, and consumer discourses surrounding these films.

While controversy often acts as a challenge or obstacle preventing more thoughtful interrogation of the relationship between these films and their spectators, it is also central to an understanding of their cultural impact, and an understanding of how cinematic "shock," delivered by form and content, is dependent on the intersection of a range of cultural and textual factors and appeals differently to spectators in varying social roles. I am aware that as an engaged scholar I might experience these films very differently than would a journalist or a representative of a classification institution.

Furthermore, because these films tend to resist simple genre classification, to approach any one of them as an "art film" might yield a very different (though equally emphatic) response than would approaching it as a "horror film," or a "pornographic" sex film. It is exceedingly difficult to categorize these films according to their content because they make a point of transgressing genre boundaries and combining the techniques of radically disparate cinematic traditions. Martine Beugnet has argued that it is less images of flesh and gore that tend to attract critical disapproval than the fact that neither flesh nor gore can be fully assimilated into the generic categories the films evoke (37). One could argue the same holds true for the challenges these films pose to censorial claims makers in a variety of contexts, which has emerged as a key theme of this study.

Finally, I wish to address the fact that many of the films highlighted in this study, as well as several of their historical counterparts, deal in some form or another with the tremendously sensitive topics of rape and sexual assault. It is not my intention to argue that the showing of rape for aesthetic purposes is a noble artistic strategy. I am aware that the moral implications of showing sexual violence are complex, and not necessarily the same as those that apply to other kinds of violence. It is highly possible that the moral outrage caused by such imagery justifiably outbalances the claims regarding its artistic merit. Yet, I believe cinematic images of rape are worth considering, at the very least for what they potentially reveal about cultural attitudes toward the topic. Because sexual violence in cinema is so frequently targeted at female characters, I have relied on female (in many cases feminist) critics such as Tanya Horeck, Linda Williams, Diane Wolfthal, and Barbara Creed for theoretical frameworks from which to approach the cinematic depictions of rape and sexual assault contained in these films.

Summary

This book examines film "classification" as a practice of regulative social labelling that relies heavily upon culturally constructed boundaries between "types" of films in distinctive national contexts. The analysis draws parallels and distinctions between governmental policies in these contexts, as well as between various social control mechanisms at work within a wide-reaching network of institutions beyond censorial bodies themselves, including news media, film festivals, and advocacy groups. The latter half of the study illustrates the means by (and ends to) which the regulation of film content persists in the "post-censorship" media landscape of Britain, Canada, Australia, and (where this model has most matured) the United States. While the case studies examined each involve distinct problematics, what links them conceptually is attention to how notions of, and related to, film classification, categorization, or labeling manifest in regulatory, artistic, and commercial market contexts: ranging from ratings institutions to journalistic criticism, film distribution, and advertising practices. The study also draws comparison between now obsolete formal censorship practices and machinations of the US "ratings" model of classification that Great Britain, Canada, and Australia moved swiftly toward during the late 1990s and early 2000s.

The aim of this research is to explore the interplay between "provocative" cinema and mechanisms of film regulation in the contemporary media landscape. This includes the conceptual link between the abrasive and self-reflexive aesthetic strategies of post-millennial "art-sploitation" cinema, and the shift from censorship to "classification" in Great Britain, Canada, and Australia. A second goal of this study is to examine how the motivations and machinations underlying the history of film censorship persist in a post-censorship cultural context. It argues that rhetorical strategies previously employed by censors to label films as "obscene" or "problematic" continue to appear elsewhere in the institutional structures and practices of cultural production. The goal is to illustrate how the social regulation of cinema, in the absence of traditional state enforcement, continues to operate in the complex interactions between alternative networks of disciplinary power and discursive practice. This involves a focus on the censure of art and genre cinema in the cultural contexts of both the longstanding US ratings model and the newly classification-oriented media landscape of the UK and commonwealth countries.

Within this broader scope of study is a particular focus on the way in which formal film censorship practices of the past, as well the post-censorship regulation and social control of cinema, rely on complex processes of "labeling": of drawing distinct boundaries between types of film content, and disciplining (with sanction and censure) those filmmakers whose work deliberately resists this rigid categorization.

PART I

1. THE ROAD TO CLASSIFICATION

Few mass media have been subject to such consistently fervent regulation as has cinema. The history of film censorship shows its modes and practices varying radically over time but remaining remarkably steadfast. From the inception of the medium, film was perceived by many as posing a potential threat to the moral well-being of its audiences, linked first and foremost to its primarily visual means of communication. As Thomas Doherty observes, motion picture morality had been monitored by guardians of civic virtue since the chaste peck between middle-aged lovebirds in Edison Studio's *The Kiss* (1896): "For progressive reformers and cultural conservatives who beheld the embryonic medium the potential for social damage and moral blight, the products of the motion picture industry warranted regulation and prohibition as a public health measure" ("Code" 6).

The first broad-scale organized attempt to implement social control of motion pictures took place in Ontario, Canada, in the form of the Ontario Theatres and Cinematographs Act of 1911. Enacted in March of that year, it led to the formation of the Ontario Censorship Board on June 27, predating both the formation of short-lived State Censor Boards in America later that year and the establishment of the British Board of Film Classification in 1912. Under the chairmanship of George G. Armstrong, the exceedingly broad evaluative criteria provided to the Ontario Board noted, "No picture of an immoral or obscene nature or depicting a crime or reproducing a prize fight shall be exhibited" (qtd. in Report 181). Given that it took until 2005 for the Ontario government to begin legislatively limiting the extent to which it would prohibit "mainstream" films from entering the public market, Ontario can be seen as serving Western cinematic censorship practices both as incubator and hospice. The explicit prohibition of "prize fight" reproductions in the Ontario Theatres and Cinematographs Act exemplifies the sometimes-peculiar subjects of focus in these earliest attempts at organized censorship (in the following year, Australia would issue a ban on any film involving "bushrangers"—escaped convicts in the early years of the British settlement of Australia—a prohibition which lasted for thirty years [McKenzie 54]). The implementation of a governmental censor board in Britain swiftly followed on the heels of its Canadian counterpart. Formed in 1912, the British Board of Film Censorship (later "Classification") (BBFC) initially administered only two purely advisory "Universal" and "Adult" categories, with which all films had to conform (Phelps 62).

In the United States, it would take until 1952 for motion pictures to be granted the protection of the First Amendment to the Constitution—the privilege of free speech guaranteed to print media. According to Tom Gunning, the basis for legalized film American censorship, which lasted nearly four decades, came very near to proclaiming motion pictures evil (22). According to the longstanding Supreme Court decision in the case of *Mutual Film Corporation v Ohio Industrial Commission* in 1915, the new medium of film was especially capable of causing harm because of its immense attractiveness to audiences, as well as its general manner of exhibition.

Beyond issues of mere censorship, Gunning argues, the 1915 decision not to overturn the film censorship law and board of censors in Ohio was part of an attempt to grapple with a new medium. Rather than address the content of a specific film, the regulation of film more generally was an attempt to wrestle with the nature of the medium itself: its relationship to its audiences, and its unique power of attraction (22).

The Production Code

In 1922, following several high-profile offscreen scandals and films containing images of rebellion, seduction, and other affronts to conservative values, US Postmaster General Will Hays was appointed chairman of the Motion Picture Producers and Distributors of America. Hays set out to rehabilitate Hollywood's image as a cesspool of immorality and sin, chiefly via the creation of a "Production Code" in 1930, a sophisticated set of moral guidelines largely dictated by Jesuit and Irish-Catholic Victorian values. The Production Code represents perhaps the best-known historical attempt at social control of the cinema. However, like its previous historical counterparts, the earlier Hays Code and the guidelines of city or state censors, the Code's ambition evolved beyond the expunging of filmic images toward the broader propagation of a particular moral vision.

This was particularly the case once Joseph I. Breen assumed the mantel of Hollywood's mediator of public morality. As Doherty writes:

> The job of the motion picture censor is to patrol the diegesis, keeping an eye and ear out for images, language, and meanings that should be banished from the world of film [. . .] More challenging is the work of textual analysis and rehabilitation that discerns and redirects hidden lesion and moral meanings. The astute and dedicated censor knows that correct images and proper words do not alone a moral universe make. [. . .] Breen saw his errand in the Hollywood wilderness in grander terms than the concealment of skin and the deletion of curses. He wanted to remake American cinema into a positive force for good, to imbue it with a transcendent sense of virtue and order. To earn Breen's imprimatur, the moral meaning of the picture needed to be clear, edifying, and preferably Catholic. ("Code" 10)

Doherty astutely highlights the degree to which processes of censorship are not limited to analysis of a film's content. Censorship in film, as well as other art forms, is symptomatic of larger cultural debates that weigh the perceived merit of an artwork against the moral outrage it has potential to incite.

An approach to modern censorship from a sociological perspective demands consideration of how specific institutional controls over cultural content benefit those who exercise them. Often, such controls act for institutions as a successful means of self-preservation via the promotion of cultural hegemony. The influence of the American Catholic Church on the dictates of the Hollywood Production Code throughout the 1930s provides a clear illustration of this dominance. The regulation of Hollywood's film representations during this period did not fall solely within the purview of a single organization (The Motion Picture Producers and Distributors Association of America) operating in isolation from external pressures. Many images that were excised from 1930s Hollywood films were indirect casualties of a larger war on secularization and modernism within which the American Catholic Church was engaged at that time. The Church used cinema to promote a distinctly Catholicized version of American morals, one that interacted with secular notions of Americanism and patriotism and was extraordinarily successful in gaining control of the means of cultural production in the decade between the onset of the Great Depression and the US entry into World War II. Catholic values designed and selected to encourage and promote trust in the forces of traditionalism thereby became the de facto regulators of Hollywood morality.

The chief principle governing the Production Code from 1934 onward, that "No Picture shall be produced which will lower the moral standards of those who see it," asserted a particularly Catholic definition of "moral standards." In the case of sexuality, for instance, the Catholic interest group the National

Legion of Decency adhered to the strictest of dogmatic guidelines when defining what constituted acceptable sexual behaviour and acceptable representations of sexuality in cinema. Female independence in matters of the body and sexual pleasure were most often portrayed as sinful, and the requirement was embedded in the code that they should be punishable in a scripted "tragic" outcome, while such themes as homosexuality or abortion were to be effaced entirely (McGregor 99). The Legion of Decency used such regulations to promote a strict, non-negotiable Catholic morality as inseparable from that of secular America. Titles that incurred the Legion's condemnation included Ernst Lubitsch's *Design for Living* (1933), in which Miriam Hopkins shares a flat (and presumably sleeps) with both Gary Cooper and Fredric March (Mank 120), as well as Josef von Sternberg's *Scarlett Empress* (Black 309). It would, of course, be overstating the case to say that the American Catholic Church was an all-powerful hegemonic force whose dogmas were publicly accepted without question, since the Church's goal of "oneness" with secular America sometimes required negotiation and compromise (McGregor 175). However, the Church's engagement with pressing issues of the day illustrates Annette Kuhn's suggestion that concrete practices of censorial intervention or prohibition are best understood as manifestations of hegemonic views on social matters.

In Britain, the BBFC introduced the X (16 and over) certificate in 1951, after which point the Board found itself routinely embroiled in contentious censorship cases, many involving high-profile Hollywood exports. In one such case, notable today in part because of the film's very intensive retrospective reputation, Nicholas Ray's *Rebel Without a Cause* (1955) was famously pruned of scenes depicting "anti-social" or "rebellious" behaviour, particularly where they reflected "discredit" on the hero's parents (Jim Backus and Ann Doran). It was "evidently not thought acceptable to suggest that adults might be in any way responsible for the unhappiness of their children" (63). Another contentious element of *Rebel Without a Cause* involved a scene in which Jim (James Dean) is seen engaged in a knife fight with fellow teenager Buzz (Corey Allen) outside the Griffith Park Observatory. Examiners requested that drastic cuts be made to the sequence, leaving only the barest amount of footage necessary to maintain narrative continuity (Pomerance, "Horse" 44). Film scholar Michael DeAngelis identifies the same elements of the sequence that the BBFC sought to expunge as greatly contributing to the "realist aesthetics" for which the film has since been so frequently celebrated (81). Despite its massive international success, *Rebel* was awarded an X certificate by the BBFC in December of 1955.

Censorship vs. Ratings

To determine the extent to which, in its broader understanding, censorship continues to restrict and constrain certain artistic voices and points of view in the wake of classification reform, the present study requires consideration of controversies in which, even following the shift to covert censorship, artistically serious films have been rejected, dismissed, or marginalized for their aggressive presentation of "pornographic" subject matter. The best contextual referent for such cases is perhaps the US, where film classification has more recently been an industry initiative. Films failing to meet classification standards necessary for theatrical exhibition have still found circulation in "unrated" exhibition, which has often garnered an audience via word-of-mouth (or, as in the case of films by such producers as Howard Hughes and Otto Preminger, even added publicity generated by the films' failure to secure a Code Seal). This longstanding model, which dates to the dismantling of the Production Code Administration's "Seal of Approval" system in 1966, gives a useful indication of trends likely to resurface in countries where the shift from censorship to classification is more recent.

The replacement of the Production Code in 1968 by the Code and Rating Administration had a dramatic effect on the content of Hollywood film, initially most apparent in the explosion of high-impact violence in R-rated films that followed, such as Sam Peckinpah's *The Wild Bunch* (1969), Francis Ford Coppola's *The Godfather* (1972), and Martin Scorsese's *Taxi Driver* (1976). The shift created a space in the market for films not intended for viewing by children without adult supervision, resulting in the ability of filmmakers to depict violence with a graphic detail that had been forbidden in Hollywood films of previous decades. The reasons for the US film industry's transition to the CARA system were numerous and complex. Foremost among them was the desire of Hollywood studios to combat the influence of regional censor boards by eliminating the necessity of age-based policies for film admission that would vary from city to city and state to state (Prince, "Classical" 252). The shift implied the abandonment of the industry's previous ideal of a mass, heterogeneous audience for films (which regional censors sought to preserve by requiring cuts to the sorts of scenes not "fit for everybody") and the move to niche audiences that the G-M-R-X system would facilitate. Filmmakers not only capitalized on this shift but, in an important sense, also precipitated it. The boundary-pushing content of 1960s Hollywood cinema, evidenced in films like Alfred Hitchcock's *Psycho* (1960) and Mike Nichols's *Who's Afraid of Virginia Woolf?* (1966), as well as an influx of European arthouse imports like Antonioni's *Blow Up* (1966), had increasingly highlighted the degree to which the rules of the Production Code were recognized openly as being rooted in the outmoded politics and mores of the 1930s (253). The disconnect between the morality of the Production Code and the social and political sensibilities of 1960s America had gradually eroded the Code's authority, resulting in its simply being ignored more and more by increasingly bold and visionary filmmakers.

FILM REGULATION IN A CULTURAL CONTEXT

As this study suggests with reference to the multiple case studies, it can often seem as though daring artists pursue their visions with a partial eye toward dismantling the sort of rigid criteria and particular sensitivities of audiences and censor boards alike. As Thomas Doherty writes of Hitchcock's infamous shower scene in *Psycho* (1960):

> The jagged incisions into the naked body of an innocent woman—with the knife thrusts shredding the victim's flesh in rhythm to the jump cuts—was a murderous frenzy without precedent in Hollywood cinema [. . .] Hitchcock's slashing ambush seemed storyboarded for the express purpose of hacking apart all the conventions and expectations of American cinema since 1934.(329)

The tendency of audacious filmmakers specifically to take aim at longstanding cultural taboos often places them at the center of discussions surrounding the boundaries and limits of free artistic expression. The replacement of regulations with ratings labels then becomes an effective way to shield vulnerable (typically younger) viewers from content deemed potentially harmful to them without resorting to prohibition of production and exhibition. Doherty continues, "The notion of motion picture ratings—classifying films according to content and restricting admission by age—had offered a middle ground between state censorship and the free market" (333). However, as this notion of "middle ground" implies, classification cedes moral ground to more prohibitive forms of censorship.

In the wake of the Production Code's collapse, John Schlesinger's 1969 Best-Picture Oscar Winner *Midnight Cowboy* (with its direct exploration of male hustling in New York) received an X rating upon release (an "adults-only" classification category traditionally reserved for pornography). Along with the critical and commercial success of Mike Nichols's *The Graduate* (with its frank sexual liaison between a twenty-year-old man and the middle-aged mother of his girlfriend), *Midnight Cowboy* forever blurred the previously distinct boundaries between mainstream and exploitation film markets.

For directors of the 1960s, the X category allowed complex, nonpornographic topics to be dealt with in US cinema in an "adult" way (Williams and Hammond 328), as the Production Code was replaced by the MPAA ratings system. The cinema of the 1970s presented audiences with a new realism and frankness in treatments of adult subject matter in cinema. The blurring between boundaries of mainstream cinema, exploitation fare, pornography, and European art cinema, which became prominent in US film culture from the mid-1960s onward, has led some commentators to identify the period between 1965 and 1979 as the golden age of so-called "trash cinema," in which "an increasingly segmented cinema marketplace catered to a plethora of sensationalist minority tastes, which defined themselves against the Hollywood mainstream"

(Shiel 133). The release by Twentieth Century Fox of Russ Meyer's X-rated *Beyond the Valley of the Dolls* (1970), the commercial success of the hardcore release *Deep Throat* (1973), and the positive US reception of *Emmanuelle* (1974) (a blend of soft-core pornography and pastiche of European cinema style) further expanded the reach and recognition of exploitation cinema styles and markets (133).

As is particularly relevant for this study, the fusing of arthouse and exploitation tradition in products of early 1970s Hollywood (released in the immediate wake of the Production Code's collapse) acted as flashpoints for debates around the increasing leniency of American film regulation. Two particularly relevant examples are Stanley Kubrick's *A Clockwork Orange* and Peckinpah's *Straw Dogs*, both released in 1971. As I. Q. Hunter has written of *A Clockwork Orange*:

> While *A Clockwork Orange* exhibited the canonical qualities of an art film—stylized, authored, self-reflexive, rather boring at times —its artiness could be seen as an elaborate "square up" intended to justify an obsessive focus on rape, voyeurism, and naked breasts [. . .] By focussing on the troublesome fault line between art and exploitation, the debate over *A Clockwork Orange* registered that such categories as art and exploitation, high and low, underground and mainstream were no longer mutually exclusive. (101)

Films engaged in this sort of resistance to cultural categorization pose particularly complex challenges to both critics and defenders of cinematic censorship through their complication of a film's intended audiences and effects. *A Clockwork Orange* and *Straw Dogs* cut across not just categorizations of art and exploitation but also class-based distinctions about different audiences. While arthouse audiences might be trusted to read such films with a certain measure of ironic distance, audiences perceived by cultural claims makers as more dangerous and vulnerable, such as typical consumers of "exploitation" films, might revel in and/or seek to imitate images of violence and non-normative sexuality.

Straw Dogs and Slippery Slopes

The ripple-effect of Hollywood's loosening restrictions became evident in censorship controversies abroad. For instance, *Straw Dogs*—while much discussed domestically—ignited one of the most contentious censorship cases in the British history. Released by Warner Bros. and starring Dustin Hoffman—following his critically acclaimed and commercially popular roles in Mike Nichols's *The Graduate* (1967) and John Schlesinger's *Midnight Cowboy* (1969)—*Straw Dogs* initially received an X-certified release in Britain, much to the chagrin of the conservative press. The X (16 and over) certificate had been introduced in 1951 as an addition to the purely advisory U (Universal—i.e., suitable for all) and A (Adult—suitable for adults only) categories (Phelps 62). By 1970, the year before the release of *Straw Dogs*, the range of films passed called for a further review of the classification cut-offs at age 14 (AA) and 18 (X) (63). Of *Straw Dogs*, BBFC examiners noted "We were all agreed upon the massive impact of this film, and we were equally agreed that it is tremendously enjoyable for the most part and compulsive viewing" (Barber 68). While appreciating the overall quality of the film however, BBFC examiners did express concerns about its rape scene, in which two men sexually assault the protagonist's wife Amy (Susan George). During the attack, Amy's body language indicates what examiners (arguably mistakenly) interpreted as pleasurable consent, because midway through her rape Amy ceases resisting, even beginning to kiss one of her attackers. The rape scene was duly cut from the film's original theatrical release (Duval 152). *Straw Dogs* was also banned entirely on British home video in 1984 under the newly implemented Video Recordings Act (Simkin "Wake" 83). This more extreme reaction was due to the fear that the rape scene was particularly vulnerable to misreading if viewed out of context.

Upon its initial release, many critics took exception to the film more generally, reading its violence as needlessly shocking and its larger narrative as a celebration of barbarity and vigilantism (Ebert "Straw"). Completely at odds with the BBFC examiners who appreciated the film, Fergus Cashin labelled it "mindless pornographic violence" in *The Sun* (qtd. in Barber 68). Such readings of *Straw Dogs* can be inextricably linked to its narrative structure, which is prototypical of the rape-revenge subgenre. Following the sexual assault, Amy's academic husband David (Hoffman) kills several local brutes besieging their West English farmhouse, her two assailants among them. Although it is never entirely clear whether David has been made aware of Amy's rape, there is an intangible (but undeniable) quality of vengeance in his unlikely outburst of aggression: a sense of a morally responsible pacifist bullied past his breaking point, defending his wife (unquestionably the film's true underdog). In response to a letter of complaint about the "bestiality" of the film, head BBFC examiner Stephen Murphy outlined the Board's position and offered a carefully articulated rationale for the BBFC's approach to the film:

> We at the Board will do all we can to stop filmmakers exploiting violence, but when a serious filmmaker makes a serious film about violence, I think we would be failing in our public duty if we prevented people from seeing it—however unpopular our decision may be. (Qtd. in Barber 68)

Murphy's comments clearly indicate the direction in which Western film censorship was already heading. Within them is an effort to make clear distinctions between films that responsibly tackled serious issues and those seeking to exploit violence in the interest of providing audiences with a cheap thrill. If a film's violence was factual or made with honourable intent, it could be permitted within reason, "whereas exploitative, thrill-seeking sensationalism such as some of the more extreme material in (films like) *Dr Jekyll and Sister Hyde* (1971) or *Twins of Evil* (1971) was not permitted" (Barber 68). The distinction between serious art and crass exploitation made little difference to the press.

Peckinpah was no stranger to violence as subject matter. The bloody and explosive climax of his previous feature, *The Wild Bunch*, revolutionized the aesthetics of screen brutality with its innovative, montage-based representation of gun violence. What became the signature style of his later work, rapid cutting between slow-motion shots of blood spraying from flailing male bodies, is on full display in the climax of *Straw Dogs*. However, Peckinpah's real interest in violence unquestionably transcended its aesthetic staging. Like *Taxi Driver*, which the BBFC would prune under the 1978 Protection of Children Act (Osborn and Sinclair 101), *Straw Dogs* is a nightmare of the Vietnam War come home. David has come to England fleeing the civil strife in America, only to discover that aggression and brutality eventually leave no place to hide. Stephen Prince has written extensively on Peckinpah's treatment of violence, acknowledging that, like Scorsese's, Peckinpah's stylization of the subject often leaves him vulnerable to misinterpretation: "If the montage-based representation of violence were Peckinpah's only contribution to the late 1960s cinema [. . .] he should be condemned as an aesthete of violence, an inciter to aggression [. . .] he would be everything his detractors have claimed him to be: a glamorizer and glorifier of violence" ("Aesthetics" 199). In truth, as Prince's research reveals, Peckinpah unequivocally viewed David as the villain of *Straw Dogs*: a figure unconsciously provoking the violence around him through his inability (or unwillingness) to communicate honestly with others and himself. In the coda to the film's bloody finale, David gets in his car and drives aimlessly. His passenger Henry Niles (David Warner) remarks "I don't know the way home." David responds: "I don't either." Violence has restored no order, no humanity.

Straw Dogs is a thrilling piece of cinema, but therein lies its conundrum. Unable to prevent themselves from sympathizing with David, in truth the perpetrator of its most strikingly and elaborately staged violence, viewers see his victims as little more than extinguished threats. The dynamic energy of the violence not only draws the spectator in but also threatens to override any meaningful critical consideration of its implications. The effect can be described not as pleasure but as ambivalence. As Vivian Sobchack recalls, "I got no pleasure at all out of watching *Straw Dogs*. I felt extraordinarily tense, upset, sick. And yet I could not leave the theater until the film was over" (115). Sobchack's dilemma, her ambivalent feelings about the film's violence, is essentially the challenge posed to BBFC reviewers by the film's central rape scene. For Peckinpah, the assault on Amy is not pleasurable, merely complex. One of her attackers is an ex-lover, for whom she may have lingering feelings. Furthermore, we may read her cooperation (as Prince does) as a strategy of self-protection from additional violence. Complexity is the true implication of the violence in *Straw Dogs*. It repels *and* attracts; restores *and* destroys; incites *and* deters; reveals *and* obscures. Sobchack continues:

> Sickened, terrified, I had to watch the film. I had to learn and know what I fear and, however painful the experience was, for the moment I found a certain security in the fact that I had not backed away from instruction. In short, I was doing my homework—trying to learn how to survive. David in that movie was much like myself, the people around me. We all just wanted to mind our own business and yet found ourselves, our homes, our lives, threatened by people and things which plainly didn't make sense. (115–16)

David may, in fact, be the true villain of *Straw Dogs*. By ignoring the seeds and suppressing the lure of violence, it is he who, in an important sense, sets the wheels of the film's brutality in motion. However, the world that *Straw Dogs* and *Taxi Driver* depict is one where only the villainous survive, even if only as hollow shells of their former selves.

Although the uncut version of *Straw Dogs* remained banned on video in Britain from 1984 until 2002, any broader moral implications of its violence were of little concern to the BBFC's reviewers. Their myopic focus on Amy's body language during the rape scene was enough to maintain the film's "legally problematic" status (Duval 152). It is typical of contemporary classification institutions that the censorial impulse emerges most aggressively when screen violence is eroticized, for reasons only partially clear. There frequently seems to be a concern that for some viewers at least, rape holds a particular capacity for transgressive appeal, perhaps due to a deep-seeded cultural linkage of sexual imagery with the evocation of fantasy, which produces an understanding of onscreen rape as more likely to inspire imitation and thus generate harm. "Harmful" is the contemporary censor's most useful substitute for "wrong." Non-eroticized violence, in holding less potential to inspire fantasy and imitation, is thus a less suitable target for explicit censorship. In this sense, the treatment of sexual violence by censorial bodies, in Britain but also more generally, seems more apparently a reflection of its sexual properties than its violent ones. For censors, it is not that non-sexual violence holds no potential for transgressive appeal, but that its appeal is not transgressive enough to warrant suppression. Yet, as screen violence moves gradually further from compelling viewers to avert their gaze, its moral implications require more and more scrupulous critical attention.

Acts of Violence

Concluding her review of *A Clockwork Orange*, released in the same year as *Straw Dogs*, Pauline Kael pleads for thoughtful analytical reasoning and awareness from critics in the face of the increased presence of brutality on cinema screens:

> There seems to be an assumption that if you're offended by movie brutality, you are somehow playing into the hands of the people who want censorship. But this would deny those of us who don't believe in censorship but only [. . .] the freedom of the press [. . .] to say that there's anything conceivably damaging in these films [. . .] If we don't use this critical freedom, we are implicitly saying that no brutality is too much for us [. . .] Yet surely, when night after night atrocities are served up to us as entertainment, it's worth some anxiety. (53)

Kael may have been overestimating the influence of critics to sway public morality, but her comments touch on something profound. If morally ambiguous and spectacularized violence is to be approached as real "art," viewers simply cannot afford to passively absorb its offerings. They are morally obligated to address its dialogues and engage its discourses, to question its intentions and remain sensitized to its effects. While Kael astutely identifies the responsibility of viewers and reviewers to think critically about the meaning and context of screen violence, she neglects a group upon whom this onus falls profoundly: subsequent artists who learn from the contingencies of the past.

It is chiefly due to the blurring of art and exploitation traditions that certain films become conduits for intensified scrutiny of censorial strictness and permissiveness. The same year that *A Clockwork Orange* and *Straw Dogs* were released, MPAA president Jack Valenti published an essay in *Harper's Bazaar* entitled "In Defense of the Voluntary Rating Program." The essay was intended to address concerns that the MPAA had become too permissive in its treatment of cinematic content, seemingly evidenced by the National Catholic Office for Motion Pictures (formerly the Legion of Decency) having withdrawn its support for the newly implemented ratings system. Valenti insisted that the MPAA sought only to make a judgement on the "suitability of the viewing of [a] film by young people" and that it was not the job of the rating programme to recommend, ban, or censor movies (Simkin, "Straw" 31). In some sense, the challenge posed by the content of *A Clockwork Orange* and *Straw Dogs* had forced the MPAA to examine its policies and gauge their effectiveness in balancing free speech rights of established filmmakers with the potential threat to (particularly younger) viewers that such films might pose.

In the mid-1970s, Australia too experienced the beginning of its longest-running and most infamous case of cinematic censorship: that of Pier Paolo Pasolini's final (and most confrontationally transgressive) film *Salò, or The 120 Days of Sodom* (1976). Based on the Marquis de Sade's "The 120 Days of Sodom," *Salò* was completed just prior to Pasolini's murder in 1976. The film was banned in Australia that same year, a decision that would remain in place for nearly two decades despite ongoing requests for the film to receive a classified release (Lacey 57). *Salò* was eventually unbanned in 1993, but the decision proved to be short-lived. Its classification was withdrawn once again in 1998, when (in accordance with new provisions in legislation for considering a film's artistic merit alongside its content), a majority of the Office of Film and Literature Classification's Review Board members voted that Pasolini had failed to "clearly establish" the metaphor at the core of *Salò*'s scathing critique of Italian Fascism (58).

Moral Panic

The 1980s offered a particularly acute example of moral panic in film censorship in the form of the BBFC's implementation of the Video Recordings Act (VRA), a policy dictating strict regulation of videocassette tapes throughout the United Kingdom, and the "video nasties" scandal which immediately preceded the policy's implementation (Petley, "Film" 61). Here we find an exemplary instance of Annette Kuhn's theorization of censorship as a product of complex relations established between heterogeneous webs of discourse, law, administrative measure, and philosophical or moral proposition.

Commencing in 1981, the "video nasty" panic refers to a bout of so-named mass anxiety regarding the circulation, especially to children, of particularly explicit horror titles on videocassette. The phenomenon displayed all the hallmarks of a classical moral panic as defined by Stanley Cohen:

> A condition, episode or group of persons becomes defined as a threat to societal values and interests; its nature is presented in a stylized and stereotypical fashion by the mass media; the moral barricades are manned by editors, bishops, politicians and other right-thinking people; socially accredited experts pronounce their diagnoses and solutions; ways of coping are evolved (or more often) resorted to; the condition then disappears, submerges, and/or deteriorates and becomes more visible. (9)

Petley suggests that if the VRA was a response to panic about horror videos being "morally corrupting," the policy itself can be considered a form of "moral regulation." He draws on the work of sociologist Alan Hunt, who outlined moral regulation as the contestation of a wide range of social issues, including the kinds of entertainment to which people expose themselves, in "strongly moralized terms" ("Film" 8). Hunt pointed out that in the wake of rapid processes of secularization and social diversification in the second half of the twentieth century, justifications for criminalizing certain forms of private behaviour "relied increasingly not simply on their alleged intrinsic wrongness, but on their apparent harmfulness" (9). This concept is fundamental to an understanding of why the issue of video censorship was so consistently framed in terms of potentially "harmful" effects of certain readily available means of visual representation. For conservative crusaders of the period, it functioned as an effective contemporary substitute for the previous labels of "evil" or "wrong."

The first major articles about the video nasties appeared in *The Sunday Times* and the *Daily Mail* in May of 1982, warning of the availability of films which, as the *Times* claimed, "specialise in sadism, mutilation and cannibalism," to children on videocassette (qtd. in Petley "Film" 24). These articles lumped together a wide range of video titles, including *Don't Answer the Phone* (1980), *Snuff* (1985), and *S.S. Experiment Camp* (1986), suggesting the definition of "video nasty" was still murky at best. While the response from members of Britain's Tory Party was swift, with socially conservative moral entrepreneur Mary Whitehouse encouraging British Members of Parliament to investigate the situation, the efforts by the press to whip up sensation grew more elaborate, frequently assuming and asserting a direct causal link between screen violence and real-life violence. The following month, the London *Evening Standard* gained attention for its reporting on the "video rapist" case, wherein a defendant claimed that video nasties had convinced him women tend to fall in love with their rapists (29). More stories followed, reporting that children as young as six were viewing video nasties, that the cost of renting a morally damaging videocassette was mere pence, and that "gangsters" were running video cassette distribution channels (29). These stories fuelled claims made by MPs and their constituents that tightening of regulative controls was urgently required. These efforts led to the prosecution of several video distributors for obscenity by the Department of Public Prosecutions in September of 1982.

While many of the titles targeted by the DPP were indeed crass exercises in horror and sexual exploitation, others beg for more nuanced contextualization. For example, in 1979 former American porn director Abel Ferrara made the switch to dramatic feature filmmaking with the release of his debut *Driller Killer*, in which a New York City artist named Reno Miller (Ferrara) struggles with his increasingly deranged mental state. Unable to find work as an artist, Reno is forced to rely on his two female roommates for rent. He is humiliated by several art dealers and deprived of sleep and the ability to concentrate by the constant rehearsals of a punk rock band occupying the loft above his. Losing his grip on reality, Reno begins stalking the streets of New York's derelict neighborhoods, murdering random homeless men with a power drill. The film is amateurish in many technical respects, but the narrative combines the psychological paranoia of Roman Polanski's *Repulsion* (1965), the abrasive gore of 1970s American horror films like Tobe Hooper's *The Texas Chainsaw Massacre* (1974), and the socially alienated anti-hero theme made popular by films such as Don Siegel's *Dirty Harry* (1971) and Martin Scorsese's *Taxi Driver* (1976). Furthermore, *Driller Killer*'s unusual stylistic touches—its largely improvised dialogue and verité staging—indicated early on Ferrara's unique approach to what is ostensibly exploitation genre material.

During the "video nasties" panic, *Driller Killer* became a target for censorial wrath, famously earning a place on the British Department of Public Prosecution's list of banned videocassettes. The "nasties" included a handful of (mainly American) horror and exploitation titles released in Britain on videocassette, including Wes Craven's *The Last House on the Left* (1972), Sam Raimi's *The Evil Dead* (1981), and the work of many European genre filmmakers like Dario Argento, Lucio Fulci, Mario Bava, and Jess Franco. The "panic" refers to mass anxiety in Britain regarding the circulation of these titles by video retailers, one that focused mainly on their availability to children, combined with the notion of horror videos being "morally corrupting" (Petley, "Film" 61). The distributors of *Driller Killer* and four other videos: *SS Experiment Camp* (1976), *Death Trap* (1977), *I Spit on Your Grave* (1978), and *Cannibal Holocaust* (1980), were charged under the Obscene Publications Act (police used Section 3 of the Act, punishable only by the forfeiture of videos, rather than Section 2, for which the penalties included fines and imprisonment) (Critcher 65). Police action was defended as necessary protection against potential copycat violence that psychologically vulnerable viewers might commit. As a London Superintendent told the *Telegraph*: "The police are here to prevent violence for violence's sake, which is precisely what these films glorify. The prospect of just one person mimicking *Driller Killer* is horrifying" (qtd. in Petley, "Insane" 88).

Ferrara and Film Regulation

With its graphic imagery, made notorious by its explicit cover-art featuring a man with a drill bit burrowing into his skull, Ferrara's *Driller Killer* was vilified and censored on unambiguously moral grounds. While many films targeted by the DPP list (and the subsequent Video Recordings Act) were indeed morally dubious exercises in crass exploitation, retrospective analysis of *Driller Killer* has prompted some critics to reconsider it as a politically and stylistically serious offering from a significant emerging artistic voice. For example, in 2003 influential film critic Mark Kermode introduced a televised broadcast of the film for Britain's Channel 4 by saying that it "owes more [. . .] to Warhol than it does to any slice and dice tradition," and calling it "tough viewing, but hardly the stuff of the traditional nasty" (qtd. in Egan 245). Such critical reappraisals of *Driller Killer* undoubtedly owe a retrospective debt to celebrations of Ferrara's subsequent output, allowing the early film's artistic credentials to be recognized by virtue of its placement within a larger body of work by a latterly recognized maverick auteur (247). However, even Ferrara's most critically lauded works have been forced to contend with censorial efforts and content restrictions.

Upon its release, his 1992 police corruption drama *Bad Lieutenant* (perhaps his best-known work) posed a challenge to the newly revised classification categories of the MPAA because of several of its scenes, including one in which a nun is raped by two Hispanic youths and another in which its titular Lieutenant (Harvey Keitel) masturbates in front of two young women he has detained in an unwarranted traffic stop. Ferrara, ever resistant to capitulation or compromise, said of *Bad Lieutenant*: "I demanded the right to make an unrated picture contractually. I told (producer Edward R. Pressman) up front it would be a triple X picture [. . .] There's one version of *Bad Lieutenant* and that's it. It's an adult film but not necessarily for a limited audience" (qtd. in Sandler, "Naked" 152). Despite this firm stance, the film's video release was drastically re-edited by MCA Home Video to obtain an R rating.

It is perhaps unsurprising that the controversial content of *Bad Lieutenant* aligns historically with revisions to a system of ratings categorization. Two years prior to the film's release, the MPAA had introduced the new category of NC-17, a classification designed to restrict the attendance of individuals under 17 to certain films while avoiding the stigma of the X rating (one traditionally reserved for hard-core pornographic films). It was thought that such a category would allow serious mainstream filmmakers to explore adult themes in a frank and realistic manner, much as the X category had done for the auteurs of the late 1960s (Williams and Hammond 328). However, the hope that the NC-17 rating would have a legitimizing effect on audacious and risqué filmmaking strategies proved more complicated in practice due to the economic structure of commercial film markets, where NC-17 films face significant challenges in procuring exhibitors and advertisers in the "ostensibly family-friendly mall-culture of mainstream contemporary cinema" (328). Because rental agreements of multiplexes in malls may forbid them from screening NC-17 films, distributors are often left with a difficult decision when faced with the rating: re-edit the film to obtain the more commercially viable R or risk their product languishing outside the stream of commerce (Semonche 133).

In *Censorship: The Knot that Binds Knowledge and Power*, Jansen writes of the process by which private interests assert their own self-interested claims about, and/or definitions of, moral values:

> In attempting to rationalize their marketing strategies, corporate decision-makers, like the censors of Rome, assume the mantle of mediators

of public morals. Those who control the productive process determine what is to be produced in the cultural arena and what will not be produced. These *market censors* decide what ideas will gain entry into the "marketplace of ideas" and what ideas will not [. . .] That is, *they decide what cultural products are likely to ensure a healthy profit margin*. (16)

Jansen's writing reflects an acute awareness of how the restricted dissemination of certain ideas, genres, and cultural forms within mainstream media is not always designed solely to accommodate the demands of consumers. How corporate entities design and deploy communication technologies often equally reflects their own interests in self-preservation, and nowhere is this dynamic more apparent than in the case of the Hollywood film industry's self-regulation in the ratings era.

The disincentive for filmmakers and distributors to deliver NC-17 material is one such mechanism of self-preservation. The task of categorizing all films released by major studios and intended for mainstream theaters into R, PG-13, PG, or G ratings, and determining what onscreen images and ideas will aide or impede this goal, remains among the MPAA and CARA's most imperative tasks. Through categorization, the industry guarantees that its products are perceived as what Kevin Sandler calls "responsible entertainment," the guidelines of which are determined by a "de facto production code" that acts as "a means of defense against external interference from politicians and moral reformers and against competition from independent distributers and exhibitors" (Sandler, "Naked" 4). In other words, the criteria that separate the R and NC-17 categories still in effect determine what images and ideas are to be considered too controversial for mainstream audiences. Thus, the distinction between the marketing strategies favoring R-rated films and the more overt moralizing of the Production Code becomes somewhat negligible. While the "mechanisms of boundary maintenance" may differ between the two systems, both essentially respond to the same external pressures that, together or separately, exercise power over "what they believe should be the function of Hollywood entertainment" (41). Thus, the same forces that, via the Production Code, shaped regulations and policies geared toward providing "harmless" entertainment continue to assert their own moral definitions of what constitutes permissible entertainment.

Perhaps the most significant difference between moral and market processes of censorship lies not within their respective motivations or outcomes but within the relative invisibility of the latter. While the economic utility of film censorship is no less significant than its social or political functions (Lewis 6), the fact that market censorship practices are based on anticipated profits makes them easier to mistake for direct outcomes of consumer choices. Market censorship practices, as Jansen argues, are "reified, naturalized and integrated into the organizational structures and routine practices of media organizations" and, over time, become objectified, "understood as 'just the way things are' or 'how things work'" ("Ambiguities" 13). The concern over "moral corruption" that landed Ferrara's debut *Driller Killer* on the DPP "video nasties" list appears to constitute a clear case of vertical censorship only because the repressive apparatus doing the censoring (i.e., the British government), as well as the moral justification it offered for doing so, were so readily identifiable.

By contrast, the economic forces behind the drastic re-edits to *Bad Lieutenant*, involving complex financial incentives and contractual agreements between private parties, could be more easily dismissed as the product of routine consumer practices within a rational market system. But this makes their effects no less problematic. The desired legitimizing effect of the newly implemented NC-17 was of little reassurance to MCA, as the film's release followed in the immediate wake of the announcement of Blockbuster Films, a massive multinational video rental chain, that it would not stock any film that carried the adults only designation. A spokesman for the company, Ron Castell, stated in the *Los Angeles Times*:

> We have always had a policy that we don't carry any movie that the Motion Picture Association of America rates X [. . .] When they revised the X rating, we said we would wait and see how they would use the new rating. But the criteria used for NC-17 was the same as the X. So, we're saying that since NC-17 is the same criteria as the X, we're not going to carry it. (Qtd. in Fox 59)

Many theater chains, video stores and newspapers had previously stated that they would judge NC-17-rated movies on a case-by-case basis before booking, stocking, or running advertisements for films carrying the designation. Blockbuster's decision was one of the first that categorically barred all movies with the NC-17 rating. Faced with this and other equally daunting economic restrictions, MCA substantially altered four key thematic scenes in *Bad Lieutenant* to obtain an R rating, mangling the original film without regard for narrative coherence (Sandler, "Naked" 52).

Even the most high-profile of Hollywood directors frequently opt to censor their own work to avoid an NC-17, a notable example being Stanley Kubrick, who allowed key scenes of his final film, *Eyes Wide Shut* (1999), to be digitally altered with the goal of removing explicit sexual action. In a scene involving an elaborate orgy, populated by shrouded upper-crust elites, additional attendees were digitally inserted to block background images of couples engaged in sex. Terry Semel, co-chairman of Warner Bros., said of the changes to Kubrick's film: "We're not in the NC-17 business. When one looks at 'Eyes Wide Shut' perhaps there was not a huge difference between what would be an R, what would be an NC-17. But NC-17 is a whole industry. It includes triple-X-rated porno films. So, to us that's just not a business that we're in. Never have been" (qtd. in Weintraub). Instances in which serious films about human sexuality, made by established and respected filmmakers, cannot be seen by adults in their intended forms indicate the extent to which in American cinema art is routinely subordinated to commercial considerations.

The banning of *Driller Killer* on expressly moral grounds in Britain, and the re-editing of *Bad Lieutenant* for the purposes of commercial viability in America, seem at first glance to be separate and distinct processes with substantially different motivations and outcomes. However, when approached through the lens of Jansen's understanding of the causes and effects of market censorship, such distinctions subtly begin to break down. (Ferrara's [non-governmentally] censored 2014 film *Welcome to New York* receives substantial analysis in Chapter 8).

Classification

In the absence of regulative censorship by religious or political regimes, censorial claims often come most stridently from a culture's media sources. Such was the case in 1990s Britain where, attempting to expand its grip on video distribution, the BBFC added several amendments to the Video Recordings Act. These came amid high-profile media stories: the murder of toddler James Bulger by two ten-year-old boys, Robert Thompson and Jon Venables; and the conservative press's efforts to get David Cronenberg's *Crash* (1996) banned. Due to the sensational nature of these stories, the British national press played a key role in processes that resulted in the tightening of video regulation throughout the country. In the case of the child's murder, conservative newspapers printed erroneous articles claiming tenuous links between details of the case and the contents of Jack Bender's *Child's Play 3* (1991) (Petley, "Film" 89). In the case of *Crash*, the *Daily Mail* and *Evening Standard* newspapers launched a campaign against the film's "obscene" content, calling for the BBFC to refuse classification (115). With both the child killing and the film, the nature of the so-called threat was construed by the press in a highly stylized fashion, "as we look towards the future with feelings almost akin to terror" as the *Daily Mail* wrote on the murder, for example (qtd. in Thompson 94), and "the point at which even a liberal society must draw the line" as the paper commented on the Cronenberg film (qtd. in Barker, Arthurs, and Harindranath 1). Just as the dense concentration of Catholics in metropolitan centers and the prevalence of antisemitic attitudes toward studio heads allowed the American Catholic Church to seize control of a major industry of cultural production in the 1930s, the rise of Thatcherism in the late 1970s and a wave of social unrest spreading through Britain cultured a conservative political atmosphere, in which issues of law and order could blur with moral judgements of personal and private behaviour. Thus, the British national press became a dominant source of pressure influencing the BBFC's regulatory practices. Despite this climate, or perhaps signalling its downturn, *Crash* was in fact classified and screened in the United Kingdom.

The process by which censor boards were able to rebrand themselves as classification institutions, their movement away from censorship and toward categorization can perhaps be identified as one of what sociologists James M. Henslen and Adie Nelson refer to as "goal displacement," one primary means by which bureaucracies, once in existence, perpetuate themselves (108). When an organization's services are no longer required by society, its old goals are often replaced with new ones. Henslen and Nelson offered the example of Ontario's March of Dimes, which, having been organized in 1951 to fight polio, reoriented its goals following Dr. Jonas Salk's discovery of a cure for the disease in 1955. Faced with the loss of their jobs, March of Dimes organizers expanded the purview of the organization to serve all adults in Ontario with physical disabilities, enabling justification for the institution's existence for many decades to follow.

A similar process has been identified by Phillip Jenkins with regards to the Federal Bureau of Investigation (FBI) and the upsurge in the visibility of serial killer cases in the 1980s. Jenkins argues that the reasons for this upsurge can be found in the bureaucratic machinations of the FBI (213). Starting in the 1970s, the FBI had been under severe financial and administrative scrutiny because of Watergate, illegal attacks on the civil rights movement, and a wide range of other forms of abuse of power. When faced with declining budgets and the threat of increased government oversight, FBI officials did what they had done so many times in the past: they constructed an "enemy within" which, it was claimed, only the FBI could defeat. During earlier periods of organizational strain, FBI propagandists had inflated the threats posed by Communists, midwestern bank robbers and Italian organized criminals (Herzberg 260). Accordingly, in the 1980s Bureau representatives claimed that serial killing was a large and growing problem, that local law enforcement had neither the resources nor the jurisdictional authority to deal with murderous felons who roamed the country, and that serial killers tended to be highly intelligent and therefore difficult to apprehend.

As early as 1970, when the BBFC introduced further classification cut-offs at age 14 (AA) and 18 (X), Britain had developed the strictest film and video censorship protocols in the European Union, a situation maintained, and even strengthened, in the 1980s and 1990s (Petley, "Film" 12). However, it was the BBFC's refusal to ban *Crash*, despite immense pressure from the British national press, that signalled a turning point in the prioritization of artistic intention, examiner discretion, and case-by-case approach to films in the institution's classification process, all changes that were mimicked in the institutional reforms of such bodies elsewhere. Answering to harsh criticism of its so-deemed lax regulatory practices, the BBFC cleverly reinvented itself as an increasingly lenient institution springing to the defense of artistic freedoms as frequently as it must impinge upon them, and impinging, when it had to, with demonstrable reluctance. The *Crash* case is comprehensively explored in Martin Barker, Jane Arthurs, and Ramaswami Harindranath's 2001 study, *The Crash Controversy*. The objections of conservative journalists included arguments for the film's potential to incite copycat behaviour, its problematically ambivalent stance toward "deviant" sexuality, and even its potential to cause offense to disabled viewers. The UK reception of *Crash* suggests that, by the late 1990s, classification boards were beginning to engage in a process of loosening their restrictive regulatory policies and emphasizing the productive aspects of their role as institutional protectors of artistic freedoms—protectors of the same freedoms, indeed, that they had hitherto blithely curtailed as leading moral entrepreneurs. The BBFC's defense of the film, as well as the ensuing backlash, signaled an unmistakable shifting in the priorities and emphases of Western cinematic regulation processes.

Film censorship and classification boards might be still viewed, in some important sense, as moral regulators of the boundaries and limits of socially acceptable artistic expression. However, the British Film Board of Classification's June 1996 defense of *Crash* against the efforts of the conservative press to have it banned suggests a loosening of restrictive regulatory policies but also a new understanding of potentially productive aspects of censorship institutions as protective of artistic freedoms. The *Crash* episode clearly illustrates that in Britain, as well as more broadly, censorial impulses should not be thought of solely as the product of specific classification and film regulation policies, operating in isolation from broader legal, discursive, and administrative processes. Equal attention must be paid to the various institutions acting upon classification bodies, with means and reason to project their own moral definitions onto classification policies.

CRASH

In the case of *Crash*, it was largely the British national press, in newspapers such as the *Daily Mail*, *Daily Telegraph*, and *Evening Standard*, which campaigned against the film's "obscene" content, and called for a refusal of its legitimation through classification. Thus, it was not the BBFC but the British conservative media that engaged in typical censorious strategies, such as construing a so-called "threat" posed by the film (in a highly stylized fashion) and providing a platform for the expression of restrictive attitudes under the guise of freely articulated "public" opinion. Writing for the *Daily Mail*, Alexander Walker called *Crash* a "movie beyond depravity," with "some of the most perverted acts and theories of sexual deviance I have ever seen propagated in mainline cinema" (qtd. in Barker, Arthurs, and Harindranath 1). Walker countered any imaginable defense of the film by its makers with claims of its being thoroughly and utterly debased. *Crash*, he summarizes, "is vulnerable on almost every level: taste, seriousness, even the public safety risk of promulgating such a perverted creed" (1). The BBFC resisted the sensational nature of such claims but took very seriously the fears of conservative commentators.

Concerns over the release of *Crash* focussed mainly on the film's potential to incite copycat behaviour. Censorial claims were made that certain viewers, upon seeing the film, might imitate characters in the story and crash their own cars for sexual pleasure. Also frequently cited was a scene in which James Spader seduces a paraplegic woman (Rosanna Arquette) and appears to penetrate an open gash in her leg with his penis. Despite the media panic implicating the film and its defenders in a perceived larger pattern of social decay, the BBFC attempted to examine every complaint against *Crash* methodically before deciding whether to pass, cut, or ban the film (Sandler, "Crash" 601). James Ferman, the board's director, enlisted judgement of many professionals to reach this decision, including a forensic scientist and eminent lawyers. Additionally, *Crash* was privately screened to a group of disabled viewers to determine if the film was offensive to disabled people (601). Almost five months after *Crash* was first shown at the London Film Festival, Ferman announced that the BBFC was passing the film uncut for release, having concluded (to the chagrin of conservative politicians and journalists) that the film was neither illegal nor harmful.

The BBFC's rebranding of itself as an increasingly lenient institution proved a successful means of countering harsh criticism of its regulation processes in more liberal circles. However, this episode did little to guarantee that films with authorship less reputable than Cronenberg's, aesthetics less conventional, and presentation of sexual activity, abhorrent or otherwise, more confrontational, would enjoy the same privileged status as artistically valuable works, worthy of the protection that *Crash* seemed ultimately to merit. The BBFC's protection of *Crash* against conservative interests might be thought of as owing a debt to two important factors. First, David Cronenberg was then, as he is now, a critically acclaimed and commercially successful filmmaker, whose twenty-year career included tax-funded (i.e., governmentally sanctioned) productions in his home country of Canada, as well as forays into Hollywood filmmaking with *The Dead Zone* (1983) and *The Fly* (1986). Thanks to his direction of numerous films utilizing large budgets and featuring popular genres, name stars, and sizable box office returns, Cronenberg has achieved an internationally acknowledged status as a commercial auteur and, even, as something of a household name. Thus, to the degree that he was a critically lauded celebrity, censoring Cronenberg meant censoring success. Secondly, the ostensibly problematic sexuality in *Crash*, while wildly graphic by Hollywood standards of the 1990s, is fairly restrained and inexplicit relative to the wide range of adult material that passes through the review processes of classification boards. There is no indication that any of the sexual activity Cronenberg presents is non-simulated, thus pornographic, and there is no clear legal basis on which to base a claim that the sexual behaviour on display is "abhorrent" and expressly problematic. As a result, the objections to the film's content put forth by the conservative press could be rooted only in its being perceived as "morally degenerate," a highly subjective characterization seen by more liberal critics as too transparently linked to religious conservatism to be given priority over liberal values of free expression. In this sense, it would perhaps have been thought more remarkable had the Board succumbed to the social pressure being placed upon its criteria; succumbed, and in succumbing, banned the film.

The Board's reaction to the controversy reveals how external agents, with their own moral and political agendas, act upon regulatory bodies and how the shift from censorship to classification began to manifest itself, but as we view it through a historical lens the case now appears as something of a low-hanging fruit. The factors listed above simplify the equation and make it immediately obvious that *Crash* is the work of a serious artist, seeking to explore disturbing and confrontational themes through relatively conventional means of storytelling.

Conclusion

The BBFC's reluctance to ban *Crash*, despite immense pressure from the conservative press, signaled a liberalization of policies and practices of regulatory bodies in the late 1990s that saw such institutions gravitating toward a classification system resembling that of the Motion Picture Association of America's rating system, an industry initiative aimed at providing consumers with information about particular films, for the purposes of identifying appropriate audience segments grouped by age. However, one significant distinction remains. The American system ultimately allows for the unconstrained release of films that have not undergone the ratings process, albeit with the handicap of having their commercial prospects dramatically reduced by the "unrated" designation. In countries and provinces where governmental review of film content is mandated, this option is not legally viable.

Appearing on a television talk show in 1981, Cronenberg stressed this freedom:

> You must understand that I live in Ontario Canada [. . .] When I came down here to talk with the MPAA about ratings, it was still a relief compared with what happens in Ontario which is, they take your picture, they take every print, they cut it, they hand it back to you and they say this is your new movie. They keep the pieces that they've taken out, and you go to jail for two years if those are projected [. . .] That's real censorship. (Qtd. in Bogani)

Cronenberg's "they" is the Ontario Film Review Board, a rotating committee of film classification experts based in Toronto, the approval of which all films must acquire before they can be distributed or exhibited in Ontario. Along with the BBFC, Australia has a comparable system: "If a film is refused classification, it is illegal to exhibit the film in Australia. Each State and Territory is responsible for enforcing the Act and has their own enforcement legislation" (Kampmark 346). Cronenberg's critical comment coldly touches upon an idea rarely presented in discourses surrounding censorship in Canada and Great Britain, and Australia: if approval by classification is mandated by law, it follows that real legal consequences must be enforceable upon any filmmaker who refuses to comply. To ignore a board's ruling must be to make oneself vulnerable to legal prosecution.

Since the Motion Picture Association of America is an industry self-monitoring organization, the American ratings system is not actually governmental. Via the Classification and Rating Administration, MPAA representatives merely provide guidelines to which filmmakers can adhere if seeking a particular ratings categorization (if they so choose). In the case of the British, Canadian, and Australian classification systems, by contrast, the legal dimension of the government regulation of film content has the inevitable effect of equating certain forms of artistic expression—often, by definition, unpopular—with punishable criminality. Even if it is rarely enforced, prosecution solidifies the idea that government power remains the ultimate arbitrator of the boundaries of cinematic acceptability. This notion can seem problematic in many senses, not least of which is reflected in the notion that political power and, by extension, ideas about the role of government in shaping culture are in a state of perpetual flux. The criteria by which cinematic expression could be declared criminal are theoretically subject to routine change, while the penalty of failing to comply with such protocols remains constant.

On the surface, the liberalization of regulatory policies that characterized the shift toward current classification practices would seem to address this problem: the principal of protecting vulnerable portions of consumer audiences, typically grouped by age, remains intact while only the parameters defining which films should be excluded through banning are subject to modification. Such practice may seem to constitute censorship only in a purely academic sense, since the idea that "offensive" or "confrontational" filmmaking strategies—which challenge audiences yet violate no law—would result in the criminal prosecution of their producers seems far-fetched in contemporary Canada, Australia, or Great Britain, where political power is largely unconsolidated and subject to extensive scrutiny. As the analyses of case studies examined in this book attempt to highlight, this theory is not always borne out in practice.

2. THE NEW FRENCH EXTREMITY EMERGES

When critic James Quandt framed a then recent grouping of French films by Gaspar Noé, Claire Denis, and Bruno Dumont, as part of what he pejoratively labeled a "New French Extremity" (18), he was reprimanding such filmmakers for what he saw as exploiting tactics traditionally associated with genres of excess, like pornography and horror. Mainly a response to Bruno Dumont's 2003 film *Twentynine Palms*, Quandt criticized what he saw as the promising young filmmaker (whose *Humanité* was awarded the Jury Prize at the 1999 Cannes Film Festival) jumping on board with an ill-advised, decidedly "commercial" arthouse trend. Ironically, defenders of the films that Quandt disparagingly labelled as the "New French Extremity" have embraced the term for its usefulness in conceptually linking certain formal characteristics and aesthetic strategies of early twentieth-century European art films (my use of the label, and its more internationally inclusive counterpart the "New Cinematic Extremism," is by no means intended to echo its pejorative use by Quandt).

The extensive reformation of the Western censorship policies and practices that took place in the early part of the twenty-first century seemed significantly to coincide with the emergence of this trend in French filmmaking, in which new and abrasive forms of cinema were dealing frankly and graphically with the body. In his book *Brutal Intimacy*, Tim Palmer offers an alternative to Quandt's label for conceptualizing these films, not by singling out their transgressive elements as the basis of new genre formation, but instead by suggesting the idea of a "cinéma du corps," whose basic agenda, "an onscreen interrogation of physicality in brutally intimate terms," offers an increasingly explicit discussion of the body through its sexual capacities, sexual conflicts (57). Palmer's categorization of the films has less to do with conventional markings of genre than with a conceptual linking of the films' unusual narrative, aesthetic, and stylistic strategies. Palmer points out that the international scrutiny provoked by these "films of the body" tends to overshadow the experimental stylistic treatment that makes them so affecting in both conception and execution (59). In other words, it has been easier for audiences and critics to dismiss the cinéma du corps for its use of graphic physicality than to gauge its status as a conceptually dynamic model of filmmaking. Importantly, while these films depict acts that may be shocking, they often work through techniques that heighten the sensory involvement of audiences and work to question spectatorial complicity in desire, as related to representations of sex and violence onscreen (Horeck and Kendall 1). In so doing, they have the effect of overhauling the traditional passive role of the film viewer and demanding, instead, a viscerally engaged participant (see Metz for critical theories of passivity).

This chapter examines four illustrative examples that typify both the aesthetic adventurousness and scandalous reception of the New French Extremity, with distinctive respective contextual focuses: *I Stand Alone* (violence), *Baise-moi* (sexuality), *Trouble Every Day* (critical response), and *Twentynine Palms* (genre experimentation).

I Stand Alone

Perhaps unsurprisingly, innovations in the stylistic presentation of violence tend to significantly coincide with changes in film content restriction, either by immediately preceding or following them. This is demonstrably true of French director Gaspar Noé's work, but also of the work of the filmmakers to whom his debut feature *Seul contre tous* (or *I Stand Alone*) (1999) owes a substantial artistic debt. *I Stand Alone* is perhaps the foundational text of the New French Extremity—with its peculiar blend of Hitchcockian immersivity and Godardian self-reflexivity (which would become the NFE's signature style). Noé's filmmaking draws heavily from traditions of European Art cinema, particularly the Brecht-inspired aesthetic strategies of the French New Wave but also, more relevantly in this context, the striking and vivid violence that permeated mainstream American film culture in the wake of the dismantling of the Production Code in the late 1960s and early 1970s.

The critical and commercial success of Arthur Penn's *Bonnie and Clyde* (1967) and Sam Peckinpah's *The Wild Bunch* (1969) signaled not only the dramatic appeal of violent spectacles, of slow-motion images of blood and flesh bursting out of bodies (made possible by new squib special effects technology), but also the increasingly blurred moral boundaries separating the villains who perpetrated and the heroes who rectified it. Since its initial implementation in 1934, the Hollywood Production Code had limited the explicitness of onscreen violence but, perhaps more significantly, ensured that its presentation upheld a system of moral rectitude, in which characters engaged in cruelty and sadism were punished for their actions. Audience identification with such characters was consciously and carefully delimited and guided. In short, the moral structure of classical Hollywood violence was relatively clear. For those critical of Hollywood's newfound fondness for explicit and hyper-stylized violence in early 1970s cinema, frequent moral ambiguity was among its most alarming aspects.

Chief among these detractors, and notably expressive, was famed *New Yorker* critic Pauline Kael, who wrote in response to Stanley Kubrick's heavily stylized dystopian sci-fi epic *A Clockwork Orange* (1971): "At the movies, we are gradually being conditioned to accept violence as a sensual pleasure [. . .] The directors used to say they were showing us its real face and how ugly it was in order to sensitize us to its horrors. You don't have to be very keen to see that they are now in fact de-sensitizing us. They are saying that everyone is brutal, and the heroes must be as brutal as the villains, or they turn into fools" (51). A wider reading of Kael's critical work clearly indicates that her concern about the increasing visibility and commercial appeal of violence in Hollywood cinema was not merely rooted in conservative prudishness. Her articulate and vociferous prose expressed profound observations regarding the changing sensibilities of audiences and filmmakers, sentiments lent considerable credibility by her status in the critical community. And Kael was prescient in her critique of *A Clockwork Orange*. Despite its wildly innovative visual presentation, the film does indeed approach onscreen violence with a flippancy and amorality that was typical of narratives gaining prevalence in the period, such as Alejandro Jodorowsky's *El Topo* (1970), Don Siegel's *Dirty Harry* (1971), and Mike Hodges's *Get Carter* (1971).

However, Kael's reasoning does obscure the impact of such violence by conflating two distinct issues: stylization and morality. The aesthetic presentation of violence popularized by 1970s Hollywood auteur filmmakers including Kubrick, Penn, Peckinpah, and Scorsese may have alarmed commentators for its potential to slip into the realm of garish spectacle, but the breakdown of distinctions between heroes and villains in their work clearly speaks to the real dilemmas of social violence plaguing American society in those years. Events like Watergate, the Vietnam War, and widespread civil rights protests resulted in increasing cultural strife and morally complex social dilemmas, in the atmosphere of which moral distinctions between corrupted heroes and self-righteous villains became difficult to draw.

It is essential to distinguish between the elements of post-Code cinematic violence upon which Noé's filmmaking draws heavily and those it thoroughly works to subvert. His debut feature *I Stand Alone* clearly channels the alienation, urban blight, and relentlessly oppressive social milieu of Scorsese's *Taxi Driver* (1976). The film's protagonist, known only as the "Butcher" (Philippe Nahon), is a disaffected anti-hero driven, like Scorsese's Travis Bickle (Robert De Niro), to violent aggression by his disgust with what he perceives as the moral degeneracy and breakdown of white, Christian, Anglo-Saxon values that characterize his social existence. The Butcher's nightly sojourns through the slums of Paris, deriding and condemning the desperate actions of impoverished (mainly immigrant) groups, recall Bickle's journeys through the crime-ridden streets of 1970s New York. Noé has ironically made the Butcher a morally contemptible being whose own self-hatred, or self-anointment, frequently manifests in displays of xenophobia, racism, and misogyny. Through his unrelenting voiceover narration and his increasingly pathetic life circumstances, the Butcher manages a perhaps surprising appeal to the viewer's investment of attention. Like *Taxi Driver*, *I Stand Alone* culminates with a shockingly bloody and disturbing (but in this case imagined) act of violence, as he vividly contemplates murdering (with compassion) his autistic, institutionalized daughter before taking his own life in a final gesture of contempt for a world he unequivocally blames for his own continued misery. Noé does not shy away from the complex ambiguity of the subject's destructive and embittered thought processes. The Butcher's defiant and venomous rejection of life, society, and love is shown to manifest simultaneously as lumpen resentment taken out against people of color, as much as against the all-empowered system that, by way of his perpetual unemployment and disenfranchisement, really is stepping on him.

While the powerfully harrowing climax of *I Stand Alone* shares certain similarities with that of *Taxi Driver*, specifically in terms of graphic bloodletting at the hands of its protagonist, a thorough understanding of their dissimilarities is crucial to a nuanced appreciation of Noé's beliefs about the place and role of violence in social existence. While the narrative (and thus moral) context for the violence is parallel in some respects—both characters are utterly alienated from social institutions like family, religion, and community, as well as profoundly disillusioned by social conditions like war and poverty—its aesthetic presentation is very different. The gory shootout that forms the climax of *Taxi Driver*, for example, in which Bickle, a damaged (likely traumatized) Vietnam veteran, murders a violent street pimp named Sport (Harvey Keitel) and several of his criminal associates, encapsulates Kael's concerns about modern cinematic heroes becoming "as brutal as the villains." And as Cynthia Fuchs notes in her analysis of the sequence, its moral distinctions become increasingly difficult to maintain: "Sport and Travis will meet at this self-reflexive crossroads as a mirror [. . .] (a place) where the cowboys look like Indians, where Americans were killing themselves as well as others in Vietnam, where difference is made similarity" ("Vietnam" 46). Linda Ruth Williams has added that the effect of this blurring is twofold: "Not only does the image of the enemy become unclear; the image of the self becomes deeply unsettling" (160). Noé takes Scorsese's theme a step further, making it explicit as visual text. The Butcher's self-hatred, so routinely camouflaged throughout *I Stand Alone* as hatred for the degenerate "Other," is entirely self-directed by the film's conclusion. His violent desires turn inward, as he and those he loves most sincerely have become the true threatening Other (or in the Butcher's case, dream of the Other).

As anti-heroes, Bickle and the Butcher are made sympathetic via similar cinematic and storytelling devices: interior monologue indicating they are always thinking to themselves; starkly photographed squalor depicting their forced abodes; allegiance to a younger and defenseless female. However, the violent outbursts that conclude their journeys are markedly different in their impacts, with *I Stand Alone* completely eschewing the emotionally cathartic and viscerally exhilarating violence of *Taxi Driver*. Scorsese and his producer, Michael Phillips, initially encountered some difficulty when submitting *Taxi Driver* for review by the MPAA. As Phillips recalls: "The ratings board wanted to give *Taxi Driver* an X rating. We played a game with them. We desaturated the color of some of the blood at the end and sent the film to them so many times that they became desensitized. We got congratulated on changes that we never made" (qtd. in Priggé 108). Phillips's recollection rather amusingly raises the question of whether censors are themselves vulnerable to the same desensitization they frequently warn against. However, upon the R-rated release of *Taxi Driver*, Scorsese himself noticed that audiences were "reacting very strongly" to the shootout sequence:

> And I was disturbed by that. It wasn't done with that intent. You can't stop people from taking it that way . . . And you can't stop people from getting exhilaration from violence because that's human. But the exhilaration of the violence that's in *Taxi Driver*—because it's shot a certain way, and I know how it's shot, because I shot it and I designed it—is also in the creation of that scene in the editing, in the camera moves, in the use of music, and the use of sound effects, and in the movement within the frame of the characters . . . And that's where the exhilaration comes in. (Qtd. in Prince, "Aesthetics" 199)

While he clearly sought to disassociate himself from the aggressive reactions of exhilarated viewers, his comments on the construction of the sequence indicate that if Scorsese was sensitive to his audience's response, he was also "keenly responsive to the physical and artistic pleasures of crafting screen violence" (199). Despite its not being intended to evoke violent fantasies in its viewers, *Taxi Driver* was at least once loudly claimed to have done so, becoming, as press reports repeatedly had it, the obsession of John Hinckley Jr., whose attempted assassination of Ronald Reagan in 1981 reinvigorated the frequent argument of censors regarding the imitability of certain presentations of screen violence.

In *I Stand Alone*, by contrast, there is no final catharsis or seductive excitement in the Butcher's descent into violence. His blunt interior monologue continues, growing more frantic as it becomes ensconced in a language of pure existential dread and terror when he watches his daughter die by his hand. The Butcher shoots her in the neck, and she falls to the floor bleeding and convulsing. The Butcher's horrified expression registers her suffering, as guttural moans and a rapid heartbeat fill the accompanying soundtrack. Noé cleverly mounts the camera on actor Philippe Nahon's chest for an extended shot, creating a disorientating effect whereby his surroundings twist and distort, while his terror and grief-stricken face fill the center of the frame. These effects combine in a truly nightmarish sequence that may fill the spectator with not exhilaration but a sense of abject dread and terror. In this respect, Noé's construction of the sequence, the visceral quality with which he communicates the existential dread and futility of the horror onscreen, suggests that he was perhaps better able than Scorsese to disengage himself from the sensuous gratifications of assembling cinematic violence. Noé's talent for showing violence as only regrettable, repulsive, and shameful renders unthinkable the capacity for viewers to derive any sort of pleasure from, or desire to imitate, the Butcher's actions.

The contrast between the implications of Noé's violence and Scorsese's is made narratively explicit in the codas of the two films. Bickle, it is revealed, was shown mercy by the courts, which saw grim but undeniable merit in his actions of liberating a teenage prostitute (Jodie Foster) from Sport's abusive subjugation. He is released and becomes a minor vigilante folk hero, while a final shot indicates that his mental instability continues. The Butcher, by contrast, is revealed to have only imagined his crime. Its vivid and horrific detail breaks him emotionally, and he weeps by his daughter's side, begging her (and by extension the spectator) for forgiveness. The resolution is at once tragic and an overwhelming relief to an audience which has endured the horror that could have been. Despite being drawn to brutality as a subject, Noé is a director in moral control of his material.

Baise-moi

The connection between self-reflexive aesthetic strategies, violent sexuality, and polarized reception, with which the "New French Extremity" is most frequently associated, is exemplified vividly by Virginie Despentes and Coralie Trinh Thi's *Baise-moi* (2000). Translated to English as "Kiss Me" and/or "Fuck Me," *Baise-moi* tells the story of two alienated young women, Nadine (Karen Lancaume) and Manu (Raffaëla Anderson), who embark upon a killing spree across France after suffering humiliation and mistreatment (mainly at the hands of men) in every aspect of their punishing social existence. The film is extremely violent and features scenes containing what appears to be non-simulated, penetrative sexual action. *Baise-moi* is also strikingly clever, offering biting social commentary on such issues as violent media, gender politics, fame, and celebrity.

The film presents a postmodern narrative in which the characters are seemingly wholly aware of the contradictions and complexities of their roles as transgressive feminist vigilantes. Like Oliver Stone's *Natural Born Killers* (1994), the film delves into the dual role of violence in contemporary society as a scourge on degenerating social morality but also a glamorized preoccupation of media attention. *Baise-moi*'s characters are obsessed with (and encouraged by) their representation in media as disenfranchised vigilantes, fighting back against repressive patriarchal suppression and rejecting hypocritical social mores and taboos. This postmodern self-reflexivity is also seen in the presence of *I Stand Alone* on a background television—which the filmmakers include to conceptually link their film to Noé's similarly abrasive and confrontational aesthetics.

Wherever *Baise-moi* premiered, firestorms of controversy followed. Its classification proving problematic in France, Britain, and Australia, it was widely censored with varying degrees of severity. The film's transgressions against social sensitivities and cultural tastes are numerous and dramatic, but the most apparently egregious was an early violent scene in which the younger of the two protagonists, Manu, is gang-raped in a dingy but brightly lit public parking garage unit. In a particularly flagrant gesture of confrontational self-reflexivity, the actual penetration of the actress, Raffaëla Anderson, is briefly shown onscreen. Captured in a medium shot, which excludes the possibility of "stunt genitalia" allowed in films such as Lars Von Trier's *The Idiots* (1998), this relatively few seconds of content had a disproportionate impact on the film's cultural status. The strategy of using actual sex is typical of the way in which New Extremity filmmakers employ distancing techniques to encourage viewers to reflect on the spectatorial experience. The scene is less shocking for its actual content—most adults acknowledge that heterosexual acts involve a penis entering a vaginal opening—than for its visual presentation of this content. Mainstream audiences are not necessarily accustomed to watching other people having sex, and so the actual visual image of penetration is something strange, and potentially shocking, for unsuspecting viewers. The inclusion of penetration puts these viewers in an extremely intimate voyeuristic stance, and if one had never thought through the implications of being a voyeur, this effect is potentially quite jarring.

From a classification standpoint, this sequence is enough to immediately place *Baise-moi* in the category of "violent pornography," a designation that piques the worst fears of moral crusaders for whom film retains potential to threaten what they celebrate as conservative values and traditional standards of decency. For example, the Ontario Film Review Board (Canada)—tasked with classifying *Baise-moi* in early 2001—demanded that twelve seconds be excised from the rape scene (Whyte A29). Comments by the Board's then chair, Robert Warren, indicate that while the content itself was problematic, the more explosive issue (as is so often the case in reception of "New French Extremity" films) was, oddly, *Baise-moi*'s transgression of genre boundaries: its resistance to distinct categorization. In an interview with a Toronto newspaper, Warren remarked as to the Board's somewhat wooden policy:

> Our criteria for mainstream movies is that any explicit sex has to be limited, brief and non-violent. If it's not limited, it goes into the adult sex category. If it's not brief, it goes into the adult sex category. If it's violent, it doesn't go anywhere. (Qtd. in MacKenzie 21)

Even following the implementation of the Film Classification Act in 2005, the Board still employs the blanket designation "mainstream" to distinguish non-pornographic films from those it still retains the remit to censor. Yet the definition of what constitutes an "adult sex" film has shifted considerably, seemingly in accordance with whether or not "audience arousal" can be seen as the primary intention of the filmmaker. Changes in classification guidelines dictated by the Act seem quite deliberately aimed at minimizing the likelihood of this category sharing any overlap with notably graphic "mainstream" films. Janet Robinson, the Board's current chair, even once cited *Baise-moi* as a film she believes would easily pass—penetration shots intact—under the revised guidelines (Davidson 9). It turns out the change in guidelines prompted by the Film Classification Act's implementation were concerned less with the actual images and content appearing onscreen than with films' (and by proxy filmmakers') "general character" and "integrity." Analysis of the OFRB's shifting policies in the early 2000s sheds some welcome light on the rationale underlying these at times puzzling and frustratingly murky semantic distinctions.

If Cronenberg's *Crash* could be defended too easily as a work of considerable artistic merit, in some sense *Baise-moi* is its antithesis. To say the film was somehow "misunderstood" by OFRB reviewers is perhaps disingenuous, as Despentes and Trinh Thi introduce many elements that call out for their film to be classified as pornography (of these the presence of actual penetration is only one). The film's cheap and, at times, tacky video aesthetic is as blatant a self-reflexive nod to the pornography genre as its use of veteran adult film actresses in the lead roles. The violence (aimed primarily though not exclusively at male characters) has a pornographic quality, too, complete with fetishizing of firearms, seductive build-ups, and climaxes of bloody, murderous "money shots." The filmmakers introduce all of this knowingly, no doubt, utilizing these elements to draw attention, negative or positive, to the film's radical feminist attitudes. For one example, after Manu's gang rape, she is asked how she can remain cavalier about her victimization. She responds: "I leave nothing precious in my cunt for those jerks. It's just a bit of cock." This line functions as an unmistakable assertion of female agency: a rejection of the idea that female victims are powerless and lose the ability to define their own circumstances. However, defending this important sentiment (exemplary of the film's undeniable merit) with the claim that it is inextricably tied to the use of actual penetration is a difficult challenge. Simulated sexual violence and non-simulated sexual activity are sufficiently confrontational in themselves to draw critical attention to deeper themes. As the Board's verdict indicates, the notion of incorporating real sex into a stylized depiction of rape may indeed be wading into morally precarious waters.

A common defense against censorial claims emphasizes that what is depicted onscreen is not reality, but fictional simulation. Were a filmmaker to instruct actors to commit actual violence upon one another, for instance, this defence would become untenable. By inserting actual penetration into a scene containing simulated violence, Despentes and Trinh Thi blur this conceptual division and complicate the spectator's ethical relationship with the images onscreen in a deliberate and highly provocative fashion (see MacKenzie).

In Australia, *Baise-Moi* was refused classification. Attorney-General Daryl Williams reported in a press release that the OFLC's Review Board "took into account the combination of: strong depictions of violence; sexual violence, frequent actual, detailed sex scenes and scenes which demean both women and men" (qtd. in Kampmark 346). The press release also describes the effect of such a decision, which argued that "strong depictions of realistic violence were shown and it was considered that some scenes were gratuitous." The same was said of the sexual violence, which was unduly "high impact" in its depictions of such scenes as Manu's rape (353). Even in the film's native France, where it initially received a "16+" rating, *Baise-moi* was reclassified as "18+" after challenges from the conservative activist group Promouvoir (Keslassy), a prime example of the external pressure applied by advocacy institutions upon the practices and processes of governmental review boards (France possesses its own national Review Board—regulated by the National Film Board and comprised of parents, psychologists, and various organizations dedicated to protecting families and children—which recommends certificates for films in four categories: all audiences; -12, [prohibiting a film to viewers under 12 years of age]; -16; and -18).

Trouble Every Day

In near equal measure, journalistic reviews fervidly complimented and vehemently countered the censorious approach of classification boards to *I Stand Alone* and *Baise-moi*. However, nowhere was the polarizing effect on critics more evident than in the notable controversies New French Extremity films proved capable of generating throughout the international film festival circuit. When Denis premièred her neo-gothic vampire art film *Trouble Every Day* at Cannes in 2001, *The Guardian* wrote: "The first full-blown scandal of the Cannes film festival erupted last night over the lurid French film *Trouble Every Day*, in which the Gallic sex symbol Beatrice Dalle has sex with, murders and cannibalises four men. Even the French critics booed and walked out" (Gibbons and Jeffries 6). The article then cites, as its primary evidence for the "full-blown" scale of this particular scandal, an excerpt from French critic Jean-Paul Marceau's review, which read: "The film is terrible. There is no redeeming context. The horror seems quite gratuitous . . . I can't admire this" (6). The language of the Marceau review suggests an uncommonly personal mode of critical engagement, yet one wholly typical of the New French Extremity's broader critical reception. Marceau's sentiments are typical not in severity alone but more precisely in focussing on *Trouble Every Day*'s apparent lack of a legitimizing contextual framework for its graphic violence, as well as in highlighting his personal stance toward his own experience of viewing the film.

Like *I Stand Alone* and *Baise-moi*, *Trouble Every Day* is ultimately an exercise in genre transgression. It draws heavily upon iconography from Hollywood horror cinema (such as, in this case, *Near Dark* [1987] and *The Lost Boys* [1987]) and, like the early work of the Nouvelle Vague filmmakers in the 1960s, reinterprets the language of mainstream genre convention through a new discursive lens. The film follows the story of Shane (Vincent Gallo), an American pharmaceutical scientist using his honeymoon in Paris as pretense to track down a former colleague (Alex Descas) in hopes that he will find a cure for his own illness, which seems sporadically to induce psychosexual cannibalistic behaviour. *Trouble Every Day*'s two relatively brief scenes of cannibalistic violence are indeed explicit (perhaps less so than its reputation suggests), but have still too often been unfairly characterized as prioritizing the visceral thrills of the mainstream over the critical element of discourse in art cinema. As Denis remarked in the film's pre-screening press conference at Cannes: "Being explicit is not what I'm interested in, and I don't think (the film) is about cannibalism. It's about desire and how close the kiss is to the bite. I think every mother wants to eat her baby with love. We just took this on to a new frontier" (qtd. in Gibbons and Jeffries 6). Although the film's striking visual allusions to Hollywood horror, as well as its highly cerebral reasoning behind including such images, provide more-than-sufficient cultural context for even the most abrasive of visceral images, *Trouble Every Day*'s oblique and measured storytelling apparently failed to offer critics a sufficient narrative framework for interpretation.

The notion of horror imagery requiring a legitimizing framework to facilitate productive criticism recalls Martine Beugnet's suggestion that when critics respond negatively to the explicit content of a film like *Trouble Every Day*, they are responding indirectly to the fact that it does not fully conform to the generic categories it evokes (37). The sex and violence are seen as too explicit *for an art film* and their de-narrativization for affective purposes (to stimulate certain experiences of embodied spectatorship through heightened sensory impact) is misread as a presentation of "shock" simply for its own sake. Approaching the self-reflexive techniques of Denis and her contemporaries from an economic standpoint, Hampus Hagman identifies them as pragmatic strategies of promotion: part of an "affect economy" in which techniques "designed to keep viewers talking about a film after it ends" compensate for the limited advertising resources available to independent arthouse filmmakers (36). Hagman elaborates:

> If these films make their mark primarily through their "gross-out"—or even "walk-out"—factor, then clearly there is another form of "branding" going on than the one traditionally associated with the art film, where the "brand name" of the auteur is what draws the audience. When the auteur becomes provocateur, the extra-filmic attraction value is shifted from the "unique vision" of the director to the effects of the spectator, which become a marketing force in its own right [. . .] By mixing traditional art-filmic markers with exploitation and genre elements, the films do not conform to any ready-made critical categories. The measure of success for these "hybrid" films instead becomes to what extent they are able to produce an audience. (37)

The combined commercial success and international notoriety of, for example, Noé's work, suggest such strategies can succeed regardless of whether they represent the true intentions of the artist. They can be useful in drawing attention from international audiences to foreign films with low production and promotional budgets. However, as Hagman astutely observes, the visceral affective impact of such embodiment strategies has the additional effect of prompting critics to discuss the films primarily in terms of "personal experiences and stances toward them" (38), frequently expressed in public performances of frustration, boredom, and revulsion.

Although it is a "genre" film of sorts, *Trouble Every Day* fails to adhere to classical standards of categorization and was thus dismissed by critics reluctant to re-evaluate their own criteria for typification. Such resistance to new and dynamic models of filmmaking can be problematic, as critics play a significant role in the shaping of an ever-evolving film culture. As an offshoot of the film industry's advertising, journalistic reviewing is part of the mass media and, accordingly, of the "corporate controlled consciousness industry," which, as Jansen argues, arbitrates between individuals and "changes of the market" to "manage consumer demands for commodities, as well as ideas, candidates, and lifestyles" (138). Journalistic reviewing not only publicizes the film industry and sustains the habit of moviegoing but (along with academic criticism) helps to define "the grounds and bounds of interpretive activity, the direction of analogical thinking, the proper goals, the permissible solutions, and the authority that can validate the interpretations produced by ordinary criticism" (Bordwell 33).

Despite the resulting potential of critical censure for damage, Denis emerged from the *Trouble Every Day* "scandal" relatively unscathed. She returned to Cannes in 2015 with *Bastards*, a similarly genre-transcending neo-noir art thriller, which received largely favorable reviews.

Twentynine Palms

It is perhaps unsurprising that it was Bruno Dumont's *Twentynine Palms* that prompted James Quandt to seek a label for its apparently new cross-categorical sub-genre. The film, perhaps more than any with which it has been conceptually linked, epitomizes the NFE's confrontational blending of stark genre contrasts—namely (but not solely) "art" and "exploitation" traditions. Dumont is more extreme in this regard than his artistic predecessors (Kubrick, Jodorowsky, Von Trier, Zulawski, Haneke, et cetera). *Twentynine Palms* goes beyond the use of surreal imagery with generic points of reference, as well as the combining of "high" and "lowbrow" influences, et cetera. Dumont himself has referred to it as an "experimental horror film" (qtd. in Coulthard 171), a somewhat perplexing construction that carries a considerable weight of cultural baggage.

The culturally and economically marginalized cinema of the avant-garde and the commercially celebrated tradition of horror (and more generally genre) filmmaking are in some ways completely at odds with one another—almost opposites; or mutually exclusive—with the implementation of one demanding, by extension, the negation of the other. Historically, genre frameworks are not especially accommodating to narratological and formal experimentation, because signifiers of genre serve a very particular purpose: to locate dramatic action with established, pre-invented modes of storytelling. The content of genre film is almost always established in existing models of fiction narrative, most often incorporating traditional elements of fantasy and mythology. Because generic models allow dramatic events to unfold with a degree of predictability, genre acts as an agreement between filmmakers and audiences ensuring that established expectations are met. While the machinery of this arrangement affords filmmakers the opportunity to produce innovative work within the boundaries of immediately familiar archetypes, genre filmmaking more often reflects a limiting of original design and structure to ensure commercial viability. As an "experimental" genre film, *Twentynine Palms* forgoes strict adherence to generic codes of representation. While elements in the narrative demonstrate a basis in genre foundations, the overall product displays a much more diverse stock of artistic inspiration and content. As such, it is a film that can (and must) be analyzed separately from antiquated and trans-historical approaches to genre.

Furthermore, the type of experimentation that characterizes Dumont's film is worth distinguishing from mere genre revisionism. From the standpoint of critical studies, revision is no less integral to notions of genre than tradition, however the extent of experimentation in revisionist genre films typically consists of exposing generic formulas, as opposed to subverting them in a valuable or experimental way. This is perhaps not surprising: genuinely subverting the expectations of audiences is a precarious strategy from both commercial and critical perspectives. If a genre film fails to cater to viewer expectation, it stands at the risk of being disregarded. A genre exercise without commercial appeals is inevitably considered a failure or redundancy. It is this inherently commercial nature of genre that has traditionally placed it at odds with artistic innovation in cinema. Rick Altman has summarized this tension concisely by stating that if spectators are to experience films in terms of their genre, "films must leave no doubt as to their generic identity; instant recognizability must be assumed" (18).

Additionally, if the borders of genres are not defined clearly enough, genre criticism becomes extremely difficult to facilitate. Genre films that fail to adhere to classical standards of controlled separation risk being ignored by critics of genre study. This may prompt the critic to re-evaluate his or her own criteria for separation; but it may just as easily result in films that fail to exhibit clear generic qualifications being "systematically disregarded" by genre film critics seeking to provide material for the theoretical frameworks adopted by genre criticism (17). As a result, genuine genre subversion tends to severely limit the likelihood of a particular film finding the commercial audience or critical reception it may well deserve. *Twentynine Palms*, an extraordinarily affecting film that has all but faded into critical and commercial obscurity since its release, is clear evidence of this phenomenon.

Dumont's filmmaking aligns more closely with the visual arts (painting, sculpture, et cetera) than with the dominant modes of narrative storytelling one is sometimes quickest to associate with commercial filmmaking. The common conception of the relationship between films and their viewers is one where the viewer interacts with the film primarily by decoding its narrative and by allowing him or herself to be wholly absorbed in the illusion of reality created by the film. This "D. W. Griffith-style" of narrative cinema is so ubiquitous, it becomes easy to forget that its emergence does not necessarily represent the development of cinema's "natural" language (but merely its most instantly recognizable commercial format). Dumont is clearly approaching cinema with a different emphasis. *Twentynine Palms* does not appear to be designed primarily to entertain or tell a story, but rather to experiment with the formal and visual properties and capabilities of the moving image.

The most engaging element of the film is its deliberate emphasis on principles of structural organization. Its compositions, editing, shot lengths, and soundtrack, are organized into patterns and structures that relate directly to sensory experience and issues of perception, more so than serving the illusory purposes of narrative cinema. The film certainly has a narrative structure (not aspiring to the non-narrative experimental cinema of Stan Brakhage or Michael Snow). However, it operates in what can perhaps be more constructively thought of as non-classical narrative form. The story being told is not the focus, but a framing device for communicating concepts and emotions.

A thirty-something couple, David (David Wissak) and Katia (Yekaterina Golubev), are traveling to Twentynine Palms, California (an actual town between Los Angeles and Las Vegas) to scout locations for a photo shoot. They stop at motels, diners, gas stations. They drift aimlessly on foot through desert landscapes. They bicker about trivial matters. They have a fair share of what appears as alienated, passionless sex. They struggle to communicate on any meaningful or intimate emotional level—partly due to a language barrier (David speaks English, Katia speaks Russian, both speak some broken French).

Then, approximately 100 minutes into a film containing huge stretches of what some viewers have labeled "nothingness," David's Humvee is rammed off the road by a pickup truck. A gang of unidentified males exit the truck and attack the couple on a stretch of deserted highway. David is sexually assaulted, while Katia is forced to watch. Shortly following the attack, David stabs Katia to death in a scene that pays visual homage to Hitchcock's *Psycho* (much as echoes of John Boorman's *Deliverance* were evoked in the previous sequence). These allusions to generic points are clear and pronounced, yet also cluttered into the last twenty minutes of the film. As mentioned, most of what precedes them is (at the narrative level) extraordinarily mundane. However, both the scenes of violence and the scenes of "nothingness" are no more about *what* one sees than *how* one sees it. Dumont organizes the actual processes of creative expression particular to cinema in ways that increase the sensory impact of the film and encourage the spectator to reflect on the experience of watching as it happens.

For example, the film's soundtrack is decidedly atypical of horror genre context. It consists exclusively of real sound, recorded on location, and a total absence of musical score or any other non-diegetic soundtrack. The film's editing likewise provides a sharp contrast to the frenetic cutting of mainstream early-2000s commercial horror films, with shots dramatically exceeding the length necessary to convey narrative information. Every shot lingers onscreen with a silence and stillness conducive to contemplation (in similar fashion to a painted artwork). This applies not only to the moments of sex and violence, but also to the large stretches of narrative "nothingness" they punctuate. It is the latter moments that are perhaps most resistant to genre typology, and to decoding within the context of myth and familiarity.

In interviews, Dumont has refused to speak on theories of the film's subtext (going as far as to deny there even is one). When asked where *Twentynine Palms* originates from conceptually, he responded that it is based on his own experiences in the American West, where he spent time as a tourist in Joshua Tree desert. While passing Twentynine Palms, he recalls how he "suddenly became afraid, and stayed that way" (qtd. in Flowers). This was apparently not a fear of anything precise or tangible, but rather an overwhelming sense of ambiguous dread and impending terror. Dumont's cinema is an extremely personal one, his films being very lyrical in style. Indeed, the limited scholarship that does exist surrounding *Twentynine Palms* does struggle to map out the film's associative organization of symbolism. Despite the intentionally thin narrative, there are certain visual motifs that might facilitate such discussions. For example, extra-textual knowledge of the real Twentynine Palms as a city with a large military and marine presence, combined with imagery including David's Humvee and the expansive landscapes of the American West, might call out for interpretation of the film as a (distinctly French) meditation on American foreign policy.

Such readings, however, neglect the film's primarily *conceptual* origin. It would seem what Dumont seeks to convey with *Twentynine Palms* (and succeeds in doing so) is the purely sensory experience of being "afraid" in the deserts of California—a fear of something coming, something unknown, something inevitable. Ironically, he achieves this effect by stripping the film of adherence to generic "horror" codes—the kind that would normally ground viewers in narrative familiarity—as well as by way of structural organization and emphasis on the forms and processes of creative expression intrinsic to cinema. In so doing, the resulting film represents an exceedingly complex negotiation of audience expectation and artistic innovation.

The "New French Extremity"—both the films it refers to and the label itself—highlights the ways in which processes of classification and labeling produce social definitions of acceptable and worthwhile art. As a new and conceptually dynamic mode of filmmaking, the NFE (or its broader, more inclusive counterpart "new cinematic extremism") required measured consideration by censors, critics, and audiences specifically because of its "newness." As Marina Vaizey has argued:

> Labelling is part and parcel of the identification of art; and commercial pressures have further encouraged the fact that in some ways this labelling must take cognizance of the newness, hence originality, hence worth, both intellectual and monetary of contemporary art. What has happened is that, particularly now, art can be accredited only when a label is invented and accepted. (332)

The identification of films examined in this study and elsewhere as part of a "new cinematic extremism" is largely one that has been implemented by theorists in a primarily academic context. It would be misleading to suggest that the films selected for this study represent a definable artistic movement or a unified trend. Their points of divergence are as useful and instructive as their similarities and extra-textual connections. However, the censorship controversies that accompanied these releases played a key role in the movement's accreditation as art, and vice versa. Only once the movement had been named, and its primary tenets theorized, were censors able and willing to modify their previous systems of categorization and make allowances for the radically unconventional content of the films in question.

PART II

3. THE BANNING OF *FAT GIRL* IN ONTARIO

Film, like most forms of cultural production, is expected to be responsive to external social control. The character of such control dynamics is contextualized by specific national and regional factors. In Ontario, Canada, the relevant body has (until recently) been the Film Review Board, a rotating committee of classification "experts." Prior to 2019, all films required the approval of the Board before being distributed or exhibited in Ontario. This approval being mandated by law, any filmmaker refusing to comply could face legal consequences.

The legal dimension of the Ontario government's regulation of film content has the effect of equating certain forms of artistic expression with punishable criminality. Though rarely enforced, prosecution re-enforced the notion that government power remained the ultimate arbitrator of cinema's bounds of acceptability. This idea was problematic in many senses, not least of which is reflected in the idea that political power exists in a state of perpetual flux. The criteria by which cinematic expression could be declared criminal were subject to change, while the penalty of failing to comply remained constant.

Such issues came to light within the discourses surrounding OFRB's most recent high-profile controversy: its temporary refusal of classification to Catherine Breillat's critically lauded coming-of-age film *À ma sœur!* (2001), released to English-speaking markets as *Fat Girl*. The controversy surrounding this case demonstrates a rare instance of narrative filmmaking strategies constituting criminality, even though no aspect of the film and no part of the production process violated criminal law.

New Extremes and Classification Reform

By virtue of the way in which *Fat Girl*'s abrasive aesthetic strategies combine with its storyline, and because of Breillat's reputation for using conventions of pornography in works such as *Romance* (1999), the film seemed to enjoy fewer grounds for protection as a controversial artwork than did *Crash*, posing what appeared to members of the OFRB to be a more serious and complex moral and ethical challenge. The film offers the story of two teenage sisters, both of whom lose their virginity (shown in sequences that are frank and explicit at times) during a weekend vacation. The film was critically lauded upon its Canadian premiere at the Toronto International Film Festival in September of 2001, where it was shown in its entirety (exhibition at TIFF is exempt from the OFRB's strict review polices pertaining to general release). However, by November of that year, the OFRB had voted against classifying the film unless the distributors—Cowboy Pictures in New York, and Lions Gate films in British Columbia—made significant and dramatic cuts to the film's key explicit scenes. These companies unsuccessfully appealed the Board's objections, which, centering on the depiction of under-aged characters (not performers: the actresses were in fact over eighteen at the time of filming) in sexually explicit situations (containing prolonged, full-frontal nudity), were sufficient to prevent the film from being shown in Ontario until the decision was eventually overturned in 2003. While the OFRB was in the midst of a structural renovation, on the pattern modeled by the BBFC, changing its name from the Ontario Censor Board to the Ontario Film Review Board in the mid-1980s and prioritizing classification over traditional censorship, the *Fat Girl* affair highlighted the limit to which reform had thus far been carried. It ultimately led to the passing of the Ontario Film Classification Act in 2005, a legislation that restricts the board's power to ban "mainstream" films containing explicit scenes of violent sexuality, as well as imposing a mandate to consider the general character and integrity of films reviewed. This chapter argues that it may be possible to gain a greater understanding of the shift from blocking to typifying and protecting films by exploring how the revisions of the OFRB's policies corresponded with the aesthetic strategies of *Fat Girl*.

The role of the OFRB in the historical development of cinema censorship cannot be overlooked, especially in its structural relation to the British model, which has consistently provided a template for Western censorship boards in their movement closer to the American classification model—a response to the cultural prioritizing of artistic freedoms and consumer rights over the perceived potential "harm" of obscene content. Thus, the initial case presented by the OFRB against *Fat Girl*'s content, as well as its eventual withdrawal of refusal to classify the film, flow from broader trends regarding free expression already in place in Western liberal democracies.

The tasking of film content regulation at the provincial level in Canada (as opposed to more common National Boards) provides an interesting case regarding the importance of local standards and regional criteria involved in forming standards of acceptability and the frequent "provincial" concerns of (what are often seen as) narrow-minded and unsophisticated censors. Variance in classification policies from province to province indicate the extent to which censorship rationales and categorization standards are highly dependent on cultural context and exceedingly far from what can be considered objective realities.

The *Fat Girl* affair demonstrates the collapse of a long-lived model in which classification boards could persist in drawing distinct lines between a film, its content, the intentions of its author, and the potential effects of its release. Preceding the extensive revisions to its policies in the early 2000s that made this shift possible, the board made the ill-advised proclamation that it felt it could excise *Fat Girl*'s "potentially harmful" (indeed criminal) elements while simultaneously preserving the power of Breillat's intended message and upholding the value and importance of freedom of artistic expression. Analysis of the film, and of the Review Board's objections to it, quickly point out the illogical thinking behind this effort, which eventually proved disastrous in a fashion that demonstrated precisely why defending government censorship of motion pictures in the context of Western liberal democracies becomes a practical impossibility. *Fat Girl* and the Film Classification Act played notable roles in the development of systems for Review Board transparency and accountability, as well as in the complication of longstanding, taken-for-granted rationales for censorship. However, while installing certain protections for filmmakers' right of free expression, the notion of a more "liberal censorship" in Ontario brought a host of complications when it was put into practice.

Rejecting the Fat Girl

Between the obvious artistic merits of *Crash* and the questionability of *Baise-moi*'s morality lies the grey area in which OFRB reviewers found themselves in March of 2001 when faced with Breillat's *Fat Girl*. The film's scenes of young, teenage characters engaged in sexually explicit activity contain no shots of penetration or other un-simulated sexual activity, but effectively conjure scenarios that some took as clear representations of child pornography, the distribution of which is a criminal offense in Ontario. Beyond the similar challenges they posed to classification boards undergoing transitions, *Fat Girl* and *Baise-moi* share an important connection: both are works by female directors seeking to confound common feminist understanding by defying the usual patterns of "progressive" gender portrayals (Beugnet 47). A central influence on the "New French Extremity," Breillat has internationally achieved a coveted status as

French "Provoc-auteur" par excellence. Her confrontational style and readiness to engage in controversy date back to the release of her first feature, *A Real Young Girl*, in 1976. Her landmark feminist film, *Romance*, famously used non-simulated sex to tell the story of a young woman's harsh sexual awakening and, in the process, became one of the most widely debated French films of the 1990s (Palmer 62). With its explicit sexuality and themes of sadomasochism, *Romance* was denied classification in Australia in January of 2000, until it was rated R-18 on appeal (Grønstad 89). *Romance* became the first Australian R-rated film to contain actual sex, and Breillat's name became inextricably linked with global debates surrounding censorship.

Fat Girl, which explores sexual rites of passage through the eyes of two teenage sisters, posed a complex challenge to the OFRB's guidelines. On its initial submission, the Board requested cuts for *Fat Girl* that were distinctly more substantial than those for *Baise-moi*, demanding the removal of approximately fifteen minutes of content from two of the film's core thematic sequences, a stark difference from the twelve seconds of "objectionable" content in the latter. Asked once again to justify the Board's recourse to censorship, Robert Warren replied:

> We did not approve the film. There is a scene where a 15-year-old is shown in full frontal nudity in a sexual situation, and also a 13-year-old girl with partial nudity in a rape scene. That contravenes a section of the Theatres Act. (Qtd. in Baillie 30)

Warren's comments refer to a section of the Act that reserves the Board's right—acting *in loco parentis*, as it were—to reject a film that depicts sex-related nudity involving someone who is, or *appears* to be, underage. The rationale underlying this requirement has its origins in a mid-century initiative to control and regulate theatrical distribution in Ontario.

Introduced in 1953, the Ontario Theatres Act, hardly envisioned at the start as a moralist tool, published legislation for the establishment of licensing fees and official approval of construction and alteration plans for theatres throughout the province (Report 484). It being applied in the case of *Fat Girl* is merely the last in a long line of (somewhat curious) deployments geared toward controlling the exhibition of sexual materials across Ontario. For instance, in the mid-1970s the Act was amended specifically to address the proliferation of "sex" films exhibited in storefront theaters on Toronto's Yonge Street, requiring expansion of the Censor Board's control over all methods of reproducing moving pictures (including 8mm and videotape exhibitions) for public viewing or financial gain (Report 485). The updated Theatres Act forbade the public exhibition of hard-core pornography throughout the province, meaning that any such title would be subjected to severe cutting if submitted to the Board. In this case, the Act was exploited for the purposes of policing commercial sex, a tactic that has been connected to the expansion and deployment of policies that regard prostitution and pornography as antithetical to the reinvention of city centers as middle-class family-oriented consumption spaces:

> For those who would reclaim the city in the name of traditional values, X-rated bookstores and movie theaters, video palaces, topless bars, and peep-show parlours rank alongside the homeless and working poor as quality-of-life issues, a euphemism for class-motivated warfare on the visible effects of poverty economic disenfranchisement and difference perceived as deviance. (Papayanis in Tyner 114)

While the relationship between cinema and measures of social control often bears this strong class dimension, more esteemed and prestigious cultural products do not always enjoy protection.

Shortly after the expansion of the Theatres Act, the Board cited the same section later used against *Fat Girl* as grounds for banning Volker Schlöndorff's *The Tin Drum* in 1979 (Veronneau 56), featuring scenes in which eleven-year-old actor David Bennent (playing a sixteen-year-old) appears to have intercourse with a sixteen-year-old girl (played by twenty-four-year-old Katharina Thalbach). Schlöndorff's film, it is worth noting, was awarded both the Palme d'Or at Cannes and the 1979 Academy Award for best Foreign Film. Despite these extremely prestigious accolades, and its resulting inarguable status as a serious work of cinematic art, *The Tin Drum*'s banning by the Ontario Censor Board meant that its exhibition would be a prosecutable offense under sections of the Criminal Code dealing with child pornography, and therefore that police action would be possible. The *Fat Girl* affair contained echoes of this previous controversy, but there is one substantial difference: unlike the case with Bennent, both lead actresses in Breillat's film are merely *portraying* under-aged characters.

The banning of *The Tin Drum* in Ontario demonstrates how, prior to the introduction of the Film Classification Act, the Board had little in the way of a system to ensure works of considerable artistic merit were afforded different review criteria than "Adult Sex Films." Their approach at the time thus implied an understanding of film content as being entirely separate, in its power and potential effects, from the intentions and reputation of the author. If an Academy Award was insufficient to relieve *The Tin Drum* of the stigma of child pornography, likely so too was anything else. Even following the Classification Act's implementation in 2005, the criteria for what separates "mainstream" and "pornographic" films in the Board's evaluation process remains somewhat ambiguous, but at least reflects concerns broader than just the content of the images onscreen. The Board defines "pornography" according to its primary intention being to arouse spectators. More specifically, the 2005 Act defines an "adult sex film" as any that has "as its main object, the depiction of explicit sexual activity," adding that "in the absence of evidence to the contrary, a film is presumed to be an adult sex film if there are words, images or a combination of them on the cassette or exterior container of the film that would lead a reasonable person to believe that the film is an adult sex film" (ontario.ca). Cinematic works designed with this purpose are, from a government standpoint, vices akin to drug use or gambling, requiring regulation to ensure that the health and safety of audiences do not become subordinate to the financial motives of filmmakers and producers. Such legislation obviously takes for granted the assumption that a film image could compromise someone's health and safety by virtue of "contaminated" content. Even if this conceit is granted, an author's intention remains a difficult thing to ascertain quantitatively, at least with any definitive certainty. If a situation presents itself in which the Board is skeptical of an artist's statements about the intention of his or her work, there is little that can be done systematically to address or disprove the claim. Thus, it seems, the Classification Act is less useful as a definitive guide to categorization of content and more fundamentally a way of formally ensuring that reviewers have some measure of discretion in deciding how to approach individual films on a case-by-case basis.

An important conceptual link remains between cinematic censorship of the past and the current classification model. As a system of categorization, classification may serve the (oft-stated) purpose of informing consumers as to the content of films they can potentially see, dictating the suitability of imagery for certain portions of a larger heterogeneous audience, but the categories it creates serve regulatory interests by leading to the establishment of different rules for different kinds of films. In short, it remains a process of sharpening and defining boundaries—between art and pornography, harmful and benign content, and between artistically serious and crassly exploitative filmmaking strategies. It is perhaps no surprise that films of the "New French Extremity" routinely presented review boards with difficult challenges. Films like *Baise-moi* and *Fat Girl* aim in completely the opposite direction, toward the dissolution of categorical boundaries. These films (perhaps intentionally) often evoke and incorporate tropes of genres of which the aesthetic goals are completely at cross-purposes to their own. Nowhere is this more obvious than in the case of Breillat's work, because to approach *Fat Girl* simplistically as child pornography is to completely neglect the context in which the film's nudity appears. That context is a new and different modality of looking that elicits neither voyeurism nor objectification, what Asbjørn Grønstad has referred to as Breillat's "de-pornofied" poetics of looking (10). Despite the film's reworking the conventions of pornography (and, to a lesser extent, horror cinema), serious critical analysis casts extreme doubt on any suggestion that its scenes of sex and violence are intended to mimic the aesthetic strategies of successful porn or horror productions, a conclusion that has continually been demonstrated by serious critical and scholarly readings of the two sequences identified as problematic by Warren and the OFRB's reviewers.

A Tale of Two Sisters

Fat Girl opens with a conversation between two sisters on rural holiday. Elena (Roxane Mesquida), the older, thinner, and more conventionally attractive of the two, is describing her desperate desire to lose her virginity and vows to pick up the next boy she meets. Her overweight, "ugly" sister, Anaïs (Anaïs Reboux), accuses her older sibling of having loose morals, a charge from Elena exempts herself on the grounds that she has, for too long, been saving her virginity for a romantically appropriate moment. Anaïs claims that she, by contrast, would rather lose her own virginity long before finding romantic love (as her first time, particularly in the mind of her imagined male suitor, "won't count").

Here, Breillat immediately establishes one of the film's main thematic concerns, that Elena, despite being the older and presumably more mature of the pair (based purely on her more extensive sexual experience), betrays a certain naivete in her understanding of love and gender relations. She envisions her "first time" as the perfect romantic moment, infused with storybook love and overwhelming passion, while Anaïs, despite her sexual inexperience, is clearly better able to separate romantic love from sex, an ability that will equip her to navigate the sometimes harsh and painful world of adolescent sexual awakening. Already, Breillat is using genre tropes to establish audience expectations that will ultimately be subverted.

Figure 3.1   Anaïs Reboux (l.) and Roxane Mesquida in Catherine Breillat's *Fat Girl* (Arte France Cinéma, CB Films, Canal+, Immagine e Cinema, et al., 2001).

As a teenage coming-of-age story, one might reasonably expect the film to relate Anaïs's overcoming of her pessimism about the intentions and nobility of future male partners by meeting a worthwhile suitor who proves to be the exception to her rule. By the end of the film, however, her negativity will be shown to be not only warranted but also essential to her emotional and psychological survival in coping with a series of traumatic events. This is one example of how the film subverts the conventions of the generic categories that its narrative is structured to evoke.

Arriving at a café, the girls meet an Italian law student named Fernando (Libero De Rienzo). Anaïs awkwardly watches Elena and Fernando engage in an overt mutual seduction, culminating in a long, impassioned kiss. Her role as a spectator of Elena's "romance" with Fernando becomes more dramatic when, a few scenes later, Elena sneaks Fernando into the bedroom of the family vacation home (a bedroom she shares with Anaïs). In a nearly twenty-minute sequence, Fernando attempts to seduce Elena with numerous false promises of love, subtly coercing her into surrendering her virginity while Anaïs secretly bears witness (pretending to be asleep). This theme of the third party (the viewer, by way of Anaïs) observing two people in lovemaking, with interest and care, is essential to the territory Breillat seeks to explore with regards to sexual awakening. The sequence provides a chilling depiction of sexual interaction seen as a site of power struggle. Fernando is initially very aggressive, removing Elena's clothes and caressing her body while professing his "love" for her. Yet, as Elena begins to display hesitation and a sudden fearful reluctance to be deflowered, his demeanour changes almost instantly. He grows despondent and acts disinterested, partly a manipulative performance but also one that betrays sincere frustration. Elena relays her concern that "sleeping" with him might cause him to lose romantic interest in her. On the surface, this seems to run counter to her faith in romantic love. However, Elena too is engaged in an act of manipulation. She is (perhaps even subconsciously) attempting to elicit a particular response from Fernando, one that will be sufficient to negate the fears she is expressing. Whether or not she truly believes his promises, she requires them if she wishes to retain any hope of placing her growing sexual desires in an appropriately "romantic" context.

Elena proceeds to lift her translucent nightgown, exposing her pubic area, as Fernando climbs on top of her. The camera briefly shifts to a shot of Anaïs watching reluctantly from across the room, her hand draped across her face, again emphasizing her spectatorship. In the next shot, Elena becomes overwhelmed with emotion and stops Fernando as he is about to enter her. She explains that she is not ready and begs him to "give her time." Fernando responds cruelly, accusing her of "ruining everything." Elena's reaction is complex, and a testament to Mesquida's tremendous acting skill. In her soft-spoken, apologetic insistence that Fernando "give her time" is the simultaneous expression of guilt for "ruining" his plan and the dismal fear of allowing him to continue. Having highlighted the moment as one of painful ambivalence for Elena, the scene then continues for several minutes as Fernando caresses her partially nude body while requesting that she allow him to enter her anally, thereby preserving her virginity. As Elena's will is eventually weakened, the camera returns to the image of Anaïs watching, where it remains for most of the rest of the scene (while the sexual activity is heard in the background).

In her analysis of the sequence, Tanya Horeck identifies as a key aesthetic effect that although Elena is the one being seduced, the drama is played out on Anaïs's face (203). Hearing her sister's moans, which indeterminately indicate pain, pleasure, or some combination of the two, Anaïs's reaction is also, fittingly, one of ambivalence. She tosses in her bed, seeking simultaneously to take in what is happening across the room and to ignore it. Despite the ambiguity of her reaction her body language offers no suggestion that she derives any sort of voyeuristic pleasure from this act of spectatorship. Thus, any such pleasure on the part of the viewer, as he or she has come to identify with Anaïs's gaze, becomes nearly impossible.

Elaborating on her designing of the sequence, Breillat stated that she decided to shoot Anaïs during its sexual climax because "violation is more strongly felt from the other's perspective" (qtd. in Horeck 203). Through this distancing, Breillat resolves the ambiguity and defines the moment as violation, whereas one is less certain of Elena's position on the matter. In a brilliant use of strategic self-reflexivity, typical of New French Extremity aesthetics, Breillat is seeking to viscerally involve the spectator by aligning his or her experience with the image of Anaïs's own spectatorship.

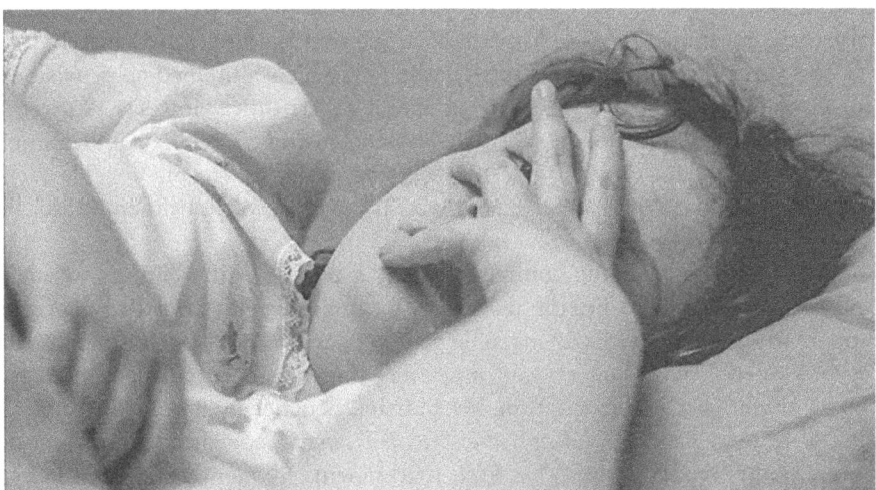

Figure 3.2 Anaïs peeking at her sister's sex in *Fat Girl*.

Instead of the viewer simply registering Elena's "violation," he or she registers Anaïs's own registration of this event. Linda Williams has astutely identified two other elements in addition to this unconventional strategy—both also frequently employed in works of the movement—that separate this sequence from countless other scenes representing the loss of innocence in Hollywood cinema: its prolonged duration and relative explicitness (281). Both qualities are central to the New French Extremity's particular use of realist techniques to viscerally engage the spectator. Breillat has insisted that, in her work, both duration and explicitness are tied to a concern for showing images in their fuller contexts: "Porn films remove sex from human dignity . . . [My films] restore female dignity by showing sex acts in their entirety" (qtd. in Horeck 203).

Critical and scholarly discussions of these elements recall the frequent debates surrounding *Baise-moi*, *Irréversible*, and other New French Extremity titles. The prolonged scenes of graphic sex and violence present in all these films tend to attract accusations of gratuitous sensationalism. However, as Williams argues, in this case the explicitness and duration of the sexual content are combined for the purposes of allowing a battle over the loss of virginity to become a more psychologically and emotionally accurate ordeal, defying in the process the "soft-focus erotic prettiness, the contained lyrical musical interlude, that has marked the 'sex scene' of mainstream Hollywood" (35).

The sequence of Elena's seduction is one of those cited by Robert Warren as having contravened the Theatres Act by containing "full frontal nudity" of under-aged characters. While it is factually accurate, this basis for the Board's objection represents a fundamental disregard for thematic concerns underlying the scene's use of prolonged nudity, which, given what Breillat herself has said, appears to have been designed not to arouse the viewer but to generate discursive meaning. One could perhaps argue that the Board was merely following the stringent criteria set forth in the Act, which contained no provisions for considering an artist's integrity or intent at the time. However, Warren's assertion was complicated by further comments justifying the board's decision: "We talked about whether (the scenes) were necessary for the picture. The feeling was that it could have been as powerful a picture without them" (qtd. in Hutsul A02).

While the rationalizing comment signals a political difference as to what "sex scenes" ought to be, the discursive meaning Breillat hoped to generate apparently remained wholly invisible to the Board. Here Warren's reasoning becomes problematic, once again indicating that the real challenge posed by such content is its categorization. As Martine Beugnet points out in *Cinema and Sensation: French Film and the Art of Transgression*, negative responses to the explicit sexuality in recent French art cinema frequently suggest it is less the images of flesh in themselves which attract disapproval, than the fact that these images cannot be fully assimilated in the generic categories that the films evoke (37). That is, the explicit sexuality is only gratuitous for an art cinema in which a relay of discourse and narrative is expected to at least counterbalance the presence of such visceral effects. What complicates this process, as Beugnet proceeds to argue, is the fact that the penchant for formal experimentation displayed in such films tends to result in the critical element of discourse becoming inseparable from the same formal strategies that complicate its decipherability (37). The content of *Fat Girl* did not merely violate the policies of the Theatres Act but confounded the criteria of controlled separation it employed to shape and promote its definitions of cinematic acceptability.

It becomes difficult to take seriously Warren's claim that removing nearly fifteen minutes of content deemed objectionable by the Board would have little or no effect on the discursive meanings that *Fat Girl* puts forth or, for that matter, on its notable affectivity in doing so. Warren's comment seems to indicate a failure to realize that tampering with the film's formal design is, invariably and fundamentally, altering its message, rendering Elena yet one more innocent girl blushingly elevated and augmented through a violent seduction. However, if one breaks down the apparent aim of the Board's extensive demands for cuts (i.e., to curb the affectivity, that is, emotional impact of certain formal elements), this reasoning quickly begins to fall apart. Taken at face value, the primary concern of the Board's reviewers was the presence of "under-age" sexuality. That presence being fully evident seconds after the seduction sequence begins (if not before), it seems unlikely they took exception specifically to the scene's duration, as other "mainstream" commercial films (such as Larry Clark's *Kids* [1995] or Sam Mendes's *American Beauty* [1999]) contained similarly prolonged scenes of minors involved in sexual situations yet were passed uncut in Ontario (Arnold 9). If the OFRB's objections were rooted in the scene's fragments of explicit sexual action, it should also be noted that nudity of teenage characters frequently goes unchallenged in mainstream high-school comedies like *American Pie* (1999). Breillat unquestionably broke no laws in the filming of *Fat Girl*: Mesquida was herself over eighteen at the time of filming, as was De Rienzo, who wore a prosthetic erection during shooting (Gerstel C04). In addition to the sexual action being entirely simulated, the nudity is never presented in close-up. As previously mentioned, the sex act itself takes place off-screen. Consideration of such factors did little to assuage the Board's concerns that *Fat Girl* carried the potential for social harm, nor did the dramatic and thematic context provided in the film's numerous benign and inexplicit other sequences.

Most of the remaining scenes in *Fat Girl* deal with the emotional dynamic in Elena and Anaïs's family. The girls' emotionally despondent parents, a passionless, CEO father and a cold, sardonic mother, seem hardly to notice the shift of mood since witnessing her sister's violation, as Anaïs becomes withdrawn and grows frustrated by Elena's putdowns. Elena oscillates between trying to cheer Anaïs up and growing irritated by her "sulking." In a way that is representative of Breillat's approach to every aspect of the narrative, from the girls' reactions when facing sexual discovery and disillusionment to the occasional abrupt shifts in tone, the relationship between the sisters is made complex, in the sense that neither character ever feels any one way only. In the interest (and perhaps at the risk) of complicating the drama of an otherwise straightforward plot, the scenario is infused with a wide range of contradictory emotions, as are articulated in an intimate moment shared between the sisters while gazing into a bathroom mirror. Commenting on their striking differences in appearance and physicality, Elena remarks: "Look at us. You'd never know we were sisters. It's funny. We really have nothing in common. Yet, when I look at you, I feel like I belong." Anaïs responds: "That's why we're sisters. When I hate you, I look at you and I can't. It's like hating myself." This notion of experiencing two incongruous emotions; a sense of always being pulled in two equally powerful and compelling directions at once, is fundamental to Breillat's goal with this story, and the sequences that the Board sought to excise are those which relay this important incongruity most clearly. For Breillat, Elena's sexual moment is the ultimate scene of extreme ambivalence. She explains, "The film image allows for a truthful vision of the world that emerges from contradictions" (in Horeck 208). *Fat Girl*, like many of her films, is expressly interested in the power of cinema specifically to capture and dramatize ambiguity.

In the context of art cinema, rape is frequently presented as a means of exploring such issues related to ambiguity (Russell 2). *Fat Girl*'s second conduit for controversy and censorship arrives late in its running time, in the form of a rape scene that initially seems to arrive from nowhere. Elena's mother quickly learns of the affair between her daughter and Fernando, and cuts short the family vacation. On the drive home, the family car pulls into a rest stop where, in an abrupt tonal shift (from teen movie to horror film), a man smashes through the windshield, killing Elena with a blow to the head and strangling her mother. Anaïs exits the car, holding the gaze of the random attacker, who proceeds to sexually assault her in a nearby wooded area (in a scene that is relatively brief compared to the preceding sequence of Elena's seduction).

Throughout the ordeal, Anaïs's body language betrays an ambivalence that has been highly debated in critical engagement with the film and often misinterpreted. The British Board of Film Classification, for example, saw fit to completely excise the sequence from home video releases, fearing it perpetuated the myth that rape can be sexually pleasurable for the victim (Barker, "Watching" 105). The ambivalence of Anaïs's body language, her lack of visible negative affect through the attack, is amplified by the scene's noticeable lack of musical accompaniment, a device conventionally used in such a sequence to guide audience feeling. As Horeck argues, however, to read Anaïs's lack of negative emotion as pleasure (as opposed to unpleasure) is to fatally oversimplify what

Figure 3.3   Anaïs returning her attacker's gaze in *Fat Girl*.

is actually taking place. Much as her sister was tempted to do when confronted with Fernando's aggressive seduction tactics, Anaïs may be trying, indeed struggling, to put the rape in the context of sentimental romance (Horeck 208). In the final moments of the film, two police officers guide her from the woods, one commenting to the other, "She said she wasn't raped." Recalling Manu's defiant rejection of a victimized status in *Baise-moi*, Anaïs adds: "Don't believe me if you don't want to." To say Breillat is suggesting rape as pleasurable violation is to completely neglect the complex thematic context that she has meticulously designed the whole of the film's preceding action to establish.

The Appeals

Writing to the OFRB in support of *Fat Girl* and in condemnation of the Board's ruling, David Cronenberg vouched for Breillat as an important artistic voice and for her film as a "serious study of sisterhood and adolescent sexuality" (F03). He adds:

> The film is not in any way pornographic or socially irresponsible. If the provisions of the Ontario Theatres Act dealing with adolescent sexuality are applied mechanically and to the letter—as they seem to be in the current case—they will in effect prevent any profound cinematic discussion of this entire field of human experience. That was not, I trust, their purpose. I respectfully request that [*Fat Girl*] be allowed to be shown uncut in the cinemas of Ontario. (F03)

This letter was included as part of the written appeal submitted by Cowboy Pictures and Lion's Gate, who vowed not to cut the film regardless of the Board's response. Five board members screened the film for a second time, and voted 3–2 in favour of upholding the refusal to classify its uncut version (Stone B1). Since Ontario law requires that all films be classified prior to exhibition or distribution, the effective ban was upheld. By this time, the film was playing to great acclaim and financial success in British Columbia, and in Quebec—where it was rated 16+ (Veranneau 56). Sarah Waxman, a member of the Ontario appeal panel who voted in favor of the film's release, expressed her disapproval of the board's decision publicly: "This intelligent handling of a controversial subject, adolescent sexuality, does not glorify or glamorize the subject . . . if anything, this is an anti-sex film" (qtd. in Hutsul A02). Cowboy and Lion's Gate announced they would be taking the Ontario provincial government to court, to argue for the film's uncut release, but also to challenge the constitutionality of the Theatres Act and to combat and draw attention to what they deemed an unjustifiable infringement on freedom of expression as guaranteed by the Canadian Charter of Rights and Freedoms.

Addressing the unsuccessful appeal, Warren cited the OFRB's regular consultation with psychologists and "ordinary" Ontario citizens to represent prevailing community standards and concluded that:

> A lot of [*Fat Girl*] is based on potentially harmful activities which shouldn't be shown to vulnerable people in our society [. . .] Ultimately, the reason why they turned it down was because underage nudity was clearly established—they were 15 and 13 and were in the nude in sexual situations [. . .] We're in the business of drawing boundaries [. . .] based on community standards. We have to ask ourselves, what kind of precedent would this set if we were to approve it? (qtd. in Hutsul A02).

Warren's envisioning of the Board's role as one of boundary delineation reveals its potential for conflict with films of the New French Extremity, the stylistic strategies of which are most transgressive in their postmodern collapsing of boundaries. As Grønstad points out: "The recurring problems of censorship with which Breillat's films have wrestled are in no small measure due to Kristevan blurring of categories held sacrosanct by the culture at large" (94). Faced with criticisms of the Board's narrow-mindedness and inability to recognize artistic value in challenging artworks (such as were leveled by not only Cronenberg but Atom Egoyan and numerous other filmmakers and academics), the board was retreating to the most well-worn and useful term in any censor's toolkit: "harmful."

In *Governing Morals: A Social History of Moral Regulation*, sociologist Alan Hunt points out that in the wake of rapid processes of secularization and social diversification in the second half of the twentieth century, justifications for criminalizing certain forms of private behaviour relied increasingly "not simply on their alleged intrinsic wrongness, but on their apparent harmfulness" (7). The underlying issue for Hunt, as for other social critics, was the increasing complexity, even impossibility, of locating "intrinsic" values in an ever-shifting, increasingly multicultural social context. In such an ideological climate, moral discourses become less and less dependent on taken-for-granted religious frameworks. This is fundamental to an understanding of why issues of film censorship are consistently framed in terms of potentially "harmful," rather than "improper," effects. For vocal conservative crusaders, "harm" functions as an effective contemporary substitute for the previous labels, "evil" and "wrong." This semantic construction highlights the degree to which censorial claims makers must tailor their arguments to the cultural sensibilities of audiences if they hope for the warrants and solutions proposed to be taken seriously.

The designation of the Ontario Film Review Board as responsible for the regulation of "harmful" materials raises some perplexing questions. First, what in the qualifications of the Board members (drawn from a range of industry, educational, and governmental occupation holders) constitutes expertise on morality? In "Watching Rape, Enjoying Watching Rape," Martin Barker interrogates what he dubs "figures of the audience," which are predictive claims built from theorizations of how film might affect audiences. Barker's research compares claims used by classification boards to regulate film content, with surveys of actual audience responses to those same films. He finds "systematic differences between the experiences which regulatory bodies impute to viewers and those which engaged viewers say that they experience" (110). Barker's study was commissioned by the BBFC, as part of an effort at reflexivity, accountability, and transparency in the policy analysis that informs their judgements. His study surveyed the online responses of real audiences to films containing sexual violence. Due to its history of controversy, *Fat Girl* was included among them. The results suggested that engaged viewers were much more likely to make the sort of thematic connections explored in this chapter (often bringing their own life experiences to bear on their engagement with the film's content) and much less likely to attribute potentially negative consequences of viewing the film to others. However, it is precisely responses imputed to disengaged viewers that tend to form the basis of demands for censorship. As audiences and review boards clearly do not agree on "social values" (depending on viewers and reviewers' level of engagement), Barker demonstrates that film review processes indeed function essentially as rationalizing camouflages for relatively idiosyncratic moral judgements.

Further, in what sense might the ruling of the Board not be made redundant by more efficient mechanisms for the enforcement of moral judgements that are already in place (in this case, sections of the Canadian Criminal Code dealing with child pornography and their enforcement by the Ontario Provincial Police)?

Concluding his nation-wide survey of Canadian censorship history in 1981, Malcolm Dean labeled such practices of closure as "misguided attempts to deal with vital social processes and to place constraints on creative individuals" and suggested they were "representing a process of judging the emerging present through a vision of the past" (24). Dean's critique could be said to characterize the prevailing sentiment of reactions to *Fat Girl*'s banning, in artistic circles and in the (predominantly liberal) Canadian Press, where discussions of the distributor's right to exhibit the film became ensconced in language reflecting the rights of adult spectators to choose their own entertainment. Unlike the *Crash* case, where the BBFC found itself defending a film against conservative calls for censorship in the press, the OFRB was forced to defend its own conservatism in the face of its perception as employing outmoded and dogmatically rigid policies and criteria, a defense that ultimately and rapidly proved untenable.

In November of 2002, Robert Warren announced his retirement from the Board "for personal reasons" (Posner R2). By January 17 of the following year, the board had approved a new policy of considering the "General Character and Integrity" of any film considered for non-approval (Ontario Film Review Board). The construction of these new provisions seemed aimed precisely at countering the criticisms of the board made throughout the *Fat Girl* case. Less than a month after these revisions to the Board's policies, Cowboy Pictures announced that the Government of Ontario had agreed to have the film resubmitted and approved, approximately one month prior to a scheduled hearing before the Ontario Superior Court of Justice (Stone B1). In a sudden and dramatic reversal of the Board's original verdict, Warren's replacement, Bill Moody, declared the scenes in question "artistic and integral to the plot" (Qtd. in Whyte A29), indicating a shifting of priorities in the board's criteria and, more directly, measures to protect against precisely the sort of rigidity that came under attack in the *Fat Girl* case. Moody added:

> We're trying to really look at our guidelines and decide if they really reflect society today. This board is not a static board. We're changing and evolving every day, and looking at our policies, because people out there are changing every day. (Qtd. in Whyte A29)

Accounting for the reversal in the board's decision, Craig Martin, who was set to represent the distributors in court, cited the government's reluctance to defend the constitutionality of its censorial powers (McKay). It remains unclear whether Warren's departure was the impetus for, or merely a symptom of, revisions to the OFRB's policies. In either case, the Board was clearly attempting to signal its capacity for flexibility and, in so doing, announcing its arrival into the twenty-first-century artistic landscape that Breillat, as well as Despentes and Trinh, had played no small part in ushering in.

What can be said with some certainty is that the challenges posed to the OFRB by the abrasive aesthetics and self-reflexive techniques of *Fat Girl* (and to a slightly lesser extent, those of *Baise-moi*) irrevocably blurred longstanding demarcations between the cultural value of transgressive artwork and the highly arguable theorizations in which the Review Board's claims of "harmfulness" were based. Due largely to Breillat's numerous risky and radical artistic sensibilities, the OFRB was forced to take measures to limit its own ability to censor works of incontestable artistic merit. However, the Film Classification Act remains far from perfect, continuing to rely on reviewers' subjective judgements of what constitutes "pornographic" and "mainstream" films, and policing a cultural Iron Curtain between the two.

Nonetheless, the *Fat Girl* case represents a leap forward in the cultural privileging of serious cinematic projects as worthy of protection, however confrontational in their formal design and subject. Most crucially, the *Fat Girl* versus the OFRB affair demonstrates that the notion of a Review Board simultaneously recognizing the cultural value of an artwork and nonetheless seeking to excise its allegedly problematic or "harmful" moments is ultimately and inherently contradictory. This is particularly true when (as is the case with *Fat Girl* and most other films in this study) such problematic moments are deliberate components of the film's formal design and its desire to provoke affective responses in the service of communicating important social insights or artistic statements.

The board's rejection and subsequent approval of *Fat Girl* suggests that the film verged on the boundaries of acceptability at a time where the processes of film regulation in Ontario were being significantly revised. Measures designed to prevent the criminal circulation of child pornography were applied to *Fat Girl* in such a way as to neglect the context in which the film's nudity appears, while critical analysis of the film's formal strategies provides a sharp contrast to its initial reception by the OFRB, one that calls into question the boundaries of acceptable cinematic expression and begs critical analysis of the film, and of its reception, as representational subjects of particular political and historical processes. Numerous lawyers, politicians, and filmmakers vocally criticized the Board's outmoded thinking and, as a potentially direct result, the OFRB amended its policies to limit its own ability to regulate "non-pornographic" cinema.

The *Fat Girl* case encapsulated the ethical and legislative complications that can arise when conservative classification policies are confronted with the abrasive aesthetic strategies of extreme art cinema filmmakers. Throughout the controversy, media pressure and public opinion were weighted heavily toward the rights of individual artists to free expression, as well as the rights of adult viewers to seek out whatever entertainment they wish, spurring a liberalization of classification policies aimed to curb the perception of the Board's practices as outmoded and puritanical. With the implementation of the Film Classification Act in 2005, the Board essentially altogether forfeited its right to demand cuts to or ban what it designated "mainstream" films, a label that reflected the increasing value it would place on artistic intention and narrative context in the film review process. While the Board retains the remit to explicitly censor "pornography," a notoriously slippery categorization to define, it has seen little in the way of media controversy or public criticism since and thus, as we may presume, the amount of "pornography" in circulation has markedly declined. More precisely, this decline is likely a result of digitalization and the growing popularity of online file-sharing platforms producing a dramatic reduction in public exhibition venues and rental outlets for pornographic films.

If viewed as a sort of pugilism between cinematic artistry on one side, and repressed public policy on the other, the case of *Fat Girl* might seem to offer a happy ending. Loosening of the Board's restrictions could be seen further in March of 2003, with Gaspar Noé's *Irréversible* testing the limits of the newly refined guidelines toward the representation of sexual violence and passing completely uncut. It would seem the intrinsic artistic merits of the New French Extremity films were key in prompting film boards to use ample discretion in their regulatory processes, the results of which find less and less opposition in the media or public discourse.

4. PROTECTING AUSTRALIANS FROM *KEN PARK*

As in Great Britain and Canada, every film made publicly available in Australia must go through a classification process before it can be legally exhibited or distributed. A national government body, the Office of Film and Literature Classification (OFLC), administrates the laws and regulations used to determine a film's classification. Also, like the BBFC in Britain and the OFRB in Ontario, Canada, the OFLC significantly refined its guidelines in the mid- to-late-1990s, shifting focus away from conventional censorship (at least in theory) and toward film classification, duly implementing the Commonwealth Classification Act in 1996. The Act (which applies to publications, films, and computer games) was introduced at a time when censorship controversies had been relatively sparse in Australia for a decade. Two of the act's prominent points are: "(a) adults should be able to read, hear, and see what they want;" and "(d) the need to *take account* of community concerns ..."—seemingly mutually exclusive points that strive for balance between acknowledging the necessity of freedom from restrictive censorship and tacitly advocating for its use (Lacey 58). Within the uneasy balance, the Act aims for—in a phrase— liberalized censorship.

The 1996 shift did not prove immediately problematic—that is until its newly expanded scope and limits were tested by the films of the New French Extremity—most notably Virginie Despentes and Coralie Trinh Thi's *Baise- moi* (2000). The intense erotic thriller's seemingly endless capacity to strike up controversy wherever it was exhibited or submitted proved especially challenging for Australian censors, who feared the social harm posed by the film's "excessive" hyper-stylized sexual violence.

Despite responsibility for enforcing its laws, the OFLC does not itself typically determine a film's classification status. This task instead falls upon the reviewers who comprise the Australian "Classification Board," a group of twenty "ordinary folk" who watch every film submitted for classification to assess the level of violence, sex, profanity, drug use, and nudity, and make recommendations for suitable age categories based on these classifiable factors (McKenzie 52). The 1995 Classification Act also includes provisions for the examination of "themes" present in a film, along with pointed consideration of the narrative context, tone, duration, frequency, and level of detail in a film's treatment of violence, sex, or nudity.

Submitted to the board in early 2002, *Baise-moi* was initially passed as an R18+ rating. The decision swiftly came under fire from Australian family groups, who lobbied (successfully) to have the film banned from cinemas. *Baise-moi* was refused classification in May 2002 and ordered to be pulled from cinema screens, though several theaters in Sydney and Melbourne continued to exhibit it (SBS). Instances in which public exhibition of cinematic artwork (or private for that matter—*Baise-moi* was likewise banned from Australian DVD home video markets in 2013) meets the legal threshold for punishable criminality can prove instructive litmus tests for both the practical capability *and* the willingness of law enforcement agencies to uphold such prohibitions. The response can inevitably determine to what extent classification status in liberal democracies functions as "strong advisory/recommendation" (secondary to the priority of protecting the rights of adult viewers) or as proscriptive "letter-of-the law" regulation and enforcement.

In the case of Australia, the reality would become clear in 2003, when New South Wales police raided and shut down an illegal protest screening of Larry Clark and Edward Lachman's independent American erotic-drama *Ken Park* (2002), hosted by Australian film critic and free speech advocate Margaret Pomeranz in Sydney. *Ken Park* had been previously submitted for review in preparation for a scheduled screening at the Sydney Film Festival, only to be refused classification in any category. In July of the following year, officers entered Balmain Town Hall, where hundreds had gathered to see the film and to show solidarity in support of its (age-restricted) release in Australia, and demanded organizers turn over the illegal DVD exhibition copy less than ten minutes into the screening, stating: "the Ken Park film has a refused classification; our sole purpose is to prevent any breach of the law" (qtd. in Sydney "We've"). As of 2022, *Ken Park* has never been resubmitted for classification review in Australia, meaning its effective banning (despite international availability in various DVD editions online) remains in place. The OFLC's rationale for refusing classification to *Ken Park* highlights umbrage taken with its "too realistic" depiction of sexual violence and psychological abuse of its young protagonists.

The discourses of sex, violence, and free expression surrounding *Ken Park* and its censorship in Australia have symbolic significance for three reasons. First, the protection of children—precious in the eyes of would-be censors as symbols of innocence and uncorrupted moral virtue—has become the last surviving rationale for film censorship in a culture largely prepared for its retirement. Classification remains a popular process of regulation precisely because young viewers (children and adolescents) are perceived as vulnerable to "psychologically damaging" (once "morally corrupting") material. Secondly, the raiding of the Sydney protest screening by police represents a rare "show of force" in matters of film classification, in which the willingness of government agencies (even in liberal democracies) to back up proscriptive regulation with binding legal enforcement is plainly showcased. Lastly, the objections of relevant censorial agents involved in the affair highlight the discrepancy between rationales for excising certain problematic visual images from films, and those for even more prohibitive treatment for cases in which no amount of excised material could soften the perception of "harm" posed by a film's broader narrative messaging.

An American Maverick

Larry Clark's name will forever be synonymous in broader film culture with his directorial debut *Kids* (1996), a realist sexual drama which, despite its arthouse leanings, achieved mainstream commercial success amidst the boom of independent American cinema in the 1990s. Written by (then nineteen-year-old) Harmony Korine and distributed by Miramax Films, *Kids* became a flashpoint for controversy when marketed and framed in popular discourse as a pseudo-documentary "exposé", capturing the hedonism and debauchery of American teenagers absorbed in the emerging "skater" sub-culture and its associated drug use and sexual promiscuity. *Kids* follows a group of New York City teenagers—Telly (Leo Fitzpatrick), Casper (Justin Pierce), and Jenny (Chloë Sevigny)—over a twenty-four-hour period, in which Telly deflowers two young girls; Jenny receives a positive HIV diagnosis (having previously slept with Telly); and Casper rapes Jenny (implying all three characters have ultimately contracted the deadly virus). Janet Maslin of *The New York Times* referred to the film as a "wake up call to the world" (C13)—which became a catchphrase echoed in posters, trailers, and other promotional and marketing materials. The implication of such a characterization was apparently aimed to suggest to the film's adult audience that "these could be *your* kids." The credibility of such a claim is highly questionable. The film's impression of authenticity is certainly very striking: due largely to its improvisational performance styles (many scenes feature extended, unscripted dialogue); its reflection of 90s youth culture (slang, music, et cetera); and its lackadaisical narrative structure (key plot points sporadically punctuate what often feels like loosely structured observational documentary). However, the deliberate characterization of the film as socially pressing "exposé" ignores the fact that its subjects are products of a very distinctive, very specific socio-economic cultural milieu (hyper-urban working-class teenagers; decidedly not the average suburban middle-class teen invoked by Maslin and others in discourses surrounding the film). Still, this marketing strategy succeeded in pushing the film into the cultural mainstream, a fact evidenced, for example, by screenwriter Harmony Korine appearing on *Late Night with David Letterman* to promote the film.

Despite a lack of frontal nudity and the presence of only one violent scene, *Kids* received the MPAA's newly implemented NC-17 rating, but (perhaps surprisingly) encountered minimal resistance from British/Commonwealth classification boards, earning the equivalent of 18+ ratings in uncut form (despite, for example, an opening scene in which Telly coldly manipulates and takes the virginity of a near-nude [as scripted] twelve-year-old girl). The critical embrace and commercial success of *Kids* are no doubt partly symptomatic of increasingly lenient discussions surrounding sexuality in the popular discourse of 1990s culture: evident elsewhere in popular television sitcoms like *Seinfeld* and *Roseanne*, the much-discussed impeachment of US President Bill Clinton for sexual liaisons with White House staffers, et cetera. However, the film was not without its vocal detractors, for example Rita Kempley, who wrote in her August 25 review for the *Washington Post* that the film is "virtually child pornography disguised as a cautionary documentary" (qtd. in Lee). Clark would follow up *Kids* with several similarly themed films about aimless, angst-ridden, sexually active teenagers (his most remarked on artistic trademark) with somewhat inconsistent results. 2001's *Bully* is a harrowing masterpiece of true-crime cinema; relentlessly confrontational as it is artfully rendered. The made-for-television *Teenage Caveman* (2002) was, by comparison, a decidedly less novel or interesting outing (a failed experiment at incorporating Clark's signature subject matter into an explicit genre—in this case post-apocalyptic sci-fi–framework).

Ken Park was completed in 2002 and screened internationally at several prestigious film festivals including Venice, Telluride, and Toronto International Film Festival. Clark shared directing credit with his cinematographer Edward Lachman and worked again from a screenplay by Korine (written concurrently with *Kids* in 1995). The film was met with polarized critical reception throughout its international film festival run, perhaps unsurprisingly. Its content is confrontational, drawing on taboo themes including (but not limited to) incest, physical and psychological abuse, intergenerational sex, teen suicide, and eroticized violence. Yet, it would be extremely difficult to argue for lack of artistic merit in its treatment of these subjects. Clark's renown in the art world dates back to the 1970s, most notably to *Tulsa*, his series of photographic essays that took American teenagers in Oklahoma—their offbeat youth sub-cultures and gritty lifestyles—as its subject. His immaculate photographic eye brought visual excitement to the "docu-drama" style of *Kids*, and the photography of *Ken Park* (with Lachman as collaborator) is perhaps even more striking—considerably slicker and more deliberately composed. The film also approaches its potentially highly exploitable narrative subject matter with remarkable sensitivity. Clark has always made a notable effort to understand his young subjects *on their own terms*, rather than as a judgemental adult looking in (Clark was sixty at the time of *Ken Park*'s production—while the film's lead actors ranged from eighteen to twenty-two).

Ken Park could perhaps constructively be thought of as a "spiritual sequel" to *Kids* (neither *Bully* or *Teenage Caveman* were penned by the narratively experimental Korine, and accordingly featured much more conventional plotting). However, one notable difference in the thematic focus distinguishes the two films. According to Clark, "the first film, *Kids*, was just about the kids' secret world where adults weren't allowed at all. And everyone said 'Where are the parents?' And I always said, 'wait until *Ken Park*'" (qtd. in Machen). Indeed, the teenage characters in *Ken Park*, as in *Kids*, are disaffected, alienated, and predisposed at times to arguably anti-social attitudes and behavior. However, the film's adult characters (namely parents) are shown substantially contributing to (if not outright precipitating) these same attitudes and behaviors. *Ken Park* is also more explicit in its treatment of sexuality than *Kids*, featuring two scenes with graphic nudity (one involving auto-erotic asphyxiation, the other group sex). It would seem to be the latter distinction that earned the ire of censors in Australia, where *Ken Park* was refused classification. However, this chapter will argue that conceptually separating the explicit staging/photographing of these two scenes from the role played by adult/parent characters in the narrative's transgressions against public tastes and cultural sensitivities is not the straightforward task it might superficially seem.

A Limited Run

Unlike the case of *Baise-Moi*, a film similarly refused Australian classification in the same year, it is difficult to draw cross-national comparisons regarding *Ken Park*'s treatment by censors. The film has never been officially distributed in Britain, America, or Canada. This has apparently less to do with its potentially objectionable content than with a series of peculiar incidents, which have acted as obstacles to its official release in these countries. The lack of official distribution in North America was apparently to do with clearances for music rights, as Clark explains: "I had a crazy producer who said he'd cleared all the songs, and he didn't. I worked for a year to clear them. I got them cleared, and they didn't pay for them. So, we either have to re-clear them or change some music or something" (qtd. in Martin). Clark has provided no update on the status of this effort since stating this claim in 2006.

An even more peculiar explanation has been cited for *Ken Park*'s failure to secure distribution in the UK. A deal had apparently been arranged with Metro Tartan for the film's British release until, at a party celebrating its gala premiere at the London Film Festival, Clark allegedly assaulted the company's owner Hamish McAlpine (reportedly following a heated discussion about the September 11 terrorist attack and its implications for US middle eastern foreign policy) (Hall). Incidentally, Alpine had been instrumental in arguing for the uncut release of *Irréversible* by the BBFC earlier that year, and potentially could have done likewise for Clark's film.

The Australian Review Board's refusal to classify *Ken Park* functioned as an effective ban, since it is expressly illegal to exhibit any film in Australia that has failed to obtain a rating from the Board. The rationales offered for the decision reference "high impact" scenes that, it was claimed, were "too realistic" in their depictions (Kampmark 354). Examples included: the auto-erotic asphyxiation of one of the protagonists, including full shots of his genitals, his orgasm, and a semen trail on his hand. The Board read this sexual activity as non-simulated, which added to its problematic nature. However, other (less confrontational) scenes were also cited, including a suicide, and a scene of a male character urinating into a toilet (354). Such images apparently exceeded the Board's tolerance as described in the classification guidelines. The focus on these "high impact" moments is perhaps expected, but no less curious given that the 1996 Classification Act included provisions encouraging Board members to consider problematic scenes within the broader context of a film's narrative. I argue that the staging and photography of these moments merely provided a convenient scapegoat for the Board's objections, which in fact can be linked to the "realism" applied more broadly to its narrative treatment of sensitive subjects.

The Kids Aren't Alright

Ken Park's narrative centers around the home lives of four teenage protagonists living in Valencia, California: Shawn (James Bullard), Claude (Stephen Jasso), Peaches (Tiffany Limos), and Tate (James Ransone). Aside from a brief but notable exception in the film's epilogue, the subplots of these four main characters never intersect. The script has their stories unfold in parallel fashion, alternating between the four sub-stories, each being comprised of roughly four or five sequences. In this sense, the screenplay is significantly more meticulously structured (at least apparently) than the comparatively loose assembly of vignettes that form the pseudo-structure of *Kids*.

Shawn appears to be the most well-adjusted of the script's four protagonists. He has a stable home life—a little brother and a caring mother—and a same-aged girlfriend. In an early scene, Shawn arrives at his girlfriend's, finding her younger sister watching television. He makes his way up to the bedroom, where his girlfriend's mother, Rhonda (Maeve Quinlan), is folding laundry. After stilted small talk, he abruptly and nonchalantly asks, "Can I eat you out?" Rhonda smiles and responds gently, "Not now, I'm folding." Subsequent scenes reveal that Shawn and Rhonda have been engaged in a sexual relationship for some time. Shawn is indeed seen performing oral sex on the woman (roughly twice his age) and confessing his passionate affection for her as they cuddle in bed after. The dialogue subtly makes it clear that this affection is not reciprocal. When Shawn admits that he thinks about Rhonda constantly and fantasizes about killing her husband so they can be together, Rhonda uncomfortably reverts to her parental role, asking if he and his brother will need a ride to their scheduled extra-curriculars.

Shawn later arrives at school and connects with his girlfriend, Hannah (Ashley Crisp), who is clearly oblivious to Shawn and Rhonda's relationship. The two appear like any other typical teenage couple. Later, Shawn is invited to dinner, where he, Hannah, Rhonda, and Rhonda's husband/Hannah's father engage in benign, pleasant chatter. It is an immensely uncomfortable scene for the viewer, as we await the shattering (no doubt psychologically devastating for all involved) revelation, which in fact never comes. Rhonda's particularly felt betrayal of daughter *and* husband remains hidden.

Figure 4.1 James Bullard (l.) and Maeve Quinlan in Larry Clark and Edward Lachman's *Ken Park* (Busy Bee Productions, 2002).

Claude is a wiry skateboarder and only child who lives with his pregnant mother (Amanda Plummer) and unemployed, alcoholic father (Wade Williams). Claude is emotionally sensitive and carries himself in slightly feminine fashion, which seemingly aggravates his burly, athletic father to no end. The atmosphere in the home is tense, but not especially abnormal. Claude is emotionally close to his mother, evidenced in his gesture of cutting her toenails in one early scene, promising not to "tickle her" in doing so. Claude's father (always with beer in hand) encourages him to "grow out" of skateboarding and stop wasting time with his "weirdo" friends. Claude resists this pressure, visibly contented with his interests and lifestyle.

The atmosphere in the home gradually sours as Claude's father's frustration with his son increases. When his efforts at providing a positive male role model (ironically perceiving himself as such) fail, he lashes out at Claude with physical violence, breaking his son's skateboard and striking him twice across the face. Claude holds back tears and remains defiant—easily seeing straight through his father's inflated sense of self-worth. In another of the film's intensely uncomfortable moments, Claude's father complains to his wife about Claude's attitude. Then, failing to coax her into sex, mentions how much she "looks like Claude." The comment subtly foreshadows a disturbing imminent turn in the family dynamic. Arriving home drunk one evening, Claude's father stumbles into Claude's bedroom, climbing clumsily into the bed where his son is sleeping. The scene is darkly lit—no explicit sexual conduct is visible—but Claude wakes up and kicks his father to the ground. Claude is then seen packing a bag, as his tearful and bewildered mother pleads with him to stay. "How you gonna make it out there if your daddy's still making you cry?" she asks with a mix of care and condescension. "You don't get it," Claude responds, "I wasn't doing anything! I was asleep!" Claude leaves the house (presumably for good) as his mother struggles either to admit, confront, or simply process the meaning of his words.

Peaches is an adolescent female who lives alone with her ultrareligious widower father (Julio Oscar Mechoso). It is never revealed which specific Christian denomination Peaches's father belongs to, but his zealotry is palpable. When Peaches invites Curtis (Mike Apaletegui), a "friend from Bible study," over to the house, the three sit down to lunch (a meal eclipsed in awkwardness only by Shawn's dinner at Hannah's). Peaches's father eats on his knees and regales the teens with a story of receiving oral surgery without the aid of anesthetics. Curtis is visibly bewildered. Peaches's father then reminisces about his deceased wife and, in a scene echoed in Claude's narrative, how much she looked like Peaches. Later, he visits his wife's gravesite as Peaches and Curtis engage in fetish-bondage sex at the house. Peaches's father returns home and finds the couple in bed, exploding in a frenzy of anger and savagely assaulting Curtis, who, still bound to the bed frame, cannot defend himself. The scene is possibly the film's most harrowing. Still reeling from the

Figure 4.2 Julio Oscar Mechoso (l.) and Tiffany Limos in *Ken Park*.

shock, Peaches's father quotes scripture in condemnation of "harlotry" as he presents her with her dead mother's wedding dress. He then leads his sobbing daughter in a bizarre makeshift home wedding ceremony.

Tate is the most observably dysfunctional of the film's four protagonists. He is an anti-social loner who lives with his grandparents (Patricia Place and Harrison Young). Tate aggressively berates his kind and well-meaning grandmother and takes any opportunity to challenge the integrity of his war veteran grandfather. In perhaps the film's most notorious sequence, Tate becomes aroused by a Serena Williams tennis match on television. He chokes himself with an improvised noose and masturbates, slipping out of consciousness as he climaxes. As previously mentioned, the scene's confrontational verité treatment was singled out as especially problematic for censors.

Tate is later shown naked in bed, dictating into a handheld tape recorder. He narrates the events of his evening, which we see in flashback. Tate, still nude, enters the kitchen and cuts himself a large piece of cake, the kind (we are told) his grandmother makes for him on "special occasions." Knife still in hand, he proceeds to enter his grandparents' bedroom, where he climbs on top of their sleeping bodies. Tate stabs both his grandmother and grandfather to death and, staring blankly at their bloodied corpses, claims that during the act, he "started to get an erection." Tate pauses his narration and opens his mouth, inserting his grandfather's false teeth.

We later see Tate handcuffed in the rear of a police car, wistfully reminiscing about random anecdotes from his youth. Despite this aggressively dark turn,

FILM REGULATION IN A CULTURAL CONTEXT

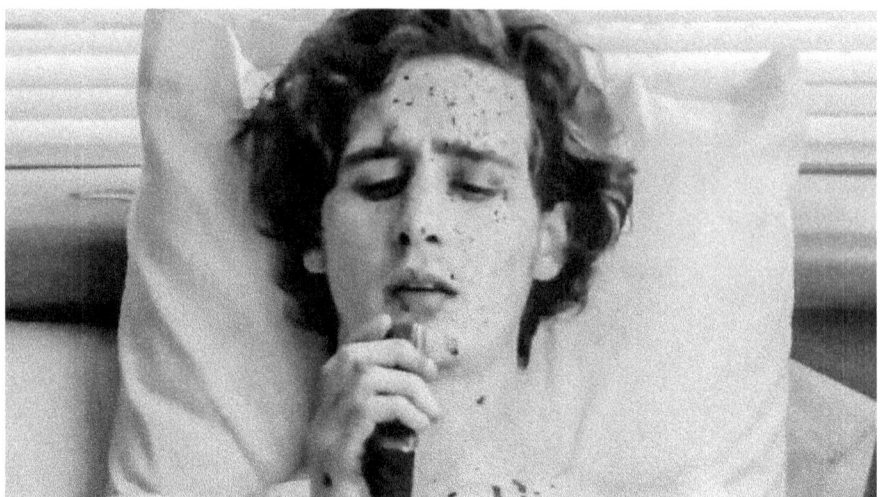

Figure 4.3   James Ransone in *Ken Park*.

Tate's subplot ironically provides virtually all the film's few moments of levity. His histrionic tirades completely bewilder his exceedingly conventional grandparents, who are thoroughly unequipped to counter his hostile and disruptive behavior. The script never references the whereabouts of Tate's actual parents, but elicits dark humor from the household's bizarre and dichotomous dynamic (there is the indication that Tate was driven to murderous rage primarily by his grandfather's cheating at Scrabble). Tate is a psychopath, left to freely indulge in his morbid devices by his well-intentioned but totally ineffectual grandparents, who inevitably fall victim to his rage.

Ken Park concludes with an epilogue in which Shawn, Claude, and Peaches are shown engaged in group sex. Despite being one of two notoriously explicit moments of sexual activity, the scene—gentle and celebratory in its staging—provides rare respite from the film's otherwise bleak and dark tonality. It is the only scene in which the characters appear together onscreen (they verbally reference Tate's absence), but also (perhaps ironically given its "adult" nature) the only instance in which they are shown embracing the carefree joy of adolescence.

The Sum of its Parts

In banning the film, the OFLC declared that *Ken Park*'s treatment of sexual matters did not meet "the standards of morality, decency and propriety generally accepted by reasonable adults" by including scenes of "child sexual abuse, actual sex by people depicted as minors, and sexualised violence" (Sydney "Filmmaker"). This rationale calls out for further clarification in several regards. The two instances of "child sexual abuse" are either notably inexplicit (Claude's father climbing into his son's bed) or wholly implied (the forced marriage of Peaches and her father). The "actual sex by people depicted as minors" perhaps loosely applies in the case of James Ransone's (Tate's) auto-erotic activity, which was in fact apparently non-simulated (Martin). However, the ages of the characters are never stated. The board apparently felt the actors *looked* young enough to be considered as depicting minors, despite Ransone and Limos being in their mid-twenties at the time of filming. In the case of the film's epilogue, all three actors appear fully nude (all were over the age of eighteen at the time of filming), but Clark maintains that the sexual activity itself was simulated (Sydney "Filmmaker"). By the standards of pornography, the scene is relatively inexplicit—there are (obviously) no shots of penetration, close-up or otherwise. The presence of "sexualized violence"— namely Tate's reference in narration to his (offscreen) erection while stabbing his grandparents—is indeed chief among the film's most provocative and confrontational elements. However, its delivery via dialogue was decidedly overshadowed in the Board's notes by the stylistic treatment of scenes depicting "actual sex."

In his thorough examination of the *Ken Park* and *Baise-moi* censorship controversies in Australia, Binoy Kampmark notes a tension between the Review Board's umbrage with *Ken Park*'s overall "message" (its confrontational portrayal of the "psychological abuse of children" and parental neglect), and the emphasis of Board members on the unduly "high impact" staging and photography of relevant scenes (354). This speaks to a much broader challenge issued to institutions tasked with protecting viewers from so-called "harmful" cinematic material: the challenge of drawing a meaningful distinction between the alleged harm posed by a film's style, and that posed by its substance or subject. In other words, will a censorial institution be content with protecting the public from "harmful" images, or must it also take stock of the film's linear movement through these images—of multiple characters moving through multiple scenes? Naturally, films are most often telling *stories* that expand beyond the content of any one shot or scene. These stories communicate *themes*, very often in a degree of complexity that makes them difficult to separate out from stylistic elements. While the censor may easily enough distinguish between the style and substance of a film, added complications arise when these concepts prove difficult to approach in entirely separate and distinct fashion.

In the very best and most effective artworks, style and substance share a symbiotic relationship—informing, influencing, or outright determining one another—and working in tandem for maximum effect or impact. The more fitting a certain style for a particular subject, the more difficult it becomes to separate out the two conceptually. In the case of *Ken Park*, Clark and Lachman's visual presentation of certain scenes (particularly Tate's auto-erotic asphyxiation and the concluding group sex scene) invoke certain structural elements of pornography (length and duration in the former, lack of conventional narrative context in the latter), which made the film particularly vulnerable as a target for censorship. Even Clark himself readily acknowledges that the frankness of *Ken Park* on subjects of sexuality warrants age-restriction measures, saying "I'm not stupid, you know . . . I wouldn't want my son, when he was thirteen, fourteen years old, to have seen an autoerotic asphyxiation scene" (qtd. in Martin). Such an admission could seem, at least on its face, like a partial concession to arguments of pro-censorship groups like the Australian Family Association ("outspoken in their opposition to abortion, gay marriage and the 'dangers' of sex education" [McKenzie 54]), who also feel that restrictive classification helps protect children from possible harm. Such groups had demonstrably proven able to exert considerable influence in classification decisions regarding *Baise-Moi* and *Irréversible*.

Clark would likewise no doubt acknowledge the decidedly "high impact" effect of his and Lachman's shooting approach in the auto-erotic asphyxiation scene (the pronounced length of the shots, the post-climax close-up and notorious "semen trail," et cetera), but unlike those who would seek to censor or ban the film outright, he clearly attaches no moral dimension to these kinds of aesthetic decisions. Of the infamous scene, Clark has said:

> People say, "Well why didn't you just show, you know, the close-up of the head, of the face?" It never occurred to me for a moment that I would do that scene and not show it the way I showed it. I come from the art world, and you can put whatever you want to on the wall and people go "Ho-hum." But when you make film, there are all these rules, you don't have rules in art. But I'm an artist. In every movie I've ever made, people have said you can't do this and can't do that. I said, "Yes I can." I don't think like a director. I'm going to do whatever I want to do. (Qtd. in Martin)

Clark's comment highlights a pervasive blind spot in censorial logic, namely a willingness to consider certain filmed images in specifically *stylistic* context. It is perhaps somewhat curious that the "ordinary folk" (McKenzie 52) who comprise the OFLC's Review Board, and the "classification experts" so frequently consulted in Australia (or elsewhere by the BBFC or OFRB), so rarely include notable artists. The result is an obvious insensitivity to logic like Clark's—filming the scene in the manner he did according to artistic instinct—no other approach was ever conceivable.

In some significant sense, the Board's objections did uphold the promise of the 1995 Commonwealth Classification Act by framing Clark's and Lachman's visually "high-impact" moments (in this case to the film's detriment) in the context of Korine's equally challenging screenplay. Perhaps the most striking feature of Clark and Korine's previous collaboration *Kids*, particularly in hindsight, is its relatively amoral approach to its social realism style. *Kids* is often characterized as "cautionary" docudrama, and its characters (it is unambiguously implied) will eventually suffer the devastating effects of their youthful indiscretions. However, the screenplay also deliberately subverts such conventional messaging, for example in Telly's closing narration:

> When you're young, not much matters. When you find something that you care about, then that's all you got. When you go to sleep at night you dream of pussy. When you wake up it's the same thing. It's there in your face. You can't escape it. Sometimes when you're young the only place to go is inside. That's just it—fucking is what I love. Take that away from me and I really got nothing.

The implication here is that Telly will continue infecting virgins with HIV until he himself dies from the virus. Despite any obvious potential moral objection from the viewer, there is no clear or explicit indication in Korine's script that Telly's proclivities are in any way (in his own eyes at least) "not worth" his own inevitable misfortune and the trail of pain and destruction it will leave in its wake. It is a chilling insight regarding the apathy and nihilism of angst-ridden adolescence.

An even more fascinating (and relevant for the purposes of this discussion) example is Korine's own directorial debut *Gummo* (1997), a narratively experimental series of grim and harrowing vignettes set against the impoverished backdrops of Xenia, Ohio. Along with its follow-up *Julien Donkey Boy* (1999), *Gummo* is as close as (arguably) mainstream American filmmaking (independent or studio) has come to the non-classical narrative forms long present in the work of European master filmmakers like Renoir, Antonioni, or Bertolucci. *Gummo* is also replete with disturbing images: a drowned cat; a developmentally disabled prostitute; a house covered in cockroaches, et cetera. Even more conspicuous, however, is the film's lack of any "morally redeeming" narrative framework for these images, an absence that proved puzzlingly problematic from a ratings perspective.

Submitting the film to the MPAA, Korine claims he was told that while any one scene of *Gummo* taken individually could pass under the guidelines for an R rating, their *culminative* effect resulted in messaging so anti-social and nihilistic as to warrant the significantly stricter NC-17:

> I was allowed to appeal, so they would say, "trim this, this is really unbearable, if you make it a little shorter we'll give you the R-rating." So, I would do it, because it was relatively insignificant. Then they would say "Oh, you know, we re-watched it, and it's really still too

hard to sit through." If you look at their rulebooks, they say that NC-17 is for graphic sex, terrible violence, or extreme profanity or drug use. *Gummo* has no sex . . . almost no "dirty" words . . . no gore . . . And the only drug use is glue out of bags. So right there, it should have gotten a G-rating. (Qtd. in Jamie and Hainley)

The case so frequently made by classification institutions that certain *individual images* carry a capacity for harm is a considerably easier one to defend than the supposition that such images, assembled in the case of *Gummo* in relatively random order, will contain a capacity for harm greater in sum than in parts. The reason for this is obvious. To target the length, or composition, or even the subject of a single shot for censorship, is to present a technical problem with an equally technical solution (shorten or remove the shot). To target the narrative broadly, by contrast, is to wade into the realm of precisely the kind of explicitly moral censorship that, for example, characterized the 1930s Hollywood Production Code. It is a regression to insistence upon the permissibility of certain narrative outcomes to the exclusion of certain others.

As previously mentioned, the lack of cross-national points of comparative reference in this case fundamentally obscures the degree to which the narrative messaging in *Ken Park* was perceived as particularly acute for Australian censors, as compared to their British or Canadian counterparts. Kampmark certainly implies a notion of distinctive "Australian-ness" in the OFLC's responses to *Baise-moi* and *Ken Park*, invoking the cultural archetype of the Australian "wowser," a pious person who "mistakes the world for a penitentiary and himself for a warder" (Kampmark 345). Certainly, the consistency in the selection of films that drew controversy amidst the shift from censorship to classification in Britain, Canada, and Australia mirrors the strong parallels in the legislative reforms themselves in each national context. It is worth noting, however, that in the case of *Baise-moi*, the OFRB in Canada and the BBFC in Britain requested specific cuts to the film's scenes of explicit sexualized violence. In Australia, by contrast, refusal to classify the film was presented in less conditional terms. In the case of *Ken Park*, too, the Board highlighted certain sequences that posed particularly threatening harm for their staging and construction, but did not recommend specific cuts. The refusal of classification was just that—outright refusal. Censorial conditions for classification would have likely proved futile in any case, as Clark has openly stated: "I think that we're really breaking new ground here, and that's one of the roles of an artist, and when people see this film, they'll see it the way it is, I'm not cutting the film for anybody, ever" (qtd. in Day).

At the same time, Clark (prior to the incident with McAlpine and the canceling of the film's UK distribution) had shown optimism about the prospect of *Ken Park*'s uncut passing in Britain, stating that he was familiar with the BBFC's "rules," and had faith in the Board's commitment to considering cinematic material within the context of: the film's broader narrative; the "seriousness" of the filmmaker's oeuvre; and the lens of artistic merit with which challenging and controversial subjects have been approached, stating:

> The rules state that you can show erect penises, you can show ejaculation, you can show oral sex, you can show intercourse, you can show anything as long as it's in context, so maybe it hasn't been done, but it can be done—there's no rules against it, and this film is all about context. (Qtd. in Day)

Given the BBFC's impressively nuanced past defence of *Crash*, and its subsequent defence of *Irréversible*, one could indeed speculate that the Board might have acted more leniently toward *Ken Park* than the OFLC, which essentially declared that "no artistic intention on the part of the director or overall message in the film could save it" (Kampmark 347). Ironically, the impetus to consider problematic images within a film's broader narrative context—precisely the thing that saved *Crash* and *Irréversible* from British censorship—was in this case the nail in the coffin of *Ken Park*'s chance of lawful exhibition and distribution in Australia.

Having acknowledged the utility of age-based ratings protections on scenes such as Tate's auto-erotic asphyxiation, Clark also makes a compelling case for the non-gratuitousness of the film's closing images of teens engaged in group sex, stating:

> Take for example the last scene in the film, the sex scene at the end. People from Venice, and film festivals all over the world, tell me that's not pornography, it feels right, it's not a dirty scene—the dirty scene is where Peaches' father kisses her. This isn't me, this is audiences everywhere, they see the film and respond and they think this is OK. I think that the people that see the film at the BBFC will see that. (Qtd. in Day)

Here, Clark raises an intriguing premise—a scene, for example, of a father kissing his own daughter (which his film also contains), can and should be thought of as "dirtier" than a scene in which legal-aged actors engage in joyful, pleasurable, simulated sexual activity. The OFLC Review Board's simultaneous disapproval of *Ken Park*'s overall messaging *and* singling out of its particularly "high impact" scenes (such as this sexually explicit climax) muddies any such attempts at meaningful moral distinction. The Board was simply unwilling to relegate its objections to *either* the film's overall narrative *or* its especially graphic/explicit moments. One might reasonably suspect that the refusal of classification ultimately had less to do with drawing conceptual distinctions between style and substance, or between individual moments and culminative effects, than with assuaging concerns of the Australian Family Association (and other such organizations), all too eager and willing to cry foul if the film saw any sort of classified release.

Censorial sentiment toward the film's "messaging" most eerily recalls the BBFC's objection to scenes of "anti-social" and "rebellious" behaviour in Nicholas Ray's *Rebel Without a Cause* (1955). Considered particularly problematic were lines of dialogue that were seen as "discrediting" the hero's parents (Jim Backus and Ann Doran). It was "evidently not thought acceptable to suggest that adults might be in any way responsible for the unhappiness of their children" (McGregor 63). *Ken Park* likewise lays much of the blame (narratively speaking) for the, at times, anti-social and abhorrent behavior of its young protagonists at the feet of dysfunctional adult characters: Rhonda essentially exploits Shawn for her own sexual gratification without apparent regard for, or sensitivity to, his still developing emotional understanding of adult sexual relationships; Claude is abused (physically and almost sexually) by his father, while being forced to squarely confront the fact that his mother—whom he loves dearly— is (for reasons never clearly elucidated) either unwilling or unable to protect him; Peaches's sado-masochistic sexual proclivities are no doubt linked to the suffocating religious repression that her father contributes to their home life; and Tate is a character (if ever there was one) desperately in need of authoritative restriction and control (which his grandparents prove totally incapable of providing). Whereas the teens in Clark's *Kids* are, in some meaningful sense, dysfunctional chiefly *because* they are still "kids" (albeit of a very specific socio-cultural milieu), the teens in *Ken Park* are dysfunctional chiefly because of the failures of their parental would-be role-models.

Vocal defenders of *Ken Park* will likely be the first to concede that the highlighted scenes of auto-erotic asphyxiation or teenage group sex are extremely shocking, challenging, abrasive, uncomfortable, confrontational, et cetera. However, reactions to the film's content are (by and large) reactions specifically to its "realism." Seeing images and scenarios that any viewer knows to exist in real life, but that so infrequently grace cinema screens—and yet appear so richly and vividly here—lends a candid authenticity to Clark and Lachman's storytelling that is far more affecting and impactful than the comparable credibility derived from the docu-verité style of *Kids*. In some meaningful sense, the OFLC's characterization of *Ken Park* is ultimately correct—the film's power is not tied expressly to its narrative broadly, or to its individual "high impact" scenes—but rather to the culminative effect of these elements working in conjunction with one another.

Of course, all of this is moot to the point of the raided protest screening. The New South Wales Police, it can be safely assumed, had no particular interest in, or especially resounding feelings toward, the challenging content of *Ken Park*. The illicitness of its exhibition was a matter of technicality—to show an unclassified film in Australia is to violate the law, regardless of the rationale for classification refusal, or how well it holds up to critical scrutiny. Thankfully, none of the screening's organizers (Pomeranz and three others) were prosecuted for criminal activity (the OFLC surely knew this would open a whole separate Pandora's box of legal, ethical, and public relations challenges). However, the thwarted screening stands as a glaring testament to the limits of so-called "liberalized" approaches to cinematic censorship—a regression to the overt, culturally invasive moral and legal film censorship of decades past. As an explicitly censorial event, it utterly belies the 1995 Classification Act's proclamation that Australian "adults should be able to read, hear, and see what they want."

Despite its unconditional banning in the only English-language market in which it ever was officially submitted for classification and/or ratings approval, *Ken Park* has gradually developed a cult following in the decades since its release. As Clark himself points out, "You can go on eBay and get a good DVD from Russia, France or the Netherlands. Don't get the Hong Kong ones; they're pixilated." (Qtd. in Martin).

5. *IRRÉVERSIBLE* AND THE CASE FOR VIOLENCE

At the turn of the millennium, the British Board of Film Classification was undergoing its own process of reform, shifting its emphasis (and public image) away from censorship and toward a model of consumer information, bringing its policies into closer alignment with the aims and processes of the Motion Picture Association of America's current ratings system. Despite this shift toward the censor's self-cleansing, important distinctions persist between the operations of government classification bodies on both sides of the Atlantic and their industry-oriented American counterpart. Chiefly, the MPAA's rating process remains a voluntary one, which filmmakers and distributors can forgo if they are willing to assume the commercial risks of doing so.

By contrast, the mandatory review processes of the OFRB, the OFLC, and BBFC render criminal the exhibition of films that have not received government certification. The rationale for the persistence of this legal stricture—that it is a safeguard, albeit flimsy, against the exposure of children to adult material—is potentially complicated by the fact that censorship processes generate continuous revenue from the filmmakers and distributors who must pay fees to have their products reviewed. Furthermore, the voluntary nature of the MPAA's rating system places the power to ban or confiscate illegal filmic materials within the jurisdiction of a given state's criminal code, highlighting the redundancy of intermediary institutions with remit to censor film content. The OFRB retains that mandate exclusively, where "pornography" is concerned, and the BBFC extends it even further by continuing to censor "mainstream" commercial films containing only allegedly lurid depictions of sexual violence (*A Serbian Film* [2009] and *Human Centipede II* [2010] being two high-profile examples). Nevertheless, the implementation of institutional protections of free expression for filmmakers, if limited, that occurred in Ontario and Britain in the wake of the *Fat Girl* controversy can certainly be viewed as progress toward a more liberal reception of films.

With its emphasis on informing consumers and its de-emphasis on suppressing "dangerous" or "harmful" materials, classification is a proposition altogether less affronting to foundational principals of Western liberal democracies than censorship. Not even the most ardent free speech fundamentalist would deny that measures should exist to prevent or regulate the access of children and adolescents to adult material, and so classification can easily be framed as not infringing on the rights of filmmakers and audiences more than is absolutely—and rationally—necessary in pursuit of this worthwhile social function. However, as this study is attempting to highlight through diverse avenues of illustration and argument, classification poses its own share of problematic and unexpected censorial challenges characterized most crucially by their invisibility. The fact that MPAA ratings criteria hold tremendous influence over a film's commercial prospects and, for various reasons, can produce a form of de-facto economic censorship is ideologically obscured by the American exhibition and distribution industry's perceived general status as a "free market" for film content. Similarly, the Ontario Film Review Board's restriction of its own censorial targets to "pornography" falls more squarely within the broader Ontario government's extensive regulation of public "vices" such as gambling or drinking, and thus doesn't stand out as a controlling process. It is perhaps in the BBFC's continued (though rare) federally implemented suppression of non-"pornographic" film content that the veiling of moral judgement, which classification has inherited from censorship, proves to be at its thinnest. Revisions to the BBFC's policies and review processes, which took place between 2001 and 2005, were less extensive in reach, and less absolute in limiting the Board's censorial powers, than was the process in Ontario.

Because the BBFC retained the remit to censor depictions of sexual violence in mainstream narrative films, many journalists and commentators were surprised by its decision in 2002 to approve—without cuts—Gaspar Noé's *Irréversible*, a film with few equals in its aggressive and punishing presentation of violence. Opening with an exceptionally graphic murder scene, swiftly followed by a notorious nine-minute anal rape scene, *Irréversible* seemed a likely candidate for the censorial wrath of British classifiers. Given the Board's preoccupation with depictions of sexual violence, the rape scene naturally became the focus of its professional consultation process and sparked concerns about the potential for repeat home-video viewing. While the film's passing uncut in Ontario merely spoke to its eluding the OFRB's criteria for pornography (visual material geared primarily toward audience arousal), its having passed uncut by the BBFC with hindsight suggests something more complex. It indicates that British reviewers saw something in the violence of *Irréversible* that was absent in the subsequent targets of its censorship (*A Serbian Film*, *Human Centipede II*). This redeeming quality cannot simply be reduced to the highly subjective notion of "artistic merit," or to an absence of potential (or a decreased potential) for societal "harm," though these factors likely played a role. More fundamentally, passing *Irréversible* reflects a proposition that this chapter pursues in detail: that even the most unpleasant and punishing scenes of violence, if they are presented within a responsible and appropriate artistic framework, hold the potential for the audience's moral edification. Violence can be artistic.

The Art of Violence

In his unfinished work *Aesthetic Theory*, Theodor Adorno laments the failure of post-war revolutionary art movements to resist cultural processes of commodification. He writes that "in the face of the abnormity into which reality is developing, art's inescapable affirmative essence has become insufferable," and that "art must turn against itself, in opposition to its own concept, and thus become uncertain of itself right into its innermost fiber" (qtd. in Grønstad 20). Through such statements, Adorno was calling for the radical formalism and reflexivity found in abstract art. To be sure, he would have rejected shock genre films for their infantile regressions rather than their aesthetical value. However, as an inescapable part of life, particularly at the time of Adorno's writing, it seems natural that violence and brutality would demand inclusion in art if it was to remain anything more than a narcotizing pleasure for the masses, and that for aesthetic form to retain its autonomy from commercialization in the wake of twentieth-century horrors, it must include visions of suffering in its creation of a parallel world.

As Adorno noted, however, any such effort is complicated in the processes by which the aesthetic techniques of vanguard artists themselves eventually become commodities, re-appropriated by the same systems they set out to critique. In the infamous opening of Luis Buñuel and Salvador Dalí's masterpiece of cinematic surrealism *Un chien andalou* (1929), an unidentified man drags the blade of a straight razor across the surface of a woman's eyeball, slicing open the soft membrane in a brief extreme close-up. The sheer violence of this moment: the graphic detail of the incision; the lack of moral or narrative context; the brazen assault on cultural sensibilities were scandalous for the time, no doubt in part for being so reflective of the psychological violence that permeated the inter-war "age of anxiety" in Europe, where writers and artists were "united in a sense of loss—of innocence, of moral certainty, of social values, of cultural confidence" (Overy 4).

Today, artistic shock tactics are familiar marketing tools, a status that inevitably strips some of their transgressive quality or rationalizes the transgression as popular, fashionable, and logical for broad audiences. Images that had the power to horrify previous generations of filmgoers have come to typify the accepted norm, now thoroughly re-contextualized, re-appropriated, and repackaged as mainstream entertainment. However, the violence in *Un chien andalou* functions very differently from that of the typical contemporary action or horror film. The cutting of the eyeball (actually a dead calf's eye), an obvious metaphorical negation of spectatorship, compels audiences primarily to look away. An involuntary aversion of the gaze is triggered by the prompt to—the garishly expressed provocation to—visceral and physical disorientation and revulsion. In a sense, the Dalí/Buñuel film is an early example of what might be labeled violence or shock "for its own sake;" Buñuel and Dalí were engaged in the conscious rejection of conventional narrative meaning, thus their presentation of the violent act bypasses any (even implicit) interpretive framework. The violence that now permeates commercial (most commonly, genre) cinema is completely the opposite in its desired effect. The violence in mainstream commercial crime, western, or horror films (such as *The Departed* [2006]; *3:10 to Yuma* [2007]; *Let the Right One In* [2008]) is typically among the major selling points of advertising campaigns. Teased in promotional materials, violence is carefully presented within specific commercial traditions and explicit moral and narrative frameworks. Posters for Scorsese's *The Departed* included the tagline "Cops or Criminals. When you're facing a loaded gun what's the difference?" With its balletic hyper-stylization, much of modern film violence is an invitation, not a challenge, to the gaze—a seductive spectacle offering viewers exhilaration, catharsis, pleasure, and a narrative pathway to order restored.

Reversing the Damage

Attending a screening of Sam Peckinpah's *Straw Dogs* in his formative years, French filmmaker Gaspar Noé claims to have "walked out" halfway through to recover from its "shocking impact" (Smith "Gaspar"). In 2002 (the year that *Straw Dogs* finally received an 18 classification without cuts in Britain), Noé issued a response by way of a harrowing film of his own. In experiencing a compulsion to leave the cinema during the rape scene of *Straw Dogs*, Gaspar Noé is perhaps the ethically and critically aware spectator with whom Pauline Kael feared Hollywood film violence was no longer aimed to engage (see Chapter 1). Where Vivian Sobchack experienced the opposite compulsion—a need to stay and confront the extreme anxieties into which the film tapped—Noé recalls thinking: "Well, if this (rape scene) is the middle of the film, I don't want to see what comes next" (qtd. in Smith "Gaspar"). There is, of course, a surface irony in Noé's recollection, because one might expect the director of *Irréversible*, often cited as the twenty-first century's most confrontational film, to have an unusually high threshold for cinematic brutality. However, his comment is profoundly telling for two reasons.

First, Noé's need to work through and make sense of the violent material in *Straw Dogs* was evidently not less imperative than Sobchack's but much more so, and presumably a key factor in his decision to explore the "rape-revenge" thriller sub-genre, which Peckinpah pioneered, and which Wes Craven's *The Last House on the Left* (1972) and Abel Ferrara's *Ms. 45* (1981) developed more fully. *Irréversible* is clearly a significant technical undertaking, which would not resemble certain narrative elements of *Straw Dogs* so closely had Noé not seen merit in Peckinpah's cinematic preoccupations. Secondly, Noé specifically (but coyly) indicates that if the order of scenes in *Straw Dogs* had been different—if the rape scene had not beckoned him onward, to further terrors lying in wait—his experience might have differed. The *real* irony, then, is in Noé's sensitivity: that he sincerely did not wish to continue watching. Its formidable reputation notwithstanding, *Irréversible* is therefore far from the product of a desensitized mind.

The plot of *Irréversible* can be summarized succinctly: a series of single long takes reveal, in reverse temporal sequence, tragic events that transpire between three friends over the course of one day in Paris. The film opens with Marcus (Vincent Cassel) and Pierre (Albert Dupontel) searching a gay nightclub, the Rectum, for a man named La Tenia (The Tapeworm), until Marcus aggressively provokes an unnamed stranger, who breaks his arm and attempts to sexually assault him. Pierre comes to Marcus's rescue, bludgeoning the assailant to death with a fire extinguisher. The plot continues backwards from this harrowing scene, showing: the chaotic trail that led the pair to the Rectum; the brutal anal rape of Marcus's girlfriend (and Pierre's ex-) Alex (Monica Belucci) in a red-painted pedestrian tunnel; a party at which Marcus's drug use causes Alex to leave alone; the trio discussing sex and philosophy on the Paris Métro; a tender scene of love between Marcus and Alex in bed; and the discovery by Alex that she is pregnant. In the final scene, Alex sprawls on a blanket in a busy public park, reading a book, while children play exuberantly in the shower of a nearby sprinkler. The image then dissolves to a vibrant white strobe light before a caption appears on screen, reading: "LE TEMPS DETRUIT TOUS" (Time destroys all things). Like the threadbare narrative details of the film's "surface" plot, the three main characters are not notably complex. The film contains little of the culturally and socio-politically specific themes of *Straw Dogs*, but primarily utilizes the language of archetype instead, suggesting the interchangeability of its key characters and scenarios.

The complexity of *Irréversible* is mainly structural. Its compositions, shot lengths, editing, soundtrack, and fragmented narrative are organized into patterns that directly relate to issues of perception and prompt the spectator to reflect on his or her own experience of viewing the film. Thus, the viewer's sense of watching is a central feature. For most, this experience is an extraordinarily unpleasant one—evidenced by the 130 rumoured walkouts at the film's première screening at the Cannes Film Festival in 2002 (West 51). Many viewers were said to have left during the opening sequence in the Rectum, not only because of the explicit violence in the scene but also because they experienced physical nausea induced by the kinetic camerawork and rumbling low-frequency soundtrack (Kerner and Knapp 27). *Irréversible*'s "high walk-out factor" (Hagman 36) speaks volumes to its presentation of violence and brutality. While Noé's script provides the minimum characterization and narrative context necessary to establish that the film's violence is, as Sobchack found with *Straw Dogs*, not wholly alien to its viewers, it also retains the visceral impact of *Un chien andalou*'s iconic eye slitting—a violence that compels viewers to look *away*. Throughout *Irréversible*, Noé employs a wealth of self-reflexive techniques that inhibit the passive absorption of violence feared by Kael, including (but not limited to): the visual abstraction of its action and space, focal identification with the victims (as opposed to the perpetrators) of its violence, and the often discussed but misinterpreted "reverse chronology" of its plot.

Like his New French Extremity contemporaries Claire Denis and Bruno Dumont, Noé has sometimes been accused of exploiting gimmickry in his filmmaking (by implication, for expressly commercial purposes). One notable example involves the appearance of onscreen text immediately prior to the violent climax of *I Stand Alone*, informing audiences that they have thirty seconds to leave the cinema and spare themselves the harrowing images to come. This moment has frequently been compared to William Castle's "Fright Break" in *Homicidal* (1961), creating something of a false equivalence. What Castle approaches as an opportunity to generate anticipation—to hype his horrors—Noé utilizes to trigger a series of ethical questions. "What might I see?" becomes "What shouldn't I see?" and then, ultimately, Kael's query: "How much is too much?" However, the content of the scene being warned about is delivered through bold and striking techniques designed to heighten sensory impact. In *Irréversible*, Noé continues (albeit differently) the strategy of drawing viewers into the violence onscreen, only to pull them out at key moments and have them question the nature of their engagement. Critical examinations of its "fire-extinguisher" sequence in the Rectum, where a man's face is brutally caved in, reveal an approach to screen violence that departs significantly from Peckinpah's in the "exhilarating" climax of *Straw Dogs*, the contrast between the films being emphasized by the scenes similarly depicting "revenge" in a particular discursive subgeneric context.

The most immediately conspicuous component of Noé's aesthetic toolkit in *Irréversible* is dynamic camerawork. From the film's opening frames, the shots move in wild spirals and arcs, at times rendering the action and players onscreen little more than a passing blur. Tim Palmer draws an aesthetic connection between the film's frenetic camera movement and the brutal content of certain scenes, a link that makes *Irréversible*, in every sense of the phrase, hard to watch:

> Vital sequences—shot upside down, most unbalanced or arbitrary in their framing, canted drastically off-kilter—segue into episodes of the camera being propelled through space, in extravagant loops and twirls. Melding digital and celluloid technologies, Noé's aesthetic design invokes avant-garde pioneer [Stan] Brakhage's efforts to create a cinema of raw and unmediated perceptual intuitions. At times, the impression is of free-form experiential data, wild and wandering visual patterns of light and darkness. (76)

At the beginning of the Rectum sequence, the viewer is given a tour of the club's labyrinthine passageways. For several minutes, the handheld camera swoops and lunges through darkened interiors, while capturing only fleeting glimpses of the clientele. The effect is extremely disorienting, as the spectator is swiftly thrust into an unfamiliar space where, as critic Stephen Hunter noted, "nothing makes sense, nothing is in focus, reality is scraps of information that refuse to assemble into a pattern" (C04). The emphasis in this prologue is on the camera movement itself, not on individual participants in the narrative (Atkinson 33).

As Marcus and Pierre enter the club, an extended tracking shot retraces the camera's previous path, this time with Marcus continually in frame as he interrogates the patrons. A semblance of narrative is beginning to form, since he seems to be looking for someone, but the camera's movements remain frenetic. Timothy Nicodemo points out that Noé's use of the tracking shot in this sequence is somewhat counterintuitive. While such shots are typically used to help the viewer to better understand the camera's surroundings, thereby allowing an unmediated view of the character's environment, in this case "the tracking shot deliberately disorients, nauseates, and confuses the viewer, aiming to subvert the very function of classical cinematography" (31). Although the camera movement continually calls attention to itself, it simultaneously serves the narrative by visually communicating Marcus's chaotic headspace and nervous energy. Because the reason for his frenzied state, not to mention the goal of his aggressive interrogations, has not yet been revealed, the viewer is denied any narrative frame of reference that might lead him or her to identify with Marcus's desperate aggression, even reluctantly. Noé is clearly not interested in helping his audience to understand the motivations of violence—but only to register its manifestation as reasonless and disordered. As Marcus, believing he has found the man he is looking for, is quickly shifted from aggressor to victim,

Pierre emerges seemingly from nowhere and begins raining blows upon the man's face, caving it into a soft puddle of tissue and bone fragments.

Pierre's gruesome murder of the unidentified man (Michel Gondoin) is utterly horrific and nightmarish, with many structural factors contributing to its shocking impact. First, in opening the film, its wholly obscured narrative context emphasizes its (diegetic) senselessness, an effect compounded by its visually chaotic build-up. Secondly, the combined use of an extended single shot and, at least for its time, seamless CGI gore, lends realism to the brutality, which is simultaneously alien in its unflinching extremity.

The formal construction and narrative context become particularly pronounced when the scene is contrasted to comparable fare from Hollywood. At the climax of Scorsese's *Casino* (1995), for example, notorious gangster Nicky Santoro (Joe Pesci) is beaten to death, his former associates sadistically pummeling him beyond recognition with baseball bats. While as disturbing as any such scene likely to be found in mainstream American cinema, the narrative and aesthetic presentation of violence differs from *Irréversible*'s in several notable ways. First, Santoro has been seen throughout *Casino* engaged in various sadistic brutalities of his own, including extracting confessions with the use of a metal vice and puncturing a random stranger's jugular with a ballpoint pen. Therefore, there is a sense of retributive justice in his violent death, a contemporary version of the "compensating moral values" evident in the Production Code's insistence that protagonists of 1930s gangster films must meet a tragic end (Wittern-Keller 278). With its reverse chronological plot, *Irréversible* denies its spectator such moral reassurance twice. Not only is the full narrative context of the Rectum scene delayed, but also when it arrives Pierre's victim is revealed to be an innocent, unconnected to the rape that prefigured it. Noé's violence is thus narratively intensively abstracted. Secondly, the moral order restored by Santoro's murder in *Casino* is reflected in Scorsese's formal and withdrawn treatment of the violence; the scene takes full advantage of its classical construction, alternating between wide, medium, and close-up shots to orient the viewer in a position standing back. By contrast, Noé's aesthetic treatment of violence is most affecting in the acuteness of his identification and camera once the viciousness has commenced.

As Pierre begins his attack, the camera settles on the ground beside the victim. Tilting up and down only slightly to follow the fire extinguisher's trajectory, the camera becomes largely stationary for the first time in the film. As Nicodemo notes, "the upward angle allows us to not only witness, but to receive Pierre's attacks" as the extinguisher blows land on the man's face directly beside the camera (34). Just as he managed to place viewers on the receiving end of the Butcher's self-directed violence in *I Stand Alone*'s climax, Noé here ensures that his oft-roaming camera is precisely where it needs to be to, itself, appear to fall victim to Pierre's explosive outburst.

Figure 5.1 Albert Dupontel (l.) and Michel Gondoin in Gaspar Noé's *Irréversible* (120 Films, Les Cinémas de la Zone, StudioCanal, 2002).

Noé would later take his use of camera technique to identify viewers with victims of violence to another level in *Enter the Void* (2009). This psychedelic exploration of reincarnation and drug culture plays out entirely from the first-person perspective of Oscar (Nathaniel Brown), a young drug dealer living in Tokyo. The viewer is granted immediate and permanent access to the subjective viewpoint of Oscar's senses. When, at the conclusion of the first act, Oscar is violently and unexpectedly shot dead by police, his death is constructed subjectively for the spectator. A gunshot rings out and the camera, which until this point had replicated Oscar's path of vision and navigation of physical space, tilts down to reveal an exit wound and a pair of blood-spattered hands. Oscar's dying thoughts can be heard trailing off as the image fades to black. The sequence is a haunting sensory experience of death presented from the subjective perspective of a dying body.

Noé's adeptness in preventing viewer identification with the perpetrators of violence is also evident in *Irréversible*'s controversial rape scene, which would prove a significant point for BBFC reviewers, who voted to pass the film uncut. In this sequence, Noé employs the same self-reflexive techniques that appeared in the fire extinguisher scene. For its entire nine-minute duration, the camera is fixed on the ground in front of Alex's face. The soundtrack is comprised entirely of Alex's raw shrieks, as well as the rapist La Tenia's brutally violent language. The spectator is disturbed first by the act, but then further by being made to endure "without cutaways, or movement to anaesthetize the violence" (34). Drawing on his experience as spectator of *Straw Dogs*, Noé's treatment of rape interrogates Peckinpah's violence, addressing its merits and mistakes.

Discussing Peckinpah's talents for rendering massacre, Richard Slotkin writes that his audience

> is engaged with an aesthetic equivalent of the ethical problem of violence: How much of this sort of thing are we willing to look at? Is looking somehow a form of 'consent'? [. . .] Are we willing to take responsibility for 'what we see' and for the curiosity—a form of wish or desire to see the unspeakable—that has brought us to this scene? (597)

By showing us the rape in its entire temporal unfolding, Noé brings such questions to the forefront of spectatorial experience. As there is little narrative or compositional motivation for showing such cruelty in its actual duration, "it could be maintained that the scene is not about the violence but about the act of looking at painful images . . . It is another way of asking, in meta-spectatorial terms, how much of this sort of thing we can endure?" (Grønstad 54). Through his punishing but conceptually dynamic techniques, Noé is confronting the significant concerns and morally precarious responses one might experience from watching Peckinpah's films, eliding their obfuscation by the experience of sensory immersion and processes of narrative decoding that typically allow cinema viewers to be wholly absorbed in the illusion of reality onscreen.

While *Irréversible* uses sex and violence to emotionally absorb the viewer, it approaches such subjects through formal strategies of disassociation. The resulting film thus demands emotional involvement while also forcing an awareness of the spectator's relationship to those emotions, as well as his or her own engagement and complicity in the visual representations of sex and violence onscreen.

Figure 5.2 Jo Prestia (l.) and Monica Belucci in *Irréversible*.

A Happy Ending?

The relationship between the depiction of violence in *Irréversible* and the reverse chronology of its plotline is a complex one. The bleakness of what at first appears to be the narrative resolution: Alex fallen into a coma from her attack; her lover Marcus in hospital himself, with serious injuries; and Pierre bound for prison for a vicious murder (the victim of which turns out to have been only a bystander), has led many to take its closing caption literally: time destroys all things. The artistic statement of Noé's film has been variously taken as profoundly fatalistic, nihilistic, and pessimistic; fearful of human nature and wary of the "civilized" discourses that oftentimes fail to conceal it. Among the most sophisticated readings of the film is David Sterritt's, which notes that its content and structure closely resemble those of the traditional apocalyptic narrative "in which perceived threats, social turmoil, and anomalous occurrences are interpreted as signs that foretell imminent worldly destruction [. . .] The effects of Noé's apocalypse may be limited to a small handful of characters, but its larger implications are inescapable" (191). Sterritt reads the film's narrative as a condemnation of the social repression that camouflages the revulsion and rage at the base of human instinct and impulse. "In *Irréversible*," he writes, "rituals like romantic love, marriage, the family, and friendship are revealed to be no more than vacant shams, and we are left with a resulting sense of anomie, disorientation, lawlessness and chaos" (192). While the element of apocalyptic revelation is indeed present throughout Noé's universe, some of Sterritt's analysis seems more ideally suited to a film like *Straw Dogs*.

Peckinpah's violence, withheld until the climax of *Straw Dogs*, permeates every social interaction contained within its narrative. In his relationship with his wife, his community, and his antagonists, David is thoroughly established as a creature of tremendous passive-aggressive habituation. When he finally breaks and overpowers his bullies (savagely and without mercy), the result is a disquieting sense of his *true*—and deeply enraged—self at last having emerged. The fact that so many viewers cheered on David's violence, much to Peckinpah's reported vexation, further suggests that his trajectory can in some sense be taken to represent that of modern man—a spiral into brutality and territorial imperative, which, as Peckinpah and Sterritt would no doubt have it, is merely delayed by hollow philosophies like pacifism and tolerance.

Irréversible's subversion of audience expectations related to rape-revenge narratives, its brutal opening (that is, conclusion) and blissful conclusion (that is, opening), not only abandon the "revenge" rationale for violence that tempts so many viewers of *Straw Dogs* but, in some real and important sense, *reverse* the morally bankrupting trajectory that gives humanity no quarter, here and across the rape-revenge sub-genre. The reverse chronology of *Irréversible*'s plot has been curtly dismissed in some quarters as a derivative gimmick (Lim AR12). However, its true purpose is a central riddle—many answers to which have been all too hastily arrived at in scholarly attempts to make sense of the film. Above all, one must keep in mind that the nonlinearity of the film's surface "plot" is by no means incidental to the moral territory it explores, and yet ultimately reducible to mere archetype and illusion. As a narrative (or more precisely meta-narrative), *Irréversible* is telling two stories at once. One is a simple tale of rape and misguided revenge. The other is the story that underlies most (if not of all) of humanity's core myths—that of beauty emerging from chaos.

In her comprehensive study of the rape-revenge sub-genre, Alexandra Heller-Nicholas writes, "By reversing the process from rape-revenge to revenge-rape [. . .] the bulk of *Irréversible* that occurs after Alex's rape is by contrast almost banal [. . .] As Noé has joked, the film actually has a happy ending because of this subversion, but the impact of the film's two opening scenes of extreme violence load that 'happy ending' with bitter irony" (168). As many have similarly contested, she adds that "the reversal of the rape-revenge story ultimately concludes in a celebration of a past that both rape and revenge destroy any possibility of returning to (hence the film's statement 'Time destroys all things')" (170). In his analysis of the film, Michael Atkinson arrives at a comparable understanding of the film's main premise: "In watching *Irréversible*, the viewer is constantly confronted with the question 'what if they had acted otherwise?' and it is easy to imagine as the film undoes each of its narrative threads that the future events did not have to happen" (28). Nick James and Mark Kermode write of the film: "The true meaning of (its) title lies ultimately in its depiction of violence as being utterly irreversible, suggesting that (contrary to generic law) a rape-revenge movie can only have a happy ending if you play it backwards" (22). While these attempts to articulate the film's real meaning are perfectly valid and defensible, they all seem quite willing to take Noé's profound pessimism as given. The reality, one could argue, is more complex.

It seems the feeling of "bitter irony" that some derive from the film's beautifully shot climax—in which Alex relaxes in a public park, surrounded by playing children—is not necessarily shared by Noé, who has referred to the power of these images to "erase" the disturbing ones that preceded them (qtd. in Smith). It seems quite likely that the absent promise of any such images at the conclusion of *Straw Dogs* chiefly precipitated Noé's walking out, his shock at the film's midway point only suggesting the further horrors to follow.

A clue to the film's statement about time can be found in the book Alex is reading—J. W. Dunne's pseudoscientific study of precognitive dreams *An Experiment in Time*—which posits that linear chronology is merely one way in which humans experience time (chiefly in the here and now of waking life). By contrast, Dunne argues, realms of dream and memory provide a different kind

Figure 5.3   Alex reading in the park in *Irréversible*.

of access to time, a "Time 2" in which past, present, and future are experienced simultaneously (Atkinson 27).

This is the experience of time that interests Noé. As the pregnant Alex ponders—almost meditates upon—Dunne's theories, the camera rises above her and, looking down, begins to spiral. The Second, Allegretto, movement of Beethoven's Seventh Symphony in A Major overwhelms the soundtrack, as the spiralling increases in speed. The camera tilts back to reveal a brightly lit sky, spinning in circles, becoming the image of a spiralling universe "metonymic of the ultimate creative act, the Big Bang" (26). A conceptual connection is thus formed between Alex's pregnancy and planetary notions of time and cosmic creation. Beneath Noé's "joke" of *Irréversible* having a happy ending is an earnest and profound truth. The film is a dream, and the reverse-order of its surface narrative is, in some sense, arbitrary. On a meta-narrative level, the beauty of life—the miracle of conception, the order of the natural world—does not follow *or* precede the pure chaos of irrational violence shown in the Rectum. These polar extremes of human experience, in fact, exist alongside one another. The "apocalypse" Sterritt finds in *Irréversible* is not imminent, now, or passed. It is always and ongoing.

Yet, the major riddle of the film remains: if the events of the film play out in "Time 2," where sequencing is arbitrary, why does Noé tell this particular story in reverse (as opposed to random) order? One explanation is that the reverse chronology allows Noé to redeem human experience for its ugliest forms. The meaning of *Irréversible* is archetypal; the meaning of many tales that came before it. As the film's intoxicating final shot proves, there is profound beauty in the universe. To glean it, however, one first must wade through (and survive) unimaginable chaos. As in life, what we most seek waits just beyond those places we are most afraid to look.

A Happier Ending?

It is all too fitting that BBFC reviewers should be presented with the confrontational brutality of *Irréversible* in the same year as their laboured reconsideration of *Straw Dogs*. Noé's own inability, or perhaps unwillingness, to stomach Peckinpah's presentation of sexual assault suggests that he too saw something in it that resembled the moral and ethical precariousness with which it was labeled by examiners, and which kept the uncut film out of home video circulation in Britain for so many years. By 2002, advice from professionals and experts had become a regular component of the Board's decision-making process—"especially where the issues were complex or the outcome likely to be controversial" (Duval 153). A clinical psychologist viewed *Straw Dogs* in its entirety, concluding that "harmful messages were unlikely to be taken from it" (153). *Irréversible* underwent a similar research process. According to the Board's press release for the film (at present the only documentation available), a clinical forensic psychiatrist was consulted: "She agreed with the Board that the scene is a harrowing and vivid portrayal of the brutality of rape. However, it contains no explicit sexual images and is not designed to titillate. The Board was satisfied, therefore, that no issue of harm arose in the context of a cinema release for adult viewing only" (qtd. in Hicklin 126). The Board ultimately released both films in their uncut forms, signaling the beginning of an increasingly liberalized form of censorship in Britain, one characterized by a greater emphasis on classification and a stronger mandate to seriously consider the artistic merit of films reviewed (117). By contemporary standards, *Irréversible* is more viscerally affecting in its presentation of rape than *Straw Dogs*, thus its "Adult Viewing Only" certification was a matter of extensive consideration for examiners.

Many critics of *Irréversible* did not agree with the BBFC's determination that the film's treatment of rape in fact constituted a brutal anti-rape message, as opposed to exploitative titillation. As Leslie Felperin, for example, wrote in the esteemed British film journal *Sight and Sound*:

> The film's S&M tactics and moral murkiness are most pronounced in the rape sequence. The fulcrum of the movie, the scene is all about provocation, from the shimmering flesh-coloured satin dress that seems painted on Monica Bellucci's perfect body (caressingly shot for maximum effect when violated), to the angle from which we watch the rape take place. Some have argued that because the camera sits unflinchingly though the nine-minute rape, and remains a few feet away during the beating, the scene is not exploitative, as if coolly discreet mise-en-scène automatically annuls identification with the rapist. Similarly, it's been argued that the very duration of the sequence drives home the atrocity of the act of rape. (48)

It seems plausible that if the BBFC had identified the issues of titillation that Felperin points to, it would have responded differently to the film. The example of these two divergent readings highlights the "difficulty of interpretation" as it pertains to censorial decision-making and the need to consider "a range of textual factors," such as shot type, duration, sound, and mise-en-scène when assessing the harm posed by cinematic depictions of sexual violence (Readman 46). However, it must be considered that the opinions of commercial critics are not necessarily representative of the reactions that engaged audiences report to experience during difficult and challenging viewing experiences.

According to the Board's press release, several factors contributed to their decision to pass *Irréversible* uncut. As with *Fat Girl* and *Baise-moi* (2000), *Irréversible* was discussed not only in terms of "serious intent" and "artistic merit," but also within the context of French art cinema, "thus providing a sense of cultural and artistic respectability that excused [the films'] explicitness and legitimized their release" (Hicklin 125). Martin Barker's audience-based research into controversial BBFC case studies has, at times, revealed a deep disconnect between the potential effects attributed to films by BBFC examiners and the experiences actual audiences claim. In the case of *Irréversible*, his findings echo the Board's press release closely:

> While it is certainly right that for many respondents, the director's Frenchness is something to discuss, it is also the case that it is [the film's] seriousness which is marked. This is spectacularly true for Noé's *Irréversible*, which is seen by many to be spoken from the "heart of a man," who has seen and understood, and wants to convey the horror of what men can do to women. ("Typically" 158)

Examiners, audiences, and a forensic clinical psychiatrist reached unanimous agreement that no pleasure could be derived from the rape scene in *Irréversible*.

The uncut release of *Irréversible* in Britain was timely evidence of the BBFC's shifting from censorship to classification, particularly its desire to publicly abandon what Janet Staiger identifies as one of the key aspects of censorship: the process of "inflicting the moral view of one group onto another" ("Interpreting" 77). Such rebranding was symptomatic of a broader trend of classification institutions failing to effectively assert their own moral viewpoint, particularly when faced with the wholly self-aware sex and violence of such filmmakers as Noé and his contemporaries. As part of an effort to distance itself from moral judgement, censorial passage of *Irréversible* was still a denial of the film's capacity for moral harm. Sexual violence remains a sensitive matter for the BBFC, but any concern over non-eroticized violence (even as confrontational as *Irréversible*'s) is effectively a thing of the past. In such a world, Pauline Kael's warning about the desensitization of moral feeling should stay with us. However, so too should Sobchack's belief in the function of cinematic violence:

> Knowledge is the magic which will save us; cataloguing or crumbling insanity; inspection will cure our anxiety. Blood and tissue, death and killing, rape and beating don't please us, don't titillate us [...] Yet we have the clear and present need to know them, to have them made significant rather than senseless [...] Our films are trying to make us feel secure about violence and death as much as possible, they are allowing us to purge our fear, to find safety in what appears to be knowledge of the unknown. To know violence is to be temporarily safe from the fear of it. (116–17)

As Alex tells the intellectualizing Pierre on the Paris Métro, "You can't explain everything." Chaos lurks beneath the surface of rationality. *Irréversible* shows the unwatchable; ponders the unknowable. It is a horror film of the first order, tapping into our most primal fears as social beings, while denying us any trace of sensual thrill in its brutality. It unmasks an ugliness that haunts the dark recesses of our world. And still, there is a bright light at the end of its red tunnel.

This analysis has attempted to posit the international release of *Irréversible* as something of a turning point in social and cultural discourses surrounding cinematic sex, violence, and censorship. Approaching the film's challenging material with a nuanced eye for narrative context and an increased emphasis on the importance of artistic intent, with fear of public censure for hyper-censorial practices and processes, classification boards passed even the film's most punishing scenes of sexual violence in their wholly uncut form. The reluctance of censors to tamper with the content of *Irréversible* demonstrated, first, that the kind of rigid adherence to film-regulation policy that had legally prevented the exhibition of certain previous films was being quickly phased out in favor of new policies geared toward imbuing the classifier with greater powers of discretion and, secondly, that while opponents of this process continued to warn of the potential "harm" that a video release of the film could conceivably cause, still the overwhelming critical consensus was far more concerned with the potential harm government interference in narrative film content might commit against institutional protections for freedom of expression. Less than two years after the censorship controversies surrounding *Fat Girl* and *Ken Park* in Britain, Canada, and Australia, it seemed that Noé's provocations had led cinematic artistry to victory in its arduous battle against repressed public policy. As in Britain, the film was passed uncut in Ontario and other Canadian provinces, and in Australia, receiving the respective version of the "18 and over" rating in both cases. The decisions were made despite complaints from the Christian Democratic Party in Australia (Lacey 57), and from select Canadian critics (Howell). To the chagrin of the relevant outraged parties, the film retained its rating.

Noé had come to represent the New French Extremity and *Irréversible*, by extension, the new benchmark for the artistic use of (and justification for) graphic film content.

In the years since the release of *Irréversible*, the trend toward extreme content in French art cinema has detectably waned. Perhaps when viewed through a historical lens, with greater critical distance, the cultural intersections between the visual politics, censorship battles, and audience experiences of the New French Extremity will become clearer.

For now, the current absence of the transgressive element from French cinema seems attributable to a complex negotiation of factors, including scholars gravitating toward the later, more "mature" works of its most promising filmmakers, liberalized censorship policies reducing the scandals that formed much of its publicity, and hardened audiences becoming increasingly shock-proof. As far as regulation, the uncut passing of *Irréversible* signaled an increasingly liberalized form of censorship in the West. The remaining chapters of this study examine how the impetus toward censoring serious art, now considered unfashionable if detected in government-mandated processes, continues elsewhere in the institutional structures and practices of cultural production.

PART III

6. CRITICAL CENSURE AND *THE BROWN BUNNY*

The cumulative controversial impact of *Fat Girl*, *Ken Park*, and *Irréversible* on international arthouse circuits became a flashpoint for the intensified scrutiny of classification policies, to much the same degree as Britain had experienced in 1971 with the near simultaneous release of Ken Russell's *The Devils* (which included masturbating nuns and the "rape" of a Christ Statue), Sam Peckinpah's *Straw Dogs* (with its uncomfortable masculinity and sexual violence), and Stanley Kubrick's *A Clockwork Orange* (showcasing extremes of anti-social behavior). While these were considerably more mainstream films in terms of studio support, director prestige, and projected audience size, their shared use of confrontational sexual violence, and especially the rapid succession of their appearances onscreen, had the inadvertent effect of making it increasingly difficult to negotiate for censorship on a case-by-case basis. Like the New French Extremity films, these New Hollywood productions collectively announced a shoddiness of pre-established standards of acceptability and a push to reconsider the role of cinematic art as a vital means of confronting the human experience—ugliness and violence notably included.

While *The Devils* was seen as a significant problem—portions of the brilliant but remarkably incendiary religious imagery remain tangled in various legal quagmires to this day—the BBFC certified *Straw Dogs* and *A Clockwork Orange* with X ratings, signaling for some commentators an inevitable demise of narrative film censorship. As *Evening Standard* critic Alexander Walker famously declared in his review of *Straw Dogs*, "What the censor has permitted onscreen ... makes one wonder whether he has any further useful role to play in the cinema industry ... For if this goes, anything goes" (qtd. in Simkin "Straw" 45). *Irréversible*, which shares many narrative and stylistic elements with *Straw Dogs*, represents a symbolic fulfilment of Walker's prediction.

As it pertained to *Straw Dogs* in 1971, the notion of an "anything goes" approach to the regulation of sex and violence in narrative cinema was little more than an abstract and wholly hypothetical construction. Filmmakers were left to read between the lines, as it were, to find whatever vague guidelines the BBFC decision might have hypothetically "drawn." However, when this sentiment of permissiveness resurfaced in critical responses to *Irréversible* it was lent considerably more weight by the extensive revision of policies making the operations of classification boards increasingly transparent. For instance, in the immediate wake of Ontario's banning of *Fat Girl* and the subsequent liberalization of OFRB's classification processes, *Toronto Star* film critic Peter Howell wrote in response to *Irréversible*: "I'm not a big fan of censors, but I do worry about what other taboos will soon be broken by attention-seeking filmmakers, now that the sluice gates have suddenly opened in Ontario" (B01). While the irony of his own attention-seeking by pointing to "attention-seeking" filmmakers appears lost on Howell, the self-imposed restrictions of censorial activity implemented by the OFRB in the Film Classification Act of 2005 did amount to a rough approximation of Walker's "anything goes" declaration: a state-sanctioned acknowledgement, protection, and perhaps even approval of precisely the kind of artistic risk-taking in which the New French Extremity filmmakers were engaged. It is worth noting, however, that Walker, like Howell, was by no means offering a value-neutral piece of sociological observation. He was, in the statement's fuller context, lamenting what he saw as the loosening of content restrictions, as certain critics in such transitional periods seem perplexingly keen to do. Perhaps as cultural commentators, critics to some degree see themselves as protectors of public tastes and sensibilities, thus become distrustful of audacious filmmakers who challenge the popular culture status quo. The dynamics of this phenomenon are complex.

Sociologically speaking, the charging of specific individuals with the task of monitoring is less significant as a means of controlling actual culture than as symbolic and ceremonial action that invites contemplation and affects the social or cultural status of those who support or reject the values of a particular lifestyle. In their examination of shifts in moral and institutional settings in the modern medical establishment, sociologists Peter Conrad and Joseph W. Schneider noted that some prestigious claims makers have greater power to define what is respectable and disrespectable, normal, and abnormal than others. Their analysis examined how claims making, in which both medical (doctors, researchers) and non-medical (corporations, professional and lay organizations) interests engage, comprises a key stage in the emergence of new deviance designations and the ensuing attempts to expand the turf of medicine's social control. In considering the adoption of new medical perspectives of deviance, they concluded that claims made by medical interests (i.e., loose professional alliances of doctors and investigatory committees) provide ammunition for the promotion of new designations by non-medical claims makers. These groups have direct economic and administrative interests in these new designations, and they can initiate activity through publicity campaigns and legislative lobbying in ways medical professionals can not (being less constrained by "professional ethics" and "scientific" credibility) (268). While inhabiting a markedly different cultural sphere, the interrelation between critics and censors operates in a way not totally dissimilar to the phenomenon Conrad and Schneider describe.

Critics, as cultural claims makers, are part of a broader hierarchy of designation in the claims making process. Along with censors and classification examiners, the subjective opinions of film critics provide a key stage in the social processes by which certain kinds of filmed content come to be designated as problematic. Mainstream criticism, conveyed via the public performance of taste, provides consumers with information about certain cinematic products, but is also constructed to shape the social and cultural status of critics themselves. While film criticism lacks the regulative and prohibitive power of governmental censorship, the claims of critics can fuel those of censors by advocating warrants and solutions that are subject to less scrutiny than are claims put forth by classification institutions. Like the claims of non-medical interests examined in Conrad and Schneider's study, the opinions of film critics are less constrained by "scientific" credibility than those of examiners, since their opinions will not become an official matter of public policy. However, the direct interest of critics in the promotion of certain ideas related to what constitutes artistic merit and worthwhile cinema should not be overlooked. As Howell's comment suggested, labeling certain cinematic strategies "problematic" can serve as a means of drawing attention to the critic as a self-appointed defender of culture against the dishonourable intentions of irresponsible and fame-hungry filmmakers.

The Censor Lives On

Any "victory" of New Cinematic Extremism filmmakers over restrictive classification policies necessarily owes a substantial debt to film critics, whose knowledge of artistic tradition and fluency in aesthetic language should ideally provide a counterpoint to the more pragmatic guidelines of classification policymakers and enforcers, one made possible by the fact that, at least superficially, critics would seem to inhabit a wholly unique sphere of professional engagement with cinema. Unlike traditional film censors, critics respond to cinematic work chiefly by way of personal taste, with no broader mandate to consider the well-being of society or the safety of citizens in rendering judgement and informing consumers. Although previous chapters of this study have suggested that censorship verdicts themselves can often be reduced to matters of personal taste, this is much more explicitly and intentionally the case with critics. One might wonder why Walker and Howell should express any interest at all in the revision of policies of which the mandates and goals fall so far outside their professional purview. One possible explanation derives from the fact that, at its core, commercial film criticism is as much a process of categorization as is censorship. As market-elected cultural representatives, critics arbitrate "good films" and "bad films" and therefore, while not engaged in traditional censorship, practice what is ultimately a process of classification. Accordingly, to the degree that censors adopt "classification" models similarly aimed at "informing" a divided audience, censors and critics are, in effect, brought closer together.

The ideological climate of a post-censorship media landscape expressly facilitates the formation of a conceptual link between film classifiers and mainstream commercial film critics. This study has thus far attempted to highlight how, despite extensive and ongoing reforms, film classification policies maintain and preserve impetuses and outcomes of traditional government censorship of cinema. However, the emphasis on informing (as opposed to protecting) consumers, particularly as carried out by federal and provincial government institutions, simply reframes familiar processes of social disciplining as operating within (as opposed to upon) the free marketplace of ideas. By 2003, as the uncut theatrical and home video release of *Irréversible* demonstrated, disruptive forms of narrative cinema like Noé's would no longer be forbidden to audiences, but merely discouraged by way of subjective categorization. Film critics, who are likewise engaged in processes of steering audiences toward certain films and away from others, may lack the power or desire to explicitly censor, but frequently engage in displays of *censure*, by way of professional performances of personal taste that publicly disapprove of certain narrative and aesthetic strategies (see for example Kael on *A Clockwork Orange* in Chapter 1). Although equating such practices to censorship is obviously contentious and problematic for several reasons, critical censure undoubtedly shares certain properties with film classification in its evident ability to impact consumer practices and, thus, to yield a degree of power over free production, distribution, and consumption of cinema.

To discuss censorship in the context of film criticism is, of course, to vastly expand its definition toward what Sue Curry Jansen calls "constituent censorships" ("Censorship" 8). Curtailment of overt regulative film censorship practices in Britain, Canada, and Australia in the early part of the twenty-first century brought their respective classification institutions into closer alignment with the Motion Picture Association of America's ratings model, an industry-initiative that remains somewhat unique in its voluntary, industry self-monitoring structure. American exhibitors and distributors are not legally compelled to submit their films for review, governmental or otherwise. They retain the option of a release designated "Unrated." However, this option inevitably carries a severe economic penalty by drastically limiting the number of theaters in which a film will screen, or stores in which it can be stocked. This is an example of "market censorship," the use of manufacturing and distribution resources to "inhibit or prohibit dissemination of ideas, information, images and other messages through a society's channels of communication" (221). In Jansen's analysis, market demands routinely place external restraints upon cultural content, despite the absence of interference by any government apparatus.

Vital to this notion of diffuse market censorship is an understanding that incentives to suppress or discourage certain kinds of content operate within, as well as externally to, the institutional structures and practices of cultural production. Even in the contemporary media landscape, with vast amounts of cinematic material available online, private and corporate interests control most distribution platforms, through which they exert broad control over audience demand (I return to this in Chapter 8 with reference to the public controversy surrounding the American distribution of Abel Ferrara's *Welcome to New York* ([2014]). This chapter focusses on mainstream film criticism as a powerful market discipline to which artists are subjected, one fully capable of inhibiting (perhaps even prohibiting) the dissemination of images.

As is the case with classification, film criticism is not inherently prohibitive. It too is based on the general assumption that providing information to individual consumers about a selection of films merely helps them navigate toward those for which they are estimated ideal viewers. Several other factors conceptually separate negative criticism from overt censorship: the fully acknowledged subjectivity of taste (an unfavorable review could as easily sway one toward a film as away from it); the precarious correlation between critical reception and box office earnings (due in part to promotional budgets that ensure an audience regardless of critical reception); and, perhaps most importantly, the touted culpability on the part of filmmakers, whom critics directly or implicitly point to as responsible for cinematic work that overwhelmingly displeases. While criticism, like classification, can impact a film's profitability, its prohibitive powers are generally restricted. However, as with classification practices, mainstream film criticism is often ill-equipped to address new and dynamic models of filmmaking deliberately designed to confound the methods of categorization upon which both systems rely. In such cases, displays of disapproval may become entirely disproportionate to the artist's perceived transgression. Such was evidently the case when American filmmaker Vincent Gallo, whose work shares an aesthetic affinity with the films of the New French Extremity, premièred his sophomore film *The Brown Bunny* at the 2003 Cannes Film Festival. What ensued was a celebrated case of acute critical censure, with ultimately censorial (in this case, self-censorial) implications.

Self-Censorship?

The scenes of explicit sexuality contained in Gallo's second feature, *The Brown Bunny*, were relatively uncontroversial from a regulative censorship standpoint, due in part to recently revised guidelines of film classification policies. Despite an explicit and reportedly non-simulated (Gibbons) scene of oral sex in the film's climax, *The Brown Bunny* was evidently acknowledged by Canadian and UK classification boards as falling squarely enough within the limits of "mainstream" narrative cinema, exempting it from the sort of regulations these institutions retain the remit to apply to "pornographic" films. While such a distinction continually threatens to dissolve into a mere matter of semantics, the fact that no concerted state-sanctioned effort has been made to censor Gallo can still be viewed as progress of a kind. Yet, in 2007 Gallo withdrew his recently completed third feature film, *Promises Written in Water*, from public circulation of any kind. Gallo has stated for the record that he has no further interest in bringing his artistic output to the market and thereby exposing it to what he has labeled the "dark energies of the public" (Leigh). Despite the absence of interference by a state-controlled classification institution in the exhibition and distribution of Gallo's films, his new work will stay "stored" for the foreseeable future. From the wording of his statement, what Gallo perceives as the crass mistreatment of his previous films exists in a somewhat different sphere than the various censorship controversies examined so far in this study.

Although Gallo's work has never been subjected to overt censorship, much of it remains inaccessible to the public—a fact that seems to demand cautious and qualified analysis. A certain temptation exists to dismiss his reluctance toward public exposure as the behavior of an overly sensitive and eccentric artist engaged in a particularly flamboyant performance of "self-censorship." Yet such an explanation too conveniently circumvents the very real external constraints placed upon market systems in which the agency of an individual artist is only part of a much larger social and cultural apparatus, one with the power to exert tremendous influence upon consumer tastes and demands. Only when examined in the context of *The Brown Bunny*'s notorious reception does Gallo's decision not to release *Promises Written in Water* become a particularly telling instance of how public and (more importantly in this case) critical censure can become akin to classification policies by way of a problematic tendency to guise subjective censorious impulses as objective realities. Accordingly, when considering the evident marginalization of certain artistic viewpoints, and the notion of "self-censorship" as a free and rational choice, we must locate some degree of agency in the institutional structures and practices of cultural production largely responsible for shaping international film markets and establishing standards of artistic value and merit. Mainstream film critics' targeting of *The Brown Bunny* upon its Cannes première clearly illustrates this phenomenon.

The scathing reactions that characterized reception of *The Brown Bunny* at Cannes can be read primarily as resistance to its brazen generic transgression and confrontational use of narratively decontextualized "shock" tactics. Its indeterminate genre status as an independent American "road"/"art"/"adult" film represents an equally challenging negotiation of audience expectation and artistic innovation, and its borrowing of aesthetic language from pornography in its climactic scene recalls *Trouble Every Day*'s use of blood-soaked images of vampirism and cannibalism for visceral but also potentially rewarding discursive purposes.

However, critical reactions to *The Brown Bunny* and *Trouble Every Day* differ in two key respects. Unlike Denis, Gallo would frequently become the subject of *ad hominem* derision, with the lambasting of his extremely personal film becoming highly personalized. The frequent accusations against the film's perceived self-indulgence seemed to open an unusually large critical space for disparagement of the particular "self" being "indulged" in the filmmaking. Gallo's lead actress Chloë Sevigny also bore a share of disparagement, with the "future" of her career (like Gallo's) being called repeatedly into question. Additionally, while critics like Marceau sought to disown *Trouble Every Day* for its perceived readiness to concede to mainstream appetites, *The Brown Bunny* seemed to draw the opposite criticism of apparently having been designed with no purpose other than to frustrate, alienate, bore, and revolt an already marginalized audience.

Boundary Issues

When addressing the challenges posed, by films like *The Brown Bunny*, to processes involving film classification, whether in government regulation or journalistic reviewing, a similar approach must be taken to any notion of cinematic "transgressions." To say Gallo's film contained a scene of un-simulated oral sex, a transgression of social standards, and was therefore subject to disciplining by critics would be too simple a rendering. In fact, the explicit sexual activity is rarely cited as an objection by mainstream critics, who seem more often to take issue with the film's pacing, and with what they perceive as Gallo's narcissism. However, as this analysis argues, neither the pacing nor Gallo's self-image can be neatly separated from *The Brown Bunny*'s graphic imagery. Gallo's real transgression is a fundamental resistance to genre delineation, and his film is ultimately an exercise in boundary transgression: in the collapsing of categorical distinctions that permeate contemporary culture. Gallo's film is structured and presented with the effect of blurring numerous perceived lines delineating various extreme binaries including life and death, narrative and pornography, reality and fantasy, and radicalism and conservatism.

It remains somewhat difficult to effectively assess immediate reactions to *The Brown Bunny*, as the version screened at Cannes in 2003 was subsequently re-edited (its length reduced by thirty minutes) before Wellspring Media acquired distribution rights in 2004. The analysis of the film to follow references the version currently available on DVD and may appear sufficiently at odds with *The Brown Bunny*'s egregious reputation to suggest that the differences between these two cuts are of paramount importance. However, the sheer dismissiveness in reviews by the film's most vocal detractors is palpable. Among these were legendary *Chicago Sun Times* critic Roger Ebert, who, when asked about *The Brown Bunny* outside of its preview screening, called it the "worst film in the history of the festival" ("Gallo's"), as well as *Entertainment Weekly* critic Lisa Schwarzbaum, who wrote, "It's unlikely that anyone will ever see a frame of Gallo's infamous folly again" (n.p.). Schwarzbaum added:

> There is little to analyze about Gallo's staggeringly self-absorbed road-trip fantasy, during which a dull guy [Gallo, oui] drives cross-country to forget the pain of a lost love and finally—the many who bolted the screening must not have known this was the reward for sticking around—demands and gets hard-core oral sex from that same love, played (if played is the word) by Chloe Sevigny. I was willing to give the filmmaker the benefit of the doubt, imagining that the road scenes belonged to a fine Iranian filmmaker, until Gallo stopped to wash his van, in real time. There is good reason to worry about a festival that, by implication, claims The Brown Bunny as among the worthiest American submissions of the year. (n.p.)

Both Ebert and Schwarzbaum's sentiments go well beyond indicating a need for trimming, having the complete opposite effect of marking the film as wholly irredeemable no matter what might have been done to remediate it. However, serious critical analysis of *The Brown Bunny* reveals it as an intensely lyrical and potent work of cinematic artistry. Following a detailed analysis of the film, this chapter offers closer examination of its fraught reception at Cannes, both to account for such a discrepancy and to highlight how the curtailment of overt "moral" censorship gives way to more diffuse "market" censorship practices in which film critics inevitably come to play a key part.

It is not difficult to form the impression that narrative storytelling is not *The Brown Bunny*'s primary focus, and that Gallo's real emphasis is on structural organization. His compositions, editing, shot lengths, and soundtrack are all clearly organized into patterns and structures that directly relate to sensory experience and issues of perception. However, the film's minimalist narrative is only deceptively straightforward. The lone protagonist, Bud Clay (Gallo) can be immediately recognized as a character at odds with himself: desperate to grow but repeatedly pulled down in emotional mire (the exact nature of which is withheld until the final moments of the film's climax). Bud is introduced in an extended motorcycle racing sequence, one de-dramatized with unbroken shots and alternating sound and silence. Handheld camerawork traces the path of his motorcycle, which moves in and out of focus, as it circles around a dirt racetrack. The sound of the roaring engine is muted partway through the sequence, as the images continue in silence. The effect is simultaneously disorienting and deeply contemplative.

Bud subsequently sets out on a south-westerly journey along the US Interstates, from New Hampshire toward his eventual destination, Los Angeles. In a mud-spattered black van, Clay joylessly stares through the windshield at passing staples of Americana: gas stations, motels, billboards, et cetera. This description fits several sequences throughout the film, comprising much of its runtime and making striking use of long static takes, facial close-ups, and melancholy musical accompaniment. These and, in fact, all the film's sequences are pervaded by a soft-spoken gloom that never truly dissipates. Indeed, the sheer consistency and (no doubt for some viewers) relentlessness of *The Brown Bunny*'s mood is perhaps its most striking achievement and greatest testament to Gallo's skills as a conceptual artist.

Figure 6.1 A characteristic shot from *The Brown Bunny* (Gray Daisy Films, 2003).

Impersonal and initially puzzling encounters with female strangers interrupt Clay's journey. His first scene of dialogue takes place in a gas station with a young clerk named Violet (Anna Vareschi). Catching sight of her nametag, he briefly emerges from his typically introspective mood to reciprocate her efforts at engagement. After they briefly exchange stilted small talk, he suddenly invites her to accompany him to Los Angeles, countering her initial hesitation with soft repetitions of the word "please." Strangely she agrees, and Clay drives her home so that she can gather her things. After a few moments of waiting outside, he becomes visibly overcome with emotion and drives away. This pattern of fleeting, sabotaged connection repeats in two subsequent sequences. One involves Clay approaching a tearful middle-aged woman (Cheryl Tiegs) at a truck stop and embracing her in a passionate kiss. Again, Clay is initially intrigued by the name "Lily" embroidered on her purse, but very little dialogue is exchanged, and the encounter ends abruptly. Later, driving through a run-down section of Las Vegas, he spots a prostitute whose beaded necklace spells "Rose" (Elizabeth Blake). He timidly requests her company, buying her lunch at McDonald's before suddenly, and apparently with no reason, asking her to leave the vehicle. Although these sequences are reserved in their revealing of narrative information, a key motif is being established. Clay is acting out a masochistic internal conflict: desperately seeking the company of a woman (with the name of a flower) but reluctant to find out where such companionship could lead him emotionally.

Figure 6.2   Vincent Gallo as Bud Clay in *The Brown Bunny*.

Discussions of *The Brown Bunny*'s use of landscape are prominent in the few worthwhile scholarly attempts at serious critical engagement with the film. In *Screening the Unwatchable*, Asbjørn Grønstad likens the film to Bruno Dumont's experimental horror piece *Twentynine Palms*, released in the same year, and relating the tale of a couple in a communicatively frustrated but highly sexually charged relationship encountering terror in the deserts of the American West. Grønstad reads both films in terms of what he perceives as an unmistakable relationship between "intricately interlaced ecologies: the desolate external landscape and the internal emotional geography of the main protagonist," a relationship in which "the condition of emotional paralysis that afflicts the characters is etched into their visual surroundings" (71). Grønstad's analysis, while pertinent, neglects to note at least one particularly stunning example of "emotional paralysis." At one point, Bud detours to the Bonneville Salt Flats in north-western Utah, a truly desolate patch of saltpan desert in which, for miles in all directions, one sees nothing but horizon. Famously used as a shooting location for Gus Van Sant's *Gerry* (2002) and P. T. Anderson's *The Master* (2012), the flats offer opportunity for a vivid representation of emptiness.

Dwarfed in the bottom center of the frame by expansive skies, Bud unloads his Honda motorcycle and rides away from the camera, gradually disappearing into the distance. The sequence is rich with terrestrial symbolism. Bud's emotional turmoil has been constantly relayed but not yet explained. Like the thick salt crust below his feet, the defensive shield surrounding his observable pain has yet to be revealed by the frustratingly minimal interaction he has had with characters thus far.

Pushing Daisy

In an early scene, Clay stops to visit briefly with an elderly couple, revealed to be the mother and father of his girlfriend from adolescence, Daisy. He informs them that Daisy and he are now living together in Los Angeles, but this news is met with disconcerting confusion on the parents' part. Daisy's mother has not heard from her and admits she has no memory of Clay. Shot in a single take with soft lines of dialogue punctuating long stretches of awkward silence, the sequence is morose and uncomfortable. The reason for Clay's visit is never made wholly clear, and subsequent narrative revelations call his claims about living with Daisy into question. However, this scene is thematically central for its introduction of the film's titular brown bunny, a tiny lop-ear quietly caged in a corner of the room. Learning that the bunny belongs to Daisy, Clay is utterly bewildered—as though if this is the case it could not possibly still be living. We sense Gallo's memory of the bunny reaches back decades. At a pet store in the following scene, as he inspects a group of caged rabbits, he learns from the clerk that creatures like this one live no more than five years; thus, perhaps the relatively small creature Clay just saw at Daisy's parents' house was not yet fully-grown. But his apparent disbelief or confusion about time signals that something is amiss. Moments later we see him softly kissing Daisy (Chloë Sevigny)—no longer a little girl, to be sure—as intentionally overexposed cinematography shrouds them in halos of white light. This blissful imagery, the only departure from the film's gloom, is revealed to constitute a dream, from which Bud awakens in a sterile beige motel room. It seems the appearance of the brown bunny has triggered something in him. His world is desolate and barren, but now it is haunted, too, by his memories of Daisy.

Very little is established of Daisy herself prior to her appearance in the film's final act. Arriving in Los Angeles, Bud drives past her house, sheepishly leaving a note. When she finally appears in the film's penultimate sequence, pieces of a complex emotional puzzle finally begin to fall into place. Bud sits on the edge of the bed while Daisy nervously approaches him. Despite his obvious reluctance, visually palpable in Gallo's stone-cold expression and understated gestures, they embrace as reunited lovers. The remarkable work of both actors infuses this sequence with an intense, foreboding quality, chiefly a result of the all-too-painful vulnerability on display. Their stilted interaction is interrupted by Daisy's frequent sojourns to the bathroom, where she smokes crack from a glass pipe stashed in her purse. Emerging higher each time, she attempts to reminisce with Bud, showing him a picture of them posing happily and reminding him of a chocolate bunny that he once bought for her. Bud appears to have no reaction, as if fighting to contain the emotional turmoil that has been swelling throughout his journey and now threatens to spill out at any moment. Daisy offers to leave and buy alcohol. With extremely grave earnestness, he informs her: "I don't drink . . . I don't drink anymore . . . ever." Here the sequence segues into the onscreen sex act with which it would prove to become synonymous. Daisy fellates Bud slowly and hungrily, while he verbally attacks her (apparently the emotional fallout from an incident still to be revealed). The scene seems to play in real time, alternating medium shots and close-ups.

Suddenly, the tone of Bud's castigation dramatically changes. His anger gives way to an apparently overwhelming wave of guilt and grief as the true fate of his relationship with Daisy is finally revealed. A flashback: shots of Bud driving in the suburbs are accompanied by Bonnie Beecher's song "Come Wander with Me." The title and lyrics suggest Gallo's cinematic invitation to the spectator to wander with him; that is, to join his aimless drifting and explore the murky terrain of both his and his protagonist's emotional headspace. However, the extra-textual context of Beecher's haunting recording highlights a brilliant instance of textual foreshadowing. The song was originally composed for a 1964 episode of *The Twilight Zone* that shared its name, in which a young rockabilly musician encountered a beautiful woman ultimately revealed to be

Figure 6.3 Daisy (Chloë Sevigny) fellating Bud in *The Brown Bunny*.

a ghost and a harbinger of the man's own death. Its deeper resonance with *The Brown Bunny* is made abundantly clear when Daisy, guiding Bud through his post-orgasmic emotional breakdown, informs him that she died from asphyxiation after he abandoned her at a party. The scene of explicit intimacy between Bud and Daisy was, then, merely an extension of his earlier dreaming of her, from which he will once again wake alone in another gloomy motel room. Like her pet brown bunny, Daisy exists in Bud's haunted imagination only as an impossibility: untouched by time and tragedy. Here, Bud's journey takes on new meaning and narrative depth. His erratic emotional makeup, melancholic contemplation, and pathological solitude are still products and processes of alienation, brooding, and anger, but now also of unimaginable guilt and grief.

Once the viewer is made aware of Daisy's death and the non-physical nature of her presence in the story, the full thematic spectrum of Gallo's experiment finally emerges. Clay's journey has not proceeded simply through the space of modern American landscapes, but was a metaphysical voyage through planes of time and spaces of memory. As the use of threadbare plot, unannounced flashbacks, and seemingly minimal character growth have been indicating, immeasurable regret has truly and permanently stunted the forward trajectory of Clay's life, dooming him to wander in a space neither wholly past nor present. The final shattering revelation, that Daisy was pregnant with his baby at the time of her death, recalls the caged bunny, the incongruous symbol of fertility, which Clay encountered earlier. It is no coincidence that "Come Wander with Me," with its ghostly connotations, accompanied Clay's winding passage through his childhood neighborhood to the house where this bunny remains (perhaps eternally) caged. This passage can be thought of as one into a purgatorial "twilight zone" of sorts, where boundaries between past and present, life and death, memory and fantasy have dissolved. The titular brown bunny, impossible in its existence yet manifest before Clay's eyes, had in fact heralded his entry into an ambiguous world of mystery and longing. The final shots of the film are of little comfort. Returning to his driver's seat, Bud steers his van alone toward some untold destination. This bleak sentiment of soldiering on, but to no clear purpose, echoes the fate of Gallo's subsequent work.

A Hard Sell

For a film typically painted as one in which "nothing" happens, *The Brown Bunny* presents an extremely complex interplay of symbolic signs and cultural concepts. It posits Clay as an outsider suffering through an internal tug-of-war. In some ways paralleling Gallo's situation itself, overwhelming negativity encumbers Bud's pursuit of fleeting redemption. His struggle remains relatable only to those with substantial time, patience, and understanding, none of which could evidently be afforded by American critics viewing the film at Cannes. In his review for *Variety*, Todd McCarthy called *The Brown Bunny* a "self-indulgent, two-hour, cross-country mope about a lost love unadorned by such niceties as psychological insight, visual flair or [intentional] humor." McCarthy apparently assumes the reasons why a mope about lost love *should* include flair or humor are self-evident. A critic for *The Village Voice* wrote at Cannes that:

> No one will ever accuse Gallo of pandering to anyone other than himself. The director treats his star's most banal activities—feeding a Coke machine or brushing his teeth—as monumental, if not world-historic, activities. Cumulatively hilarious, and perhaps the most narcissistic psychodrama in film history, *The Brown Bunny* features a borderline-autistic performance at once self-aggrandizing and withholding. (Hoberman)

Roger Ebert's print review was no more forgiving than his post-screening remarks:

> "The worst film in the history of the festival," I told a TV crew posted outside the theater. I have not seen every film in the history of the festival, yet I feel my judgment will stand. Imagine 90 tedious minutes of a man driving across America in a van. Imagine long shots through a windshield as it collects bug splats. Imagine not one but two scenes in which he stops

for gas. Imagine a long shot on the Bonneville Salt Flats where he races his motorcycle until it disappears as a speck in the distance, followed by another shot in which a speck in the distance becomes his motorcycle. Imagine a film so unendurably boring that at one point, when he gets out of his van to change his shirt, there is applause. ("Gallo's")

The validity of these criticisms aside, the language is oddly hostile: characterizations of the film as "unintentionally humorous" and "unendurable" seem rather overblown. They recall complaints of *Trouble Every Day*'s lack of "redeeming context" and fail to recognize *The Brown Bunny*'s minimalist treatment of its main character and exceedingly measured pacing as deliberate components of its formal design. Curiously, McCarthy also echoes Ebert's judgement of the film as the worst in Cannes history by stating that its mere presence in competition "prompts major questioning."

These—and Schwarzbaum's—clear attempts to invalidate the film's artistic credibility and see it, as well as other similar films, stripped from future Cannes programming seem motivated by more than simple experiences of boredom. While these critics rarely cited the sexually explicit climax as a point of objection, their disparagement of *The Brown Bunny*'s minimal narrative cannot be neatly untangled from its use of graphic physicality onscreen. The film's deliberate pacing and minimal narrative are not operating in isolation, but are working in tandem with the explicitness of the sexual action as a means of evoking affective responses. The withholding of "plot" details, which would place the sex in a clearer emotional context, results not in aggravated display but in dedramatization, both evoking and pinpointing hard-core pornography and its systems of automatic bodily response. In the face of skeptical questions about the sexual activity and the filmmaking process, both Gallo and Sevigny have suggested that the scene was entirely non-simulated (Gibbons). While such a claim is impossible to verify (for obvious reasons), it is lent tremendous credibility by the conventions of hard-core pornography incorporated into, even featured in, the scene, particularly in the close-up nature of some of the compositions and the real time duration and confrontational explicitness of the action. The scene's allusions to hard-core pornography knowingly and boldly transgress a cultural boundary that, as Slavoj Žižek has argued, implicitly prohibits the inclusion of emotionally engaging narrative within that genre (TIFF LIVE). In Gallo's own words:

> I'm using traditional iconic images. Pornography is the ability for somebody to have enhanced sexual pleasure or sexual fantasy free from responsibility, guilt, insecurity, consequence, etc. etc. What I've done is taken those icons of pornography and juxtaposed them against responsibility, insecurity, resentment, hate, greed, mourning—together. There's

no way to separate them in my film. There's no way to look at that scene and be titillated or sexually aroused. People who get off on pornography are revolted just by the kissing scenes because they can't take the level of intimacy and complex issues surrounding intimacy in that film. The graphic images are used to enhance those sequences. (Qtd. in Murray)

Thus, the film establishes a (perhaps culturally unwelcome) connection between graphic physicality (typically geared toward arousal) and intense emotional experiences of regret, guilt, and grief.

By 2003, of course, non-simulated sex scenes were nothing new to cinema. The scene in *The Brown Bunny* is unique mainly for its involvement of two reasonably well-known actors in the explicit action onscreen, a strategy that other filmmakers such as Lars Von Trier and Noé have consciously avoided in their explorations of similar territory with *Nymphomaniac* (2013) and *Love* (2015), respectively (Noé by casting unknowns and Von Trier by digitally compositing the faces of stars with the bodies of stunt performers). And while nude scenes involving female stars are less frequently remarked upon by viewers and reviewers, the decrying of Gallo's exposed genitalia in *The Brown Bunny* is reflective of a "greater resistance to male bodies onscreen than female bodies" (Readman 42). As Tom Dewe Matthews writes:

> For the film censors . . . male genitalia are the most taboo-ridden area of human anatomy. Probably this is because of the masculine monopoly of the [censors]—not to mention the establishment at large—and the notorious heterosexual male aversion to the exposure and resultant demystification of the male crotch. (178)

The sexual element of the controversy surrounding *The Brown Bunny* was mirrored in that of Michael Winterbottom's *9 Songs*, released the same year and described by *The Guardian* as "a non-pornographic film with two actors playing lovers and having real sex on film" (Jeffries). Both films successfully passed the test of censor boards' discretionary powers to distinguish, via tone, intention, and treatment, between works intended primarily to arouse and works seeking new ways of exploring human emotion and relationships. Winterbottom's *9 Songs* ran similarly afoul of critics, which may perhaps have been due in larger part to its many narrative and aesthetic weaknesses. *The Brown Bunny*, though controversial for similar reasons, is a decidedly more adventurous piece of experimental cinema.

It is somewhat difficult to accept that the censorious critical response to *The Brown Bunny* bore no relation to its frank and gloomy sexuality, especially where the objections cited by critics were less than self-evidently problematic. The tenor of Roger Ebert's comments is especially curious when contrasted with his notably appreciative reviews of the other two American films in competition that year. Of Gus Van Sant's *Elephant* (2003), which would go on to win the Palme D'or, Ebert writes that Van Sant "avoids the film grammar that goes along with medium shots and close-ups ... and so his visual strategy doesn't load the dice or try to tell us anything. It simply watches" ("Elephant"). Likewise, of Clint Eastwood's *Mystic River* (2003), Ebert fawns: "In a time of flashy directors who slice and dice their films in a dizzy editing rhythm, it is important to remember that films can look and listen and attentively sympathize with their characters" ("Mystic"). The lack of clarity as to why "simple watching" and "attentive sympathizing" is apparently impossible with Bud complicates the deployment of Ebert's "good"/"bad" classification model evident in his consideration of the competition's fare. The criteria delineating between, on one hand, "simply watching" or, on the other "attentively sympathizing" with "90 tedious minutes of a man driving across America in a van" ("Gallo's") are not immediately self-apparent, due in part to the primary focus of Ebert's review of *The Brown Bunny* being his own experience of boredom while viewing it. Uninspired by the film, the critic could still be inspired to pronounce. Instead, Ebert joined in the rhetorical admonishment of Gallo's film, proclaiming that "by no standard, through no lens, in any interpretation, does it qualify for Cannes" ("Gallo's"). By challenging the legitimizing effect of *The Brown Bunny*'s selection by festival programmers, Ebert struck a blow to Gallo's credibility that was no doubt salted by the well-established Hollywood credentials of Van Sant and Eastwood.

There could not have been a more appropriate backdrop for such drama than Cannes, which institutionally functions as a microcosm for much broader practices and processes of cultural production and distribution. Large film festivals act as "central sites" within a global film system, offering, "in their opposition to the vertical integration of Hollywood's film industry ... alternative and secondary platforms for marketing and negotiation" (De Valck 87). For decades, Cannes had been virtually synonymous with such opposition, and its acceptance of *The Brown Bunny* (an independently funded feature) was, in some respects, an audacious decision for its organizers. The modest success of Gallo's debut *Buffalo 66* (1998) had done little to establish him as a powerful presence in Hollywood or world cinema. However, such a risk entails certain reward, as controversy has long been key to Cannes's marketing purposes of signifying it as a place where bold aesthetic risks are taken (Hagman 34). To suggest that reviews of *The Brown Bunny* reflected a failure of the festival's programming staff assumes the significant attention garnered by the reaction to be as potentially detrimental to the festival as to the film itself, and this simply may not be the case, as media spectacle is a vital component of film festival networks, Cannes in particular. Like the (much more economically powerful) Hollywood film industry, the international film festival circuit relies on a necessarily "spectacular mode of conduct" (De Valck 119). In other words, Cannes, like Hollywood, remains a powerful force in world cinema through its power to create spectacular images and circulate these globally via the media.

One such image emerged two days after *The Brown Bunny*'s première, when British film journal *Screen International* ran a story quoting Gallo as saying: "I accept what they say, it's a disaster and a waste of time . . . It was never my intention to make a pretentious film, a self-indulgent film, an unengaging film, a useless film" (qtd. in Gibbons). Word quickly spread that Gallo had apologized for *The Brown Bunny*, despite his immediate insistence that the report was fabricated. No audio or video clip has been offered to contradict his claim; however, the Associated Press immediately began distributing the Gallo quote worldwide (with Ebert being one of the first to reprint it). For some, the idea of a contrite filmmaker publicly shamed into apologizing for a pretentious artistic stumble may promise a certain Schadenfreude. However, the effort by market forces to discredit Gallo's radical aesthetic ideas—indeed to posit that he himself discredits them—is made more troubling by a concurrent increase in Hollywood's practice of flooding the film festival circuit with mainstream American films, part of its larger general bulldozing of international film markets (Hagman 32). The following year, Cannes had increased the number of high-profile Hollywood filmmakers in its competition (among them Michael Moore, Stephen Hopkins, and the Coen Brothers), and selected as its opening film the $125 million Hollywood blockbuster *The Da Vinci Code* (2004) (a notable contrast from the 2003 opening film, the $22 million French adventure-comedy *Fanfan la Tulipe*). By 2006, critics and commentators were already lamenting the lack of dissent being provoked at Cannes (Mazdon 9).

A Question of Character

When we consider the evident importance of controversy and spectacle to Cannes's continued relevance on the world stage, the functional utility of *The Brown Bunny*'s disparagement becomes apparent. It was neither bombastic nor adventurous nor visually bizarre enough to please the new Cannes mainstream. However, the film's character does not explain why the film was singled out from all those in competition that year. When asked to comment on this scandalous reception at Cannes, Seiichi Tsukada, an executive at Kinetique (the film's financiers), told *The Observer*: "The bashing is not for *The Brown Bunny*. I think they're bashing Vincent. I don't know why" (qtd. in DiGiacomo). It is possible that Gallo's moderate recognizability and boisterous reputation as a Hollywood actor perfectly suited him to the "role" of an alienated artist. It has been suggested that Gallo's onscreen protagonists are involved in symbiotic relationships with his offscreen persona (Léger 90). In this instance, "offscreen" is perhaps a more constructive term than "real-life," as one might speculate that Gallo's often scathing and harsh outspokenness about critics, collaborators, and mainstream cinema audiences is a performance as meticulously calculated as anything we see on film. His distinctive Gen-X New York hipster sensibility, idiosyncratic vocal cadences, and vintage-chic fashion sense (all present but less consistently visible in his acting work for other directors) certainly infuse his fictional protagonists with a remarkably distinctive artistic signature. More importantly, Gallo, like Bud Clay, presents himself publicly as an alienated loner whose complexity is misunderstood and internalized, frequently resulting in intense feelings of ostracism and exile.

In some ways, Gallo's performances (both behind and in front of the camera) can be read as being replete with contrarian gestures, symptomatic of his broader embracing of unusual cinematic techniques and obscure motifs tailored to the refined tastes of a sophisticated few and wholly incongruous with mainstream appetites. His notable offscreen behaviors include frequent declarations of his own greatness, the occasional use of antisemitic and homophobic language, and active support for neoconservative politicians (somewhat rare in liberal artistic circles). When asked in 2004 by Howard Stern to explain his defense of unpopular policies being carried out by the Bush Administration at the time, Gallo defended himself: "It seems to me one would have to be slightly unpopular to have profound vision" (ceasestoexist). One can imagine him responding quite similarly in defense against *The Brown Bunny*'s more aggressive detractors. Some critics have argued Gallo's conservative personal politics are evident in the morality of his protagonists. For instance, of *The Brown Bunny*'s climax, where a series of flashbacks-within-the-flashback reveals that Bud and Daisy's relationship dissolved when several men took sexual advantage of her while she was intoxicated, Cynthia Fuchs writes:

> This changes everything that came before, in a startling and frankly innovative way. It is his awful, ugly fantasy, vengeful and cheerless, and invites you to dislike Bud (and perhaps Gallo) with a newfound urgency. He's the most heinous sort of "conservative," monstrous in his judgments and condemnations, unable to budge from his preconceptions. That he has reasons—primarily rage, fear, and guilt—doesn't excuse his behaviour or his ugliness. At the same time, Bud's sadness and sense of responsibility make him believe himself a victim, whether of his own moral tyranny or his love of an indecent woman. ("Brown")

As Bud re-lives the experience in his mind, he chastises Daisy as drug-dependent and promiscuous. Offscreen, Gallo has spoken passionately of his hatred of drugs and drug-induced behavior (Takano). However, given his use of pornographic aesthetics in this scene, there is a certain irony in Fuchs reading Clay's condemnation of Daisy as being morally puritanical.

Like Bud Clay, Gallo appears as something of a walking contradiction. One may be tempted to understand his work as simultaneously avant-garde and right-wing, exploiting the freedoms of liberal artistic traditions to propagate deeply held conservative values. If this is the case, *The Brown Bunny* foreshadows the contrarian sensibility of provocative "republicanism," which combines social liberalism (a certain queering of the masculine persona and celebration of decadent hedonism) with fiscal conservatism (advocating of free trade and closed borders). Yet, while Gallo's unapologetic and, at times, incendiary personal attitudes and politics may have made him a more suitable whipping boy for criticism at Cannes, they do not seem in themselves capable of generating the intensity of ire that characterized *The Brown Bunny*'s reception. As previously mentioned, *Mystic River* was embraced at the same Cannes market, despite Eastwood's own penchant for right-wing politics, self-aggrandizement, and occasionally apparent bigotry. Worth noting, however, is an allegation that the booing and jeering in both the press and public screenings of *The Brown Bunny* at Cannes (Takano) began no later than the second title card, which read "written, directed, edited and produced by Vincent Gallo." Unlike most independent filmmakers, who delegate creative decisions to multiple individuals, Gallo exerts an unusual degree of control over almost every facet of his films, which are products of a much more singular artistic vision than the practical constraints of filmmaking typically allow for.

Most unusual is Gallo's refusal to employ any agents, publicists, or managers to handle his affairs, which solidifies the perception of him as a "non-player" who can afford to be unguarded in his frequently harsh criticism of mainstream audiences, former co-stars, and other members of his artistic peer group. At the film's pre-screening press conference, Gallo jokingly boasted about firing both Kirsten Dunst (because of harassment from her "nasty" agent Theresa Peters) and Winona Ryder (because of her addiction to "tablets which seemed to have impact on her behavior") before hastily recasting both roles with help from his "crew of two" (qtd. in AP Archive). In this instance, Gallo advertises his circumvention of the Hollywood system but goes further, playfully exposing and satirizing it. In this sense, one might expect Gallo and his work to be embraced as personifying Cannes and the international festival market's (dwindling) opposition to Hollywood. Instead, mainstream critics whose livelihood is (not coincidentally) generated by and dependent upon this very system attacked Gallo's apparent brazen self-reliance and irreverence toward the established "way of doing things," purporting him to be showing nothing more than unabashed narcissism, as evidenced most outrageously by his willingness (or desire) to receive non-simulated fellatio onscreen. Gallo took exceptional offense to his characterization as a narcissist:

To call that film narcissistic or self-indulgent because I multi-task? Do you think it's fun to work without an assistant? Do you think it's fun to work without support, a production office? To sit there in a fucking van with three guys, driving through the desert? A van packed with camera equipment that I have to unload every day, that I have to fix every day, that I have to reload into the van because God forbid one of them should lift one fucking case on the film. Do you think that was self-indulgent? ... I was interested in the film for the purpose of the film, and I moved past my insecurities, my self-doubt, my self-hate, my incredible privacy that I value. I pushed that aside to achieve the goals that I had in the movie. And I think they're very clear in the film. I think if you see that film, it's clear that my intentions were to create disturbing effects around intimacies—both metaphysical and personal intimacies with this character's life. (Qtd. in Murray)

Janet Staiger argues that censorship (in its broad understanding) can be seen as a form of "social disciplining" and a "significant social response to representations" ("Bad" 5–6). Seemingly, market forces sought to discipline Gallo's various offscreen transgressions by attacking their visual equivalent onscreen. Gallo's abrasiveness may explain *The Brown Bunny*'s desirability as a target of critical censure. Its suitability for targeting, however, lies squarely in its refusal to adhere to classical standards of controlled separation: between art cinema and pornography; road film and adult film; narrative and experimental cinema; mainstream and fringe.

A PROBLEM OF CLASSIFICATION

The Brown Bunny has been largely ignored by genre critics and scholars who, as Rick Altman claims, "systematically disregard" films that fail to exhibit clear generic qualifications (17). Even Linda Williams, writing of pornographic cinema, dismissed Gallo's film as "a poor imitation of European angst" (284) (thinking, perhaps, of Antonioni). As an artful, sombre study of a disaffected male, *The Brown Bunny* does perhaps owe a large debt to *L'Eclisse* (1962) and *Zabriskie Point* (1970), films that also faced scrutiny at Cannes and from Roger Ebert, respectively (Balio 196; Pomerance "Antonioni" 180). Shot on 16mm color reversal film and prominently featuring elements of motorcycle culture, *The Brown Bunny* also pays substantial tribute to the experimental cinema of Kenneth Anger, whose 16mm films *Inauguration of the Pleasure Dome* (1954), *Scorpio Rising* (1964), and *Lucifer Rising* (1972) are visually similar in their dense and highly saturated colors. However, Gallo's film operates most aptly in the mode of the late 1960s "sexual alienation" film, which Raymond Durgnat identified with reference to *The Graduate* (1967) and *Midnight Cowboy* (1969) (95). In a sense that runs counter to its lurid reputation, the film possesses an unexpected quality of innocence, made manifest in its grainy nostalgic appearance, its conservative gender politics, and its charmed fetishizing of flowers, kissing, and motorcycles. Gallo's preoccupations and sensibilities place *The Brown Bunny*, seemingly a messy intersection of art and hard-core, amongst realist adult classics like *Midnight Cowboy*. Bud Clay, like Joe Buck, is a figure on the margins of society, one whose misguided journey feeds upon and eventually shatters his boyish naiveté.

In an eerie final burst of synergistic effect, it seems Gallo's own naiveté was shattered by the mechanics of the Cannes market. Critics with tremendous power to influence audience sensibilities and revise the rules of interpretive activity received his deeply personal cinematic expression with ridicule and censorial rhetoric. Lisa Schwarzbaum's prediction was premature as it applied to *The Brown Bunny* but has since come to pass. Gallo's cinematic artistry has forfeited its battle with cultural hegemony and the conditions of production and consumption that produce it. Or perhaps this interpretation is itself naïve. Just as films of the New French Extremity confounded the policies of classification boards, provoking the censorial wrath of the moral entrepreneurs to whose standards of tastefulness and decency they posed a threat, so too at some level did *The Brown Bunny* perhaps knowingly upset the criteria of mainstream critics and trigger elaborate performances of censure. The years since its release have seen the democratizing effect of online film reviewing lessen the profile and influence of mainstream critics. Since Roger Ebert's death in 2013, it is unlikely the personal taste of one individual will ever hold as much sway in guiding cinema audiences toward certain films (and away from others). Cannes continues to manufacture spectacles of glamor and disaster. The cinematic work around which these spectacles center is frequently more explicit but (for a host of reasons) rarely as audacious. In the contemporary media landscape, free of government censors and domineering critics, one can see virtually anything onscreen . . . Anything, that is, but the latest Vincent Gallo film.

The mechanics of advertising and circulation, as well as the cultural understanding of the film festival as marketplace, produces an economic configuration in which influential critics hold a more significant degree of control over what films get sold and/or seen than they are perhaps generally perceived to do. Films totally unsuccessful in the Cannes marketplace tend not to get marketed—that is, picked up in distribution deals—which constitute the end purpose of Cannes and of most commercial film festivals. With its confrontational aesthetic and minimal concessions to narrative convention, *The Brown Bunny* was declared an unfit commodity for the Cannes marketplace; a label that transcended the specifics of its origin and that manifested as a more far-reaching suggestion that Gallo himself deserved no place in the broader cultural marketplace of ideas.

The censure of provocative artworks and the resulting economic, cultural, and critical marginalization of their creators is by no means a rare occurrence in the contemporary media landscape. However, Gallo's case is atypical of Jansen's market censorship framework in certain important respects. His personal agency in making his recent work unavailable, despite its complex causal relationship with the market discipline of mainstream film criticism, can be considered clear-cut "self-censorship"—a term that many theorists prefer to apply, based on the naïve assumption that individual artists bear the sole responsibility for ensuring that their output is viable and competitive in a free and open market, or that it is doomed.

7. *WOLF CREEK*'S HOSTILE AUDIENCE

The horror genre has always been a particularly vulnerable target for formal censorship, as well as for social disciplining in a broader discursive context; a flashpoint for cultural control of the cinema. This was particularly the case in the latter part of the twentieth century when the genre's associated conventions and expectations were increasingly bound up and wrapped in the presentation of "high impact" violence. Perceived by cultural critics as lacking the artistic merit apparently self-evident in the more mainstream genres of drama and comedy, the intentions of horror filmmakers have often been perceived as exceptionally cynical; a business model for generating box office revenue by exploiting abhorrent tastes and proclivities. Even in the "post-classification" twenty-first-century media environment, horror films (particularly those containing "sexual violence") remain the exception to the rule that viewing rights of adult audiences should supersede the perceived threat of indecent or potentially corrupting cinematic material. This thinking is evidenced in the BBFC's censorship of notorious early millennial horror films including *A Serbian Film* (2010) and *Human Centipede II: Full Sequence* (2011). Both films were granted classification in Britain only if distributors agreed to remove certain sequences depicting "abhorrent" sexual violence. A comparable Australian example can be found in the OFLC Review Board's censorship of Canadian filmmaking collective Astron 6's horror-comedy film *Father's Day* (2011), similarly censored for abhorrent sexual violence.

Conventions of the horror genre were also instrumental in the abrasive strategies of the New French Extremity. *Trouble Every Day* draws on the literary gothic vampire in its themes and motifs, while Gaspar Noé's *I Stand Alone* famously draws its pre-climax "gimmick"—warning the audience of impending violence with flashing onscreen text—from 1950s shock merchant William Castle. The NFE movement also produced the peculiar case of Bruno Dumont's *Twentynine Palms*, the rare example of, as Dumont himself called it, an "experimental horror film" (see Chapter 2). For the sake of precision, one could consider the NFE's initial wave as concluding with *Twentynine Palms* in 2003, although the reality is slightly more complex. The filmmakers responsible for its formidable status (Denis, Noé, Dumont), pivoted their attention in more "mature" directions. Denis continues to blend genre and arthouse tradition to great effect, as seen in *Bastards* (2013) (art-neo-noir) and *High Life* (2018) (art-sci-fi). Noé pursued sci-fi in a psychedelic vein in *Enter the Void*, and Dumont returned to more conventional arthouse fair in *Hadewijch* (2006). Notably though, the French industry continued to flirt with largely American and British traditions of commercial horror filmmaking—with decidedly mixed results.

A series of internationally successful horror films emerged from France in the latter part of the 2010s—films including Alexandre Aja's *High Tension* (2003), Alexandre Bustillo and Julien Maury's *Inside* (2008), and Pascal Laugier's *Marytrs* (2008). Such titles have often (unproductively in my opinion) been counted in surveys of the New French Extremity, despite departing significantly from the criteria outlined even in James Quandt's original identification of the trend. Namely, the NFE was characterized chiefly by the incorporation of horror and pornography conventions into what were *unmistakably* art films. These latter titles reversed the dynamic by including art film conventions (albeit few and far between) into the firmly genre-oriented thrills of horror filmmaking. Art film is chiefly about the subversion of the very sorts of expectations that genre entertainment is meant to fulfill, and these latter French horror films—though still in some sense "extreme" in their presentation of high-impact violence, are exceedingly more conventional in terms of their approach to genre convention. The highly cerebral quality of Denis, Dumont, and even Noé (whose work is perhaps the most purely visceral of the bunch) is notably stripped from these latter titles. They sometimes allude to the former category, especially in terms of casting (*I Stand Alone*'s "Butcher" Phillipe Nahon appears as the slasher in *High Tension*, *Trouble Every Day*'s sultry cannibal-vampire Beatrice Dalle does likewise in *Inside*), but the critical element of discourse is non-existent (Aja in particular is almost aggressively brainless in his storytelling—which would later prove a suitable fit for Hollywood commercial horror remakes of *The Hills Have Eyes* and *Piranha*).

Genres and Audiences

As the seminal genre theories of Altman and Neale remind us, genre is fundamentally about the interplay between narrative convention and audience expectation.

Indeed, genre acts in a manner akin to an informal agreement between audience and filmmaker that, within certain "categories" of narrative or stylistic presentation, certain pre-established expectations will be dutifully met. One could argue even that genre as a cultural construct is much more useful to audiences (seeking out cinematic material to enjoy based on repeatability of past results) than to filmmakers, for whom the dictates of genre convention can appear as shackles to commercial tradition. In this sense, true "art cinema" invites critical interrogation of the artist primarily—their intention, approach, perspective. Pure "genre" cinema, by the same token, begs critical engagement with the subject of "the audience"—who perhaps more so than the artist, or even the studio executive or the promotional agent—rely on cultural constructions of systems for classifying an endless flood of heterogenous content.

Censors, who likewise traffic in the "classification" of content that is diverse in character, invoke the hypothetical audience with regularity. It is the job of the censor or "classifier"—not unlike the genre theorist—to create significant and meaningful distinctions between "types" or "kinds" of artistic and entertainment content. This is achieved, appropriately enough, through the simultaneous creation of reasonably clear distinctions between "types" or "kinds" of audiences, individual and collective. It is the additional duty of the censor or "classifier"—not unlike the marketing executive—to create significant and meaningful distinctions between diverse groups and demographics within a broader heterogenous audience. Classification, then, is a two-part process: the fragmentation of content, and the fragmentation of audiences. The most obvious example of the latter is a rating system: which classifies content specifically according to its fragmentation of a broader audience explicitly along the lines of age.

The horror genre reveals some puzzling contradictions, routine within the classification process. Horror, like the comparable "escapist" genres of fantasy and sci-fi, has always appealed to children, a fact plainly reflected in its marketing traditions and cultural legacy. This was reflected too in the largely bloodless and sexless content of even pre-Code horror films of Hollywood's Golden Age. The dissolving of the Hollywood Production Code in 1968, and the New Hollywood of the 1970s which followed, created a brief period in which horror was considered adult fare—*Rosemary's Baby* (1969), *The Exorcist* (1973), et cetera, duly enforced by the newly implemented *CARA* ratings system. The introduction of home video in the 1980s complicated the situation. The means by which invested industry and governmental institutions could restrict the access of children to horror violence were suddenly and significantly hampered. Controlling for age in the VHS era was largely untenable.

One of horror's main points of contention with censors is its combining of conventions that appeal expressly to children (supernatural realities, et cetera)—with those frequently cited as potential threats to the safety and innocence of vulnerable audiences (simulated but high-impact violence). Children are perceived as limited in their ability to safely process simulated violence and are thus considered an especially vulnerable age group. However, discursive analysis of certain horror film censorship controversies has highlighted another, equally allegedly vulnerable category of filmgoer. Several such controversies, particularly those concerning depictions of sexual violence, invoke a spectator made vulnerable not by his age, but by his anti-social disposition. This hypothetical (typically male) viewer may be a fully grown adult, but one perceived as no more capable than a child of being fully trusted to "safely" process the violent images that horror audiences expect or demand from the genre. As Theresa Cronin has argued with reference to Australian director Greg McLean's 2005 horror film *Wolf Creek*:

> *Wolf Creek* represented a significant cause for concern for a number of viewers in both the United States and Great Britain. These commentators did not call for the film to be cut or banned by an institutional authority. Instead, efforts were directed toward the problematization, stigmatization, or even pathologization of those who may enjoy, embrace, or simply want to see the film (Cronin 19).

That horror would appeal to any number of audience categories conjured up by classifiers or would-be censors is perhaps unsurprising given that, albeit cyclically and sporadically, the genre has shown its incontestable *mass* appeal. The Universal Monsters films of the Depression, the box office record-shattering success of *The Exorcist* and *Jaws* (1975) in the 1970s, the "slasher" boom in the 1980s, the low-budget success stories of *The Blair Witch Project* and *The Sixth Sense* in 1999—would seem at least in theory sufficient to remove the stigma of horror as either "kid's stuff," or pornographic presentations of violence strictly for various twisted "anti-social" types. Indeed, if any cultural or market trend exists to counter this assumption, it is to be found in the phenomenal mainstream success that low-budget horror films, including those that made high-impact violence the focal point of their marketing, experienced in the early years of the new millennium. Even the average consumer could note the toothlessness of Hollywood's self-censorship system (as well as that of formal censor boards elsewhere) in the mass advertising of wide cinematic releases for what would become known as "torture porn" titles, namely *Saw* (2004)—and its eight (and running) sequels—and Eli Roth's *Hostel* (2005) and *Hostel: Part II* (2007).

"Torture Porn"

Much has already been written about the immediate post-9/11 period as a curious moment in horror's contemporary cultural history. Fans and defenders of

Saw and *Hostel* were quick to reject the label of "torture porn"—granted to these films by a proceeding wave of mainstream critical editorials and journalistic opinion pieces—on the grounds that it (likely consciously and intentionally) implies sexual gratification on the part of any engaged viewer of such titles. This is indeed a misconception—horror entertainment of any kind need not sexually arouse the spectator to engage them viscerally in scenes of violence and terror. However, the term is not without its elucidating properties. Its users are correct in the sense that "high impact" violence and, especially in this case, creative bodily mutilation and punishment was indeed the focus of promotional campaigns—notably at the expense of narrative or thematic "substance." *Saw*, the posters for which displayed various severed human limbs alongside the teeth of a rusted hand saw, become synonymous in popular culture with the image (emphasized in trailers and TV spots) of an imprisoned man (Cary Elwes) sawing off his own leg. *Hostel* went further in inviting the "torture porn" nomenclature, with posters and teasers carefully layering its elaborate promotional campaign with sexually suggestive overtones—perhaps justified given the film's narrative (involving backpackers looking for high-class prostitutes in Eastern Europe, only to find themselves "sold" in an underground torture-for-pay syndicate)—but nonetheless granting a certain legitimacy to the "torture porn" label.

Critics and scholars were quick to frame the "torture porn" horror trend in relation to the much remarked upon "post-9/11" American cultural milieu—in which fear, suspicion, paranoia, and brutal violence were more present and pervasive in news and media discourses than they had been in the 1990s. Similar arguments have been made about the comparable success of gritty, low-budget American horror titles like *Night of the Living Dead* (1968), *The Last House on the Left* (1972), and *The Texas Chain Saw Massacre* (1974) in the late 1960s and early 1970s (see Lowenstein). As technological advancement flooded images of violence and cultural strife into living rooms across America—the Vietnam War, the Kent State massacre, the assassinations of Martin Luther King Jr. and Robert F. Kennedy—it would seem a portion of the filmgoing public turned to horror films for catharsis—perhaps as a means of confronting and processing the violence and trauma of the period. The "post-9/11" era likewise had its share of disturbing and iconic images, which were reflected in the conventions of "torture porn" in even more direct fashion (Graham-Dixon), namely the torture of suspected terrorists-cum-prisoners in Guantanamo Bay, and the videotaped beheadings of Nick Berg and other American journalists or soldiers by the Sunni extremist network Al-Qaeda (the latter, though too graphic for mainstream media, were widely searchable on the Internet).

Appearing in 2004, the promotional materials for *Saw* (again, centered squarely around severed limbs and the jagged teeth of various instruments for cutting) align both visually and chronologically with Berg's beheading.

Hostel—which featured scenes of gleeful torture and humiliation—likewise begs for contextual analysis within this climate. However, the films that *Hostel* would directly inspire reflect an even more potent and pressing theme of the cultural moment: terror-age xenophobia.

Holiday of Horrors

Hostel—a "fish out of water" story of US backpackers sadistically and methodically victimized in Eastern Europe—birthed a sub-genre of what might be thought of as "tourism horror," in which tourists encounter and/or uncover—and ultimately fall victim to—criminal syndicates, local customs, ritual practices, et cetera, which prey upon the ignorance of Western travelers abroad. Notable post-*Hostel* examples include: *Turistas* (2006) (in which black market organ harvesters target a group of teenage backpackers in Brazil); *The Ruins* (2008) (in which a group of friends on holiday in Mexico are ritually sacrificed at the ruins of an ancient pyramid); and—perhaps the sub-genre's finest offering—*Wolf Creek*, a low-budget Australian horror film written and directed by Greg McLean.

First screened at the Sundance Film Festival in January 2005, *Wolf Creek* was picked up for international distribution by the Weinstein-owned Miramax Films (under the shared control of the Weinstein brothers and the Walt Disney Corporation) for US $3.5 million and granted a wide release through Dimension Films (a horror-focussed Miramax subsidiary) in the US on Christmas Day 2005 (Blackwood 489). The film would go on to become one of the most successful in which Australia's Film Finance Corp. had invested, and Miramax's involvement in North American distribution, according to Gary Hamilton—whose company Arclight represented the film in Australia—made *Wolf Creek* "the biggest release of an Australian film" in decades (Chai A4).

Wolf Creek proved a major financial success, earning over $50 million worldwide in gross revenue from a budget of $1.4 million (Ryan 24): becoming one of the top-grossing independent Australian films of all time, eventually spawning a bigger-budgeted sequel (*Wolf Creek 2*) in 2013, and finally adapted as a spin-off television series in 2016. At the time of this writing, *Wolf Creek 3*, a third installment in the franchise, is currently in pre-production. The continued growth and increased visibility of the franchise confirms the cult appreciation that the original film has garnered in the years since its release. However, this long trajectory was not as explicitly foreshadowed as one might have expected. The original film divided critics—virtually down the middle. It holds a score of 54% on RottenTomatoes.com, with the "Critical Conesus" summary reading: "Though *Wolf Creek* is effectively horrific, it is still tasteless exploitation" (RottenTomatoes). The split critical response is perhaps to be expected, with *Saw*, *Hostel*, and *The Ruins* all scoring in the 45–55% range on the same website. Some critics came down hard and swiftly on the film, among them Roger Ebert, who included *Wolf Creek* on his list of most "Hated Movies" of 2005. In his review, Ebert flags the narrative and stylistic elements that would characterize the (relatively minor) controversy that accompanied both the original film, as well as its slow-ensuing legacy: sadism, perversion, and perceived "misogyny." Ebert also makes a point of claiming in his review that he actually "likes horror," apparently careful to keep his judgement of *Wolf Creek* distinct from the various inherent cultural stigmas surrounding the genre, even "extreme horror" as he deliberately states ("A slough").

Wolf Creek met with minimal resistance from censor boards—with one notable exception: a brief temporary banning in particular Northern Territories of Australia—for less than typical reasons (to be addressed later in this chapter). By and large, the film sailed toward uncut classification in Canada and Britain, and managed an R rating in America. One might have reasonably expected more interference from classification boards, given the sadistic "sexual violence" that critics would claim characterized the film. In fact, this critique refers to a single decidedly inexplicit moment, complicated by its narrative and stylistic relationship to the rest of the film. However, *Wolf Creek*'s controversial reception illuminates the application of social control mechanisms in cinema culture, not as much in its treatment by censors or critics, but specifically via its engagement with audiences, both niche and mass. This reception has been written about regarding the former, particularly the discursive construction in critical and consumer reviews of its "questionable" target audience—its apparently self-evidently sadistic and perverted hypothetical engaged male viewer. My analysis here, by contrast, is of *Wolf Creek* as it engaged a *mass commercial* audience—a most revealing case study in the relay of commercial strategy, genre convention, "extreme" content, and audience intelligence research.

Genre and Sub-genre

Particularly as compared to the quasi-horror films of the early New French Extremity, *Wolf Creek* is exceedingly conventional. Its violence is relatively mild compared to that of *Irréversible*, and its approach to genre convention is relatively straightforward compared to the highly cerebral vampire/cannibal musings of *Trouble Every Day*. It is, most significantly and decidedly, *not* the "experimental horror" of Bruno Dumont's *Twentynine Palms*, the film which originally prompted Quandt's derisive label. *Twentynine Palms* aggressively resists convention—evoking a purely sensory dread that both denies and defies narrative explanation. The film stands more than any other as the New French Extremity's truly visceral horror "experience"—but its forcefully "anti-genre" approach saw it largely ignored by audiences, critics, and scholars—along with a great many genre films that fail to adhere to classical standards of controlled separation. Genre and experimentation are, in some significant sense, mutually exclusive. *Twentynine Palms* is the extremely rare "experimental genre film." *Wolf Creek* is not. Its approach to horror convention caters decisively and deliberately to very particular expectations within very particular horror sub-genres (though as I argue, the film itself and its North American promotional campaign obscured the signifying power of certain of its genre elements).

As far as sub-genre, *Wolf Creek* certainly shares narrative elements with *Hostel* and its myriad imitators. However, exploiting xenophobia would be a complicated if not dubious charge in this case. *Wolf Creek* is an Australian-made film about the violent and horrifying fates befalling a pair of backpacking British tourists in the (unmistakably) Australian outback. In other words, its horrors are domestic in nature, and its *victims* are otherized—perhaps even more so than its horrific but ultimately "home grown" antagonist. *Wolf Creek* has even been accused of impacting on rural Australia's appeal as a tourist destination (Yang, Bergh, and Lee 315). The film's namesake, Wolf(e) Creek itself, is the actual site of a prehistoric meteor crater—the world's second largest and, as evidenced by McLean's location shooting, flooring to behold. It appears some Australian media commentators feared the film might be taken globally as a cautionary travel tale—the result of culturally irresponsible action on the part of its Australian filmmakers. In contrast, horror fans immediately recognized *Wolf Creek* as a direct descendent of the classic American "rural horror" of the 1970s, most notably *The Texas Chain Saw Massacre* and *Deliverance* (1972). A precursor to the "tourism horror" of *Hostel*, "rural horror" places unassuming and "yuppie" urban characters at the mercy of an isolated and gothic "backwoods" setting and its denizens. *Wolf Creek* substitutes the Australian Outback for the boondocks of Texas or the swamps of Georgia, and adds a third protagonist to its pair of female backpackers—a young male from Sydney (a sharp contrast to the rural Australians they will encounter throughout the film). It has been argued that *Wolf Creek* constitutes the continuation of a trend in the New Australian Cinema toward representing the rural in one of two ways: as a place of idyll or, in the case of *Wolf Creek*, horrific depictions of outback Australia, in either case relying upon mythological interpretations of the landscape and its inhabitants (Scott and Biron 308). These elements contain strong echoes of *Hostel*'s "tourism" horror premise (McLennan 48).

The film has also been contextualized, with varying degrees of precision, as falling within other notable and oft-used labels invoking not only sub-genre qualifiers, but national identity. *Wolf Creek* has been called "Ozploitation," a term variously used to refer to Australia's genre filmmaking heritage in the 1970s and 1980s, contemporary genre filmmaking, as well as a national style of exploitation filmmaking (Ryan and Goldsmith 2). It has also been labeled "Australian Gothic," a designation typically applied to those "high-art, often government-sanctioned films of the 1970s New Wave," with landmark works such as Nicholas Roeg's *Walkabout* (1971), Ted Kotcheff's *Wake in Fright* (1971), and Peter Weir's *Picnic at Hanging Rock* (1979), "traditionally understood as classic Australian Gothic films" (Balanzategui 23). These terms are obviously useful as conceptual categories for (particularly Australian) scholars, but offer little in terms of recognizability or familiarity for the international audiences that *Wolf Creek*'s global distribution agents were tasked with attracting.

In North America, *Wolf Creek* was granted a wide release. However, a potent but commercially precarious advertizing campaign muddied its direct engagement with audience expectations. Dimension's promotional strategy worked cleverly in tandem with the film's plot structure—obscuring (presumably intentionally) the film's specific genre leanings. The result was a pure thrill for any fans of its particular sub-genre who found themselves in cinemas for its Christmas opening weekend. Nevertheless, the strategy proved fatal with broader mainstream audiences in at least one tangible, quantitative measurement. *Wolf Creek* received a score of "F" from the research firm Cinemascore, becoming one of only eighteen films to earn the distinction since the firm's founding in 1979 (Busch).

As a mechanism for "actionable intelligence" gathering by Hollywood Studios, CinemaScore uses thirty-five to forty-five pollster teams in twenty-five cities scattered across the US at any one time. These pollsters randomly choose five theaters in five cities to collect anywhere from four to 600 ballots from audiences, who rate a film they have just seen, typically on its opening night, with a score from A to F (Lawrence). These ratings are then collated, and the film is given a score—represented by a letter grade. As indicated, the F score is exceedingly rare—eighteen titles among presumably tens of thousands. This begs a perplexing question: how does a genre horror film apparently popular enough with audiences to spawn two sequels and a spin-off television series simultaneously draw such fervent censure from a mainstream American audience? How best does one account for such a stark and striking discrepancy?

One might look to *Wolf Creek*'s company in this rare distinction. The eighteen films to receive an F score since the firm's founding are, no doubt, a curious mix of cinematic "failures." Some are perhaps easy targets—films more-or-less universally ridiculed (Uwe Boll's disastrous video game adaptation *Alone in the Dark* [2005], or Neil Labute's ill-advised *The Wicker Man* [2006] remake starring Nicholas Cage). Other titles include works by celebrated filmmakers William Friedkin or Steven Soderberg (*Bug* [2006], directed by the former, is an effective but grim and minimalist adaptation of a play by Tracy Letts, while *Solaris* [2002], directed by the latter, narratively tested the patience of anyone drawn in by the elaborate sci-fi production design showcased in its posters and promos). What sharply distinguishes *Wolf Creek* from other titles in the list is its formidable box office success. In plain fact, the audience scores collated by Cinemascore do tend to conform quite closely to average box office grosses (Busch), suggesting that despite being drawn from a relatively small sample size, the scores do still provide a reasonably accurate gauge of public opinion. Most of the eighteen films that received the "F" score were indeed commercial flops. *Wolf Creek* is the notable exception—suggesting something wholly atypical characterized its reception.

Invoking the Audience

The censorship discourses surrounding "extreme cinema" tend to focus on three constituent spheres: the official policy of censorial institutions, the character or approach of the filmmaker, and the reactionary opinions of professional critics. Spectatorship theory has proven a relatively methodical means for interrogating the relationship between text and hypothetical "viewer"—frequently invoked as a cloak for the analyzer's own speculation on the nature of audience engagement. This can serve as a valuable and versatile basis for criticism: description, analysis, interpretation, and evaluation. However, critical reflection on the audience—not as individuals but as collective groups—is more challenging to facilitate. In the case of censorial policy, the legislation itself provides a concrete subject for analysis. The statements of filmmakers and reviews of critics do likewise. The cinematic text itself provides a clear subject for spectatorship theory. When it comes to the subject of mass audiences, however, discussion tends to turn broad and imprecise. Yet, the effectiveness or value of a film is obviously contingent on its ability to engage an audience, and the decision of that audience whether to take a film seriously. A holistic picture of "extreme cinema" thereby implies mass audiences deserve at least some nuanced critical attention.

The challenges of audience-based research are obvious and numerous. The researcher must, for example, avoid treating "the audience" as a given—particularly as a homogeneous group of passive undiscerning consumers. Mass audiences are made up of diverse individuals and groups who do not just passively consume, but who willingly seek out and use cinema as a means of understanding their societies and cultures. Further, groups within audiences differ from one another in their engagement with film in any number of ways. Groups may differ in terms of their criteria for evaluation; in their attentiveness to film generally; and in their perceived importance as potential consumers. Not all audience groups are equally vital to the discourse—because not all groups have equal inclination or influence when responding to art. Mainly, however, there is the obvious challenge of accurately assessing what audiences are thinking and feeling. Again, spectatorship theory will substitute the analyst's own experiences as spectator for generalized engagement, but this limits acknowledgement of the diverse habits and circumstances of individuals and groups that collectively form the broader audience.

The goal here is not to suggest that Cinemascore's evaluation system provides a comprehensive snapshot of audience engagement. Most obviously, the data fails to account for the multiple alternate ways that cinematic content is consumed: after opening night, home video; streaming services; video-sharing websites like YouTube and Dailymotion, et cetera. More importantly, the firm's polling results are comprised of purely quantitative data, and thus provide no official or even speculative accounting for why a film will score what it does. In the case of extreme cinema, rigorous qualitative work on the subject of audiences has been performed in a scholarly context. Most notably, Martin Barker's illuminative research on the subject reveals significant and telling discrepancies in the reactions of "engaged" versus "disengaged" viewers to titles targeted by BBFC censorship, including *Baise-moi* and *Fat Girl*. Barker's study also included several horror films, mainly those containing sexual violence, such as Ruggero Deodato's *House on the Edge of the Park* (1980). The question of audience engagement is especially pertinent as it concerns "genre" entertainment. Genre informs and shapes audience expectation. Censors are not necessarily "horror fans"—and thus engage differently with the text. Engaged viewers, by contrast, will interpret horror images in a very particular context. Barker's results bear this out via detailed interviews with viewing subjects—contrasted with censorial policy and rhetorical claims. Though not a broad and immediate target for censorship (and thus not included in Barker's study), *Wolf Creek* raises numerous compelling questions about audience engagement.

While *Wolf Creek* was an unmistakable commercial success, its divided critical responses were frequently punctuated by emphatic censure, not only of the film itself (and the perceived intentions of the filmmaker), but also its demonstrably captivated audience. Ebert's review paints a vivid image of a maladjusted male viewer seeking gratification in the cynical exploitation of misogynist violence ("Slough"). In the case of the "F" rating from Cinemascore, however, it would seem audiences—at least in some measure—likewise attacked the film (the same audience that, conceived of broadly, went on to comprise its commercial following). This begs the obvious question: were the opening night viewers who declared the film a resounding "failure" (among the most severe eighteen in three decades) engaged or disengaged viewers? Why was the film's target demographic (enthused horror fans—now still watching new iterations of the franchise) not represented in Cinemascore's polling? Why might a relatively conventional and inarguably commercially successful film generate such a hostile response from a random sample audience? Perhaps the answer has more to do with mechanisms of promotion, and the relay between genre convention and commercial expectation in *Wolf Creek*'s style and narrative, than with "problematic content."

A "Cinematic Hand Grenade"

Director Greg McLean has called *Wolf Creek* a "cinematic hand grenade" (certainly an evocative conceptual image): "an intense, shocking and genuinely scary movie that was distinctly Australian, yet subverted the cliches of the outback—the Crocodile Dundees and Steve Irwins—benign larrikins with a naïve, childish view of the world" (qtd. in Sydney "Australian"). McLean seems to suggest that the film, by design, is deliberately unassuming until it "explodes"—in a sense, stunning or "attacking" the viewer. It would seem the film draws inspiration not only from the rural horror of *The Texas Chain Saw Massacre*, but also from the disorienting narrative and stylistic misdirection of Hitchcock's *Psycho* (1960). This would be a fitting homage, given that *Psycho* served as a prototype for the "serial killer" sub-genre, to which *Wolf Creek* has also been assigned (Kakmi 74). One could argue that *Wolf Creek* goes even further in its playful approach to expectation, at one point even sacrificing internal narrative logic to conceal its sub-genre conceit. While not the quasi-formalist "experimental horror" of *Twentynine Palms*, there is a certain striking subversion of expectation at play in the film. More accurately, *Wolf Creek* subverts the commercial utility of expectation itself (rather than any convention within the pre-established dictates of its very particular sub-genre). Perhaps surprisingly, the film's international advertizing campaign dutifully honored this strategy—withholding or obscuring *Wolf Creek*'s narrative and stylistic sub-genre leanings from North American promotional materials.

One might then speculate that *Wolf Creek* received the very rare "F" on Cinemascore not because it was a poorly made film, or a film that failed to deliver on typical established horror expectations (the film delivers ample horror thrills and does so in rather artful fashion). It is not only an effective and stylish horror film, but a well-made film generally. Its divided critical reception was also not unlike that of *Saw* (2004), *Hostel* (2005), *The Devil's Rejects* (2005), and other of its "torture porn" contemporaries, none of which earned the distinction of a failing score in Cinemascore polling. This suggests further that *Wolf Creek* did not receive the "F" grade simply for being "torture porn"—and in fact is arguably less deserving of this label than its contemporaries (having more thorough character development and less explicit gore than virtually any other prominent title in the sub-genre). However, it posed an altogether different affront to audiences. *Wolf Creek* scored poorly with Cinemascore's sample base not for being "torture porn," but for being torture porn delivered via "cinematic hand grenade." Polled audiences reacted to a gritty, decidedly "un-Hollywood" horror film in the trojan horse of a glossy Hollywood supernatural horror package, and all the accompanying commercial baggage.

The implications of such a theory are undoubtedly loaded. As mentioned, Cinemascore polls random audiences specifically on opening night screenings. Audiences in attendance on opening night, one might assume, are as likely as any to be considered "engaged" (their mere presence on opening night suggests a level of anticipation, which by extension suggests relatively clearly defined expectations). The polling results therefore suggest that as often as audience polling scores are reflective of a film's quality, they might just as often serve as a reflection of how closely the film aligned with pre-established expectations. This is clearly and especially the case for a film like *Wolf Creek*—the "F" score being not a representation of the film's quality, nor its adherence to genre convention, but a reaction to its ambiguous advertizing and narrative misdirection. This raises potential concerns about how Cinemascore's findings are used as "actionable intelligence" by studios, utilizing these scores in arbitrating what future projects are greenlit (Busch). The films that score highest on the firm's polling tend to be those that are part of well-known franchises, where there is far less ambiguity about what audiences can and should expect for their price of admission. Furthermore, the sharp uptick in franchise filmmaking in Hollywood in the period since *Wolf Creek* would seem to be an indication that such means of actionable intelligence gathering are indeed shaping the role and character of Hollywood's studio output.

Imprecise Promotion

The North American promotional trailer for *Wolf Creek* gives no clear indication of the film's antagonist. Its slick, stylish, and narratively efficient editing—typical of Hollywood trailers of the early 2000s—consolidates the events of the film's first act with precision. The trailer begins with a rapid montage of excerpts from early scenes, with images of main characters—a pair of twenty-something female British backpackers, Liz (Cassandra McGrath) and Kristy (Kestie Morassi), and a similarly-aged Australian male, Ben (Nathan Phillips)—indulging in excessive nightlife partying in Broome, Western Australia. We see the trio purchase a dilapidated car and set out toward Wolf Creek meteor crater, the next slated step on their camping sojourn through rural Australia. The landscapes featured in the trailer (the crater, desert roads, bush) are associated with internationally known Australian films—the Crocodile Dundee movies, Baz Luhrmann's *Australia* (2008)—but have also appeared in countless tourism commercials: "the types of landscape (that) enhance (an Australian film's) credibility, as they are consistent with internationally accepted perceptions about Australian cinema" (Leotta 217).

The trio is shown arriving at the Wolf Creek site, taking in its spectacular scenery, and then preparing to leave at dusk. However, the engine in their newly purchased car will not start. As night falls, the teaser loops audio of Ben regaling his two female companions with tales of rumored nearby alien abductions, while all three huddle in a small tent amidst the vast and expansive darkness of the Western Australian desert at night. Then, bright white lights appear in the distance, slowly and steadily approaching the site. At this point, there is a distinct pivot in tone.

What follows is a decidedly less narratively precise (no doubt by design) montage, featuring fragments of largely indecipherable horror action—close-ups on bloodied appendages, darkened on-foot escape attempts, piercing screams, et cetera. These intense and highly visceral fragments are all captured in the film's distinctive realist style, with dimly lit, shaky handheld camera—in conjunction with the now more frenzied editing—making the images difficult for the spectator to place in any meaningful or illuminative narrative context. As this abrasive intensity peaks, the film's cryptic but evocative title finally appears onscreen: *Wolf Creek* (evoking an immediate and pronounced sense of place—a rural site of danger, and direct allusion to the predatory nature of wolves—but no precise hint as to the substantive nature of its specific sinister connotation). As the trailer concludes, a punchy tag line appears onscreen in bolded text, providing the following coda: "HOW CAN YOU BE FOUND IF NO ONE KNOWS YOU ARE MISSING?" The trailer was widely seen in North America, expressly targeting its presumed fanbase by appearing in cinemas before high-profile independent horror titles released earlier in 2005, including *Hostel* and *The Devil's Rejects*.

The deliberate obscuring of *Wolf Creek*'s antagonist provides a sharp contrast to these contemporaneous titles. *Hostel*'s marketing campaign centered around its "high-concept" pitch: an Eastern European syndicate of torture-for-pay tourism; while ads for *The Devil's Rejects*, an all-but-direct sequel to 2003's *House of 1000 Corpses*, exploited familiarity (the foundational concept of genre) with its narrative predecessor's already near-iconic villains (the "Firefly" family). The unseen forces of antagonism in *Wolf Creek*'s trailer, by comparison, limit the audience's ability to formulate predictive ideas about the film's content. This is a markedly precarious strategy from a commercial perspective, though effective for the narrative purposes of the film itself. The trailer's fragments of violent action do serve functionally as genre (in this case horror) iconography. Combined with carefully constructed tone and atmosphere, they signal *Wolf Creek* unmistakably as "horror," certainly enough to fulfill Altman's theoretical stipulation that if spectators are to experience films in terms of their genre, "films must leave no doubt as to their generic identity; instant recognizability must be assumed" (Altman 18). One could argue this holds equally true, in the twenty-first-century media landscape especially, for a film's promotional materials. Further, amidst the postmodern (or post-postmodern) breakdown of distinct boundaries and generic categories, *sub-genre* is more than ever worthy of attention from marketing strategists. Prospective viewers would recognize *Wolf Creek* as a horror film ostensibly, but not necessarily as occupying a clear place within the infinite regression of horror sub-genres (zombie films, haunted house films, alien films, et cetera); many of which attract a devoted fanbase as much as or more than the larger umbrella term "horror" under which they might fall.

Genre (and indeed sub-genre) familiarity is core to understanding what Steve Neale calls the "intertextual relay" that Hollywood employs to point audiences and reviewers toward the most appropriate framework for viewing a film (39). Indeed, Neale's notion of the "generic image," the basic narrative "idea" of a film, is undeniably borne out in the industry's use of advertising copy, posters, stills, and trailers. Neale argues it is this relay itself that provides the primary evidence for the social and cultural existence of genres (40). Hollywood studios use genre categories primarily to replicate circumstances of audience interest and satisfaction for profit maximization. It is possible to think of genre in this sense (as an institutionalized practice of normalization) as ideological in its direct subordination to studio goals. However, such a blunt formulation runs the risk of oversimplifying the complex interactive exchange that takes place between studios and audiences. For Thomas Schatz, "the genre film reaffirms what the audience believes both on individual and communal levels" (Schatz 38). This approach sees genres primarily as narrative patterns growing out of social practices, providing opportunities to imaginatively conquer timeless inconsistencies and negations within these practices.

It is this conception of genre not solely as a product of studios, but rather of studio-audience interaction, which informs some of the most sophisticated horror genre criticism, such as that of theorist Robin Wood. Wood famously spoke of the popular horror film as a site for the return of the repressed, a relatively safe environment for audiences to confront those forces they would otherwise seek to expel from civilization (Wood). Horror scholar Adam Lowenstein's work further cuts against the notion of genres as singular studio creations, pointing out that many modern horror films are critical of contemporary social ideals and values—yet succeed as often as those reflecting or espousing them (Lowenstein 23). This would seem to suggest that genres, horror included, serve an important social function for the cultures that generate them (a relationship that persists even as their economic utility drives them toward repetition and parody). These various understandings of genre can be challenging to reconcile, particularly in a marketing context, and perhaps even more particularly in the case of horror (where the spectre of the psychologically repressed, and where criticism of social ideals and values, are so often sold couched in the visual language of escapist thrills).

Despite the explicit allusions to aliens and meteors in its marketing materials, *Wolf Creek* is far from conventional escapist fare. While not overtly indicated in the theatrical trailer, much of the interest and discourse surrounding the film has invoked the claims, stated on promotional print materials, in statements by McLean, that the narrative is (at least loosely) "based on actual events," a premise that represents a major trend in contemporary feature films. Coincident with the growth of reality television and the "found footage" genre, these films claim to offer their audiences fact as well as drama, action, or comedy. While all popular genres of film, including those which focus on war, romance, adventure, or in this case horror, have exploited the "actual events" formula, it is perhaps in the case of crime narratives that the approach has been most extensively employed. This is a generic designation with some significant relevance to *Wolf Creek*. The screenplay is a composite of (again, ultimately quite loose) inspirations drawn from criminal cases of recent decades in Australia, in particular two high-profile true crime stories "that have haunted the popular cultural imaginary of Australian society"; firstly, the Ivan Milat hitchhiker murders from the early 1990s; and secondly, the violent abduction and murder of British tourist Peter Falconio in the Northern Territory in 1996, a case resolved with Bradley John Murdoch convicted for his murder and sentenced to life imprisonment on December 13, 2005 (Blackwood 489).

Cinematically, *Wolf Creek* leans with enthusiasm into "true crime" territory, employing a quasi-documentary aesthetic. The camerawork is exclusively handheld, and several rounds of bleach bypass result in a deliberately washed-out palette—as reminiscent of low budget genre classics such as *The Texas Chain Saw Massacre* as its (albeit tenuous) claims of historical verisimilitude. While the "based on actual events" claim is not explicitly invoked in *Wolf Creek*'s trailer, this may have more to do with a negligible effect on sub-genre expectation than with narrative concealment. Ironically, seasoned horror audiences know such a statement does not preclude the possibility of supernatural horror-based narratives. Films about aliens (*The Fourth Kind* [2009]), hauntings (*The Amityville Horror* [1979]), demonic possession (*The Exorcism of Emily Rose* [2005]) et cetera have all employed the "true story" strategy to great commercial effect. Further, the "backpacker murders" was a high-profile media story in Australia, but considerably less so in North America. Invoking the Milat case would reveal the film's sub-genre conceit, while providing extremely limited appeal to audience familiarity. There is no official record of the rationale underlying Dimension's decision to promote the film as ambiguous rural horror, including deliberate misdirection to suggest extraterrestrial horror. There may have been concern that the stigma surrounding the "torture porn" label previously applied to *Saw* and *Hostel* would hinder *Wolf Creek*'s chances of garnering mainstream credibility. As an Australian export, the film had neither the relatively well-known

American cast members of *Saw* (Danny Glover, Cary Elwes) or the "splatter auteur" notoriety of Eli Roth (whose *Cabin Fever* [2002] was a vastly profitable independent film). It may also have been that Dimension's promotional strategists feared audience fatigue within the highly saturated "serial killer" sub-genre market, one with substantial and highly visible precedents in American pop culture.

The 1980s witnessed an explosion of both scholarly and popular interest in the problem of serial murder. Indicators of this increased popularity include the large numbers of novels, "true crime" and academic books, countless television documentaries, and, most relevant for present purposes, the start of a film trend which focussed on the exploits and apprehension of real and fictional serial killers. Importantly, the level of public interest in films of this kind remains high decades later. This feature film output includes the full range of cinematic offerings. At one end of a continuum are those films which are viewed as serious offerings, and which feature major stars and boast the backing of large studios. These include films such as *Se7en* (1995), *American Psycho* (2001), *The Summer of Sam* (1999), and perhaps most notably, *The Silence of the Lambs* (1991). At the other end is a very large number of films which aim for financial rather than artistic success. This category includes several films which claim to document the real-life stories of famous serial murderers. *Bundy* (2002), *Dahmer* (2002), and *Ed Gein: The Butcher of Plainfield* (2007) are representative titles. While some of these lower-budget films had theatrical release, most were intended for the home video market. As Nicole Rafter argues, however, serial crime films differ in emphasis from other related sub-genres including the "slasher film" and the "psycho film." Unlike these offerings, the serial killer film focusses more narrowly on the murderer and his (or less commonly her) exploits. As Rafter suggests, the serial killer film promotes a stereotype of the "super-predator who murders on the installment plan and scatters bones in his wake" (93). *Wolf Creek*'s antagonist is arguably one such figure.

Surprise Attack

Dimension's play to market *Wolf Creek* in North America—not as a "true story" serial killer film (or even as a psycho/slasher film) but as a mysterious "disappearance" rural horror film—obscures its sub-genre conceit. In so doing, however, it honors the "cinematic hand grenade" strategy of McLean's surprise attack narrative. Like the North American trailer, the first half of the film itself plays its sub-genre narrative cards extremely close to the chest. There is no "cold open" or pre-title horror "teaser," which horror filmmakers typically adopt to strategically signal to the audience that the establishing narrative setup to follow will eventually wind into overt horror convention. We do see stark white text on a black background: "30 000 people are reported missing in Australia every year. 90% are found within a month. Some are never seen again." Clearly, not specifying the exact number of people who disappear permanently or providing a regional breakdown of these disappearances is intended to imply that some 3,000 people a year might perish in similar fashion to the victims in *Wolf Creek*'s narrative (Blackwood 391). Here, the film immediately invokes the particular "Australian-ness" of its horror, which the North American trailer obscured (largely featuring dialogue from the two British female leads—and again, no explicit indication of the film's antagonist). The film itself—made by Australians, partially funded by the Australian Film Finance Corporation (the film originally faced numerous rejections by funding agencies—although it did eventually acquire government funding) (Bertram 36), and presumably designed at least initially for domestic audiences—more fully embraces Australian national identity, albeit in twisted and irreverent fashion. This would become a major source of contention in discourses surrounding the film.

Wolf Creek's first act provides ample character development between its three leads, acknowledged by notable genre scholars like Alexandra Heller-Nicholas, stating "I also loved the way Greg McLean engaged the viewer in the first act of Wolf Creek; so often, slasher films throw the beginning away and present a bunch of boring people who you can't wait to see killed. This is so disrespectful to the viewer" ("Red" 29).

Liz, more reserved than her close friend and travel companion Kristy, has developed a romantic crush on Ben, a Sydney-born surfer with whom the women have recently connected. Ben is only slightly less the "fish out of water" in rural Western Australia. As the trio stops for gas, we see him taunted and emasculated by a vulgar and aggressive local. This is perhaps the closest this first act comes to the horror "harbinger" archetype—who typically foreshadows the danger and, if necessary, provides expository narrative context or backstory about the local legend or "curse." There is no such directed foreshadowing here—beyond the trio feeling ill at ease in their rural surroundings.

Soon, they arrive at Wolf Creek—a stunningly well-preserved meteorite crater (in actuality, Wolfe Creek Crater in Western Australia). Liz and Ben awkwardly kiss, as rain (literally and figuratively) dampens the occasion. The trio pack the car and prepare to leave the site, at which point (approximately halfway through the runtime) McLean's plotting becomes rather playful. As seen in the trailer, their car will not start (we will later learn that the engine was sabotaged while the trio was exploring the crater). More curiously though, Liz and Ben's watches have likewise stopped working. No explanation is posited, here or throughout the remainder of the film. Shortly after, Ben begins his discussion of UFO sightings. While rarely remarked upon in negative reviews or complaints, this sequence is potentially a problematic one for audiences.

McLean's screenplay is (presumably intentionally and perhaps somewhat aggressively) misdirecting its audience. The crater itself resembles a UFO landing site, and the very idea of a meteor teases a distinctly alien or "other-worldly" presence. The failure of mechanical devices, like the desert surroundings, is an oft-used sci-fi trope (the two of these both notably feature prominently in Spielberg's *Close Encounters of the Third Kind* [1977]). Combined with the text and promotional motif of mysterious disappearance, the spectre of alien abduction is being deliberately invoked. And then suddenly, as if on cue, white light cuts through the darkness, appearing in the distance and then slowly approaching the tent of the vulnerable, stranded, and isolated protagonists. The moment is wonderfully suspenseful—a rare instance of horror cinema *truly* exploiting its audience's profound fear of the ultimate "unknown"—made possible by the meticulously guarded promotion and first act storytelling.

Because Cinemascore polls its audiences on opening night, one can speculate with some degree of confidence that North American audiences who rated the film had not been exposed to any "spoiler" summary material or reviews that would indicate (at least in any meaningful or precise sense) the direction in which the script's plotting is about to veer. The approaching white light turns out to be the headlights of a rusted pickup truck. Mick Taylor (Jim Jarret), a burly and jovial, but no less rugged and intimidating middle-aged outback hunter, parks and exits the vehicle. Seemingly sympathetic to the stranded trio's plight, Mick offers to tow their car to his nearby camp and repair the engine. They accept, Ben joking with relief about their fear of aliens. The tension of the prior scene is broken.

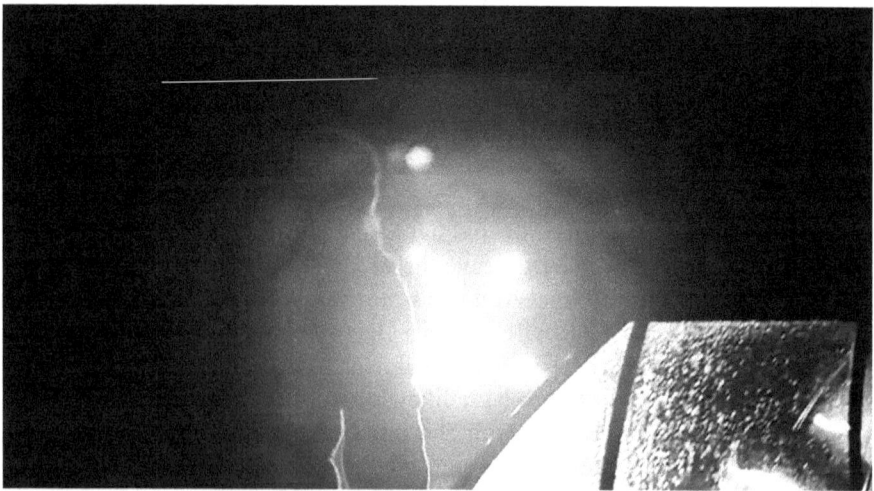

Figure 7.1   Greg McLean's *Wolf Creek* (Emu Creek Pictures Pty Ltd, 2005).

The film is about to pivot sub-genres, but not before one more masterful exercise in narrative misdirection. Before setting to work on the disabled engine as promised, Mick pours rounds of drinks for his guests, who join him around a bonfire at the rustic abandoned mining camp where he apparently resides. He is hospitable and seemingly good-natured, as he regales the trio with fond memories of his many decades as a hunter. The exchange faintly recalls the pantry scene between Marion Crane and Norman Bates in *Psycho* (albeit in complex fashion). McLean is perhaps engaging in meta-allusion with the scene, evoking Hitchcock in form and style along with content. Mick's "Larrikan" demeanor, given pitch perfect life by Jarrett (a relatively well-known character actor in his native Australia), puts his guests at immediate ease. Mick, like Norman Bates, is initially unassuming. McLean is also invoking Hitchcock's own notorious and aggressive embrace of narrative misdirection—famously killing off his protagonist halfway through the narrative and shifting focus toward Norman (all while carefully managing expectation and guarding narrative twists extra-textually as well as textually).

However, the campfire scene does provide a strong hint of the film's actual sub-genre leanings, with intertextual reference to another classic in the sub-genre. As he wistfully reflects on his occupational history, Mick explains that his services as a "head-hunter"—a hunter of vermin in vast outback farms—is no longer in demand as farmers now use poison to clear wildlife pests from their properties. This motif of the redundant butcher, not unlike the film purporting to be "based on actual events," echoes the influence of Hooper's *The Texas Chain Saw Massacre*, in which the backwoods cannibal antagonists were former slaughterhouse employees, displaced by more humane and automated methods of slaughter. The reference is a fitting one: *Chain Saw Massacre* can be considered the prototype for the rural-serial-killer horror sub-genre that most accurately characterizes *Wolf Creek*'s particular blend of thrills.

Then, as the campfire chatter dies down, the scene offers one more (much more explicit) cinematic reference. In an awkward blend of flattery and condescension, Ben admiringly imagines Mick's life of freedom, telling his host: "You get to run around the outback saying cool things like 'that's not a knife . . . *this* is a knife!'" Liz and Kristy laugh in response, but Mick stares silently at Ben. With a slightly ambiguous but no-less menacing expression of offense, anger, contempt, psychotic rage—or some combination of these—Mick holds Ben's stare for several uncomfortable seconds. Ben's careless reference to *Crocodile Dundee* (1986) has mockingly reduced Mick to a broad and crass stereotype. His disdainful stare in response is one of the most chilling moments in this (or any other) horror film.

As Mick excuses himself to work on the engine, Liz, Kristy, and Ben lay back and close their eyes. Later, Liz wakes up shackled and confined in a darkened makeshift cell. She manages, with some difficulty, to free herself and follows

FILM REGULATION IN A CULTURAL CONTEXT

Figure 7.2   Mick (John Jarratt) stares disdainfully in *Wolf Creek*.

in the direction of piercing screams. Spying into an enclosed warehouse space through a broken window, she sees Kristy—bloodied and half naked—chained by the wrists to a pillar. Mick, his belly protruding through a dirty undershirt, is seen loading his rifle nearby. He points it at the hysterical Kristy and fires—a deliberate near miss. Mick chuckles sadistically, verbally berating Kristy (notably still in the same breezy and jovial tone he has used in previous scenes, now twisted and perverted by the shifting narrative context).

No doubt this scene springs quickly to mind when the film is discussed in the context of "torture porn." Though the torture onscreen is, still at this stage, primarily psychological, the image is undeniably grotesque. Then, having finished his tirade, Mick runs his hand over his groin, grunting with ugly satisfaction. While certainly a discomforting moment for the spectator, this relatively inexplicit gesture is also the extent of the "sexual violence" that detractors of the film would all too eagerly evoke. Before Mick can carry on, Liz creates a diversion by setting a fire. Extinguishing the flames distracts Mick sufficiently for Liz to free Kristy. Most of the rest of the film is an extended chase between Mick and the two women (Ben is still nowhere to be seen—perhaps why some critics felt the film's violence betrays a thinly-veiled "misogyny.")

Liz and Kristy's escape attempts prove futile. Mick is a hunter on his own familiar terrain. He catches both women, though not before Liz finds a cache of diverse personal belongings. Among them, a camcorder displays a home video of a family of tourists likewise ensnared by Mick's predation. Their car motor, too, has been sabotaged. We realize Mick habitually preys on tourists.

WOLF CREEK'S HOSTILE AUDIENCE

Figure 7.3   Mick loads his rifle in *Wolf Creek*.

While *Wolf Creek*'s climactic third act then goes on to supply the violence and/or sadism that sub-genre convention demands, the "murder" scenes are, once again, relatively inexplicit. The most "violent" moment—the one that Ebert claimed made him want to walk out of the theater and "keep on walking" ("A slough")—is largely psychological in effect. Having captured Liz, Mick drives a hunting knife into her back (echoing Ben's earlier invoking of *Crocodile Dundee*). We see Mick's forearm make thrusting motions as he describes a method of punishment (or security) apparently used in Japanese prisoner-of-war camps. The method involves severing the spine, so the surviving prisoner cannot physically attempt escape. Mick refers to the procedure as making a "head on a stick." We see Liz collapse, presumably paralyzed. Her fate beyond this is not revealed, suggesting she may continue suffering as Mick's physically helpless prisoner. It is a thoroughly disturbing horror moment—but the severing itself happens offscreen. It is unmistakably Jarrett's performance, combined with meticulous sound design, that provides the scene's impact. Mick later shoots Kristy dead with his hunting rifle—in more definitive (but similarly inexplicit) fashion: the murder is captured from a distance, dwarfed in a wide angle shot of expansive skies over deserted outback highway.

In an epilogue of sorts, Ben wakes up nailed to a makeshift crucifix. He wriggles frees and staggers off Mick's property and into the blazing mid-day outback. We await Mick's sadistic intervention, but it never arrives. Instead, Ben collapses from exhaustion and dehydration, and is rescued by a passing couple who drive him to a hospital. Ben is then seen bruised and scarred, being escorted by government officials into a private plane. Intertitles once more appear onscreen, referencing police reports and a subsequent (fruitless) investigation into Ben's account of the incident (implying his characterization of a "super-predator" serial hunter of tourists was ultimately dismissed by Australian law enforcement agencies on the grounds of implausibility). This final sequence again invokes the "true-crime" genre, employing a documentary-like aesthetic tone that one might expect from a crime recreation television show. This tone highlights, as Gemma Blackwood has noted, how *Wolf Creek*:

> ... skilfully mixes its narrative with factual information to suggest that its events are plausible. The presence of the tourist as naïve victim in many of Australia's most notorious crimes in recent decades—from the disappearance of Azaria Chamberlain at an Uluru campsite in 1980 to the Port Arthur massacre in Tasmania in 1996—lends extra legitimacy to the film's narrative. (491)

This perceived authenticity of the events depicted in *Wolf Creek* was apparently sufficient to prompt its sole brush with formal censorship: when the defense team in the trial of Bradley John Murdoch—accused of violently abducting and murdering British tourist Peter Falconio in 1996—successfully lobbied for postponement of the film's release in the Northern Territory of Australia (where the crime had occurred) until after the trial was resolved (ABC Staff). Murdoch's attorneys evidently feared that the film's attention-grabbing content would influence the trial's outcome. The decision apparently surprised McLean, who claimed the film "isn't really that story," adding: "I guess it's a kind of a testament to the perceived impact that the film could have made, because at the end of the day it's a horror movie that's designed to scare the hell out of people" (qtd. in ABC Staff). His reaction conspicuously fails to acknowledge that *Wolf Creek* is *also* a film deliberately designed to evoke the substantial and enduring cultural interest in non-fictional serial murder—in this case in a distinctive national context—through several elements of its aesthetic construction and stylistic presentation.

A Passing "F"

Perhaps more relevant for the purposes of this study than *Wolf Creek*'s delayed release in the Northern Territory of Australia, however, is its surprisingly harsh treatment by Cinemascore's American voters. Such a focus may seem superficial, but it should be noted that exit polling represents more than a passive "rear-view mirror" look at how movies were received by the moviegoing public. According to Paul Dergarabidian, senior media analyst at

Rentrak, comprehensive exit polling "offers studios actionable future intelligence, which can be predictive of a film's longevity or be used for advanced demographic planning of upcoming releases" (qtd. in Busch). Incidents like the release of *Wolf Creek* might contribute to an understanding of why, for instance, ambiguity has been all but scrubbed out from Hollywood's promotional machine in the decades since. Studios have become averse to precisely the sort of risk-taking that eventually yielded such rich reward for the engaged target audience for *Wolf Creek*'s particular horrors.

Ed Mintz, the Cinemascore's founder, has publicly characterized the connotative meaning of the firm's ratings, saying: "A's generally are good, B's generally are shaky, and C's are terrible. D's and F's, they shouldn't have made the movie, or they promoted it funny, and the absolute wrong crowd got into it" (qtd. in Lawrence). As the rare "F" rated film (one of eighteen since the firm's founding in 1979), *Wolf Creek* may indeed fall into one of these categories: either a film that audiences felt should not have been made, or a film that was "marketed funny," resulting in failure to align with expectations that randomly selected viewers brought to cinemas on opening night.

The phenomenal commercial success of *Wolf Creek*—both as a standalone film and subsequent franchise—suggests it fell into the latter category: a film that was marketed ambiguously enough (as supernatural horror or possibly even sci-fi) to fail at drawing its target North American audience on opening night. The film's affecting "hand grenade" horror was detonated in a mass commercial context, scorching an audience apparently unprepared (or unwilling) to withstand its assault. At the same time, the ambiguity of Dimension's promotional materials preserved the shock of the film's meticulously calculated narrative, which accounts for much of its impact. The US promotional teaser misleads the viewer no more than McLean's own plotting (which commits so fully to misdirection that it never explains why Liz and Ben's watches—unlike the car that Mick sabotaged—spontaneously stop working).

Ultimately though, the striking discrepancy between *Wolf Creek*'s reception from Cinemascore voters and its eventual embrace by horror audiences and phenomenal subsequent commercial success did little to slow the displacement of nuanced film criticism and discourse in North America by research firms and aggregator websites. This shift will continue to accelerate the process by which Hollywood cinema comes more and more to resemble other kinds of mass manufactured content—reflecting a limiting of original design, a sharper clarity in sub-genre distinction, and a reluctance to gamble on filmmakers outside of the American cultural mainstream.

8. CENSORSHIP, DISTRIBUTION, AND CONTROL

Interference in the exhibition and distribution of radically unconventional, non-commercial, or "problematic" artworks can be seen to be precipitated more explicitly by economic forces upon which the individual artist has little control. These forces include not only the practical considerations of supply and demand (inherent in any conception of a self-regulating market) but also, frequently, the systems of classification and ratings that have come to replace regulative vertical censorship of film in Western liberal democracies. Classification practices do not merely compound the effects of supply and demand, they also interact with and shape these effects in significant ways, namely by generating demand for content that is intended for as large a consumer base as possible.

What exacerbates the effects of classification processes is the increased privatization (more specifically corporatization and oligopolistic patterns) of the distribution channels by which consumers can potentially access artworks. As John Keane writes:

> Communications markets restrict freedom of communication by generating barriers to entry, monopoly and restrictions upon choice, and by shifting the prevailing definition of information from that of a public good to that of a privately appropriable commodity . . . Those who control the market sphere of producing and distributing information determine, prior to publication, what products (such as books, magazines,

newspapers, television programmes, computer software) will be mass produced and, thus, which opinions officially gain entry in the "marketplace of opinions." (90)

A particularly telling example of market censorship comes from the American music industry, which in the mid-1990s instituted "Parental Advisory" labels for albums containing what were goadingly referred to as "explicit" lyrics. Like contemporary film ratings, these labels were designed to inform consumers (particularly parents) as to the "severity" of the lyrical content of albums, thereby directing adults and children away from "inappropriate" products and toward others, for which they could be presumed to form a "suitable" audience. However, when, in keeping with the company's public image of family-friendliness Wal-Mart categorically refused to carry albums bearing the provocative "Parental Advisory" label, the result was de-facto censorship, in that the music was simply unavailable for purchase in many areas, particularly more rural communities where Wal-Mart had forced the closure of local record retailers unable to compete with the multinational company.

In the case of film, the Motion Picture Association of America's industry-initiated ratings model remains somewhat unique in that producers use it on a voluntary basis. American film distributors are not legally compelled to submit their films for classification review, governmental or otherwise, always remaining free, at least theoretically, to retain the option of a release designated simply "unrated." However, the "unrated" option can carry a severe economic penalty by drastically limiting the number of theaters in which a film will be screened or stores in which it is stocked. The most severe categorization, NC-17 (no one admitted under 17), is potentially penalizing in the same way. When the demands of potential exhibitors and advertisers place external restraints upon film content, and these restraints are dictated partly by the subjective ideas of arbiters of classification criteria, familiar processes of cinematic censorship can be reframed as operating within (as opposed to upon) the private marketplace of ideas and the institutional structures and practices of cultural production.

In the contemporary media landscape, where private and corporate economic interests control most cinematic distribution platforms, from AMC Theatres to Netflix to iTunes, artists can face numerous powerful censorial obstacles in the form of market regulations, typically dictated by those with sufficient control of manufacturing resources to significantly shape consumer access to material goods. The classification procedures of the MPAA via CARA (Classification and Ratings Administration, based in Sherman Oaks, California), while explicitly informing viewers as to the content of films, also provide significant economic incentives for individual filmmakers who self-censor, as well as for distributors who demand that films they circulate adhere to content regulations that are arbitrary and restrictive at times. While the financial structure of the global film market by necessity implies some degree of routine economic censorship, the effects become problematic when censorious motives overlap with, and ultimately augment those of moral censors.

One notable example of contemporary censorial market phenomena is the public censorship controversy surrounding Abel Ferrara's perceivably fact-based drama *Welcome to New York* (2014) and its distribution in America by IFC Films, a company owned and operated by AMC networks, which also owns the cable channels AMC, WE tv, BBC America (with BBC Worldwide), and Sundance TV. Several significant players were part of the complex transactions involving *Welcome to New York*. Ferrara is a well-established independent filmmaker from New York City. His directing career spans forty years and includes such critically acclaimed works as *King of New York* (1990), *The Addiction* (1995), and *The Funeral* (1996), all gritty crime films with substantial cult audiences. Ferrara's normal agency for distribution and international sales is Wild Bunch Films, founded in 2002 and headquartered in Berlin, Germany.

In March of 2015, Ferrara initiated a cease-and-desist against Wild Bunch for supplying IFC Films with not the version he gave them to circulate, but an R-rated version of *Welcome to New York*, which Wild Bunch's co-chief, Vincent Maraval, had assembled without the filmmaker's cooperation or consent. The "fixed" version omits much of what would be euphemised by the MPAA as "graphic sexuality"—scenes in the original cut involving full frontal nudity and explicit sexual activity—thereby addressing the various practical demands for wider theatrical exhibition and video distribution. These cuts fundamentally alter the meaning of the film's narrative, but even more changes were made, as we will see.

Welcome to New York is a dramatic treatment of the Dominique Strauss-Kahn case, a prosecution for rape conducted in New York City in 2011. French politician Dominique Strauss-Kahn, then managing director for the International Monetary Fund, was accused of sexually assaulting a member of a high-end hotel's housekeeping staff. Despite Ferrara not having used his name, Strauss-Kahn threatened the filmmakers with a defamation suit in May of 2014. Through comparative analysis of the original and recut versions, this chapter will argue that the R-rated cut, distributed on DVD and Video on Demand in America by IFC, notably increases the ambiguity of the film's stance toward Strauss-Kahn's guilt by altering the narrative context—in this case temporal order—of certain sequences.

The most immediately obvious and problematic change made to Ferrara's original film involves the temporal placement of the sequence depicting the sexual assault referenced above. While originally presented from an omniscient perspective—that is, as a direct occurrence subject to the filmgoer's direct observation—the attack is re-ordered so as finally to be presented in the Wild Bunch recut as the maid's subjective flashback under interrogation, this shift evidencing the express intent of reducing the film's vulnerability to legal action. Strauss-Kahn's extensive political and economic resources resulted in the charges against him being dropped. Strauss-Kahn's lawyers were successfully able to discredit the testimony of his alleged victim, casting uncertainty on the exact nature of his sexual encounter with the hotel's housekeeper. The changes made to Ferrara's original film perform roughly the same function, presenting the housekeeper's version of the event as wholly subjective, and as dubious. As a result, the recut version thoroughly undermines Ferrara's audacious attempt at "vigilante filmmaking;" in this case an effort to highlight what he considered the failure of the justice system to successfully prosecute a guilty offender who possessed sufficient means to deflect the serious allegations.

The *Welcome to New York* controversy becomes a revealing case study in how the processes of economic censorship—in this case IFC's working to increase its profits from screenings—can come to operate as a cloak for moral and political censorship. Ferrara had wanted to take up a moral position in opposition to Strauss-Kahn, who was himself something of a profiteer; the IFC recut took the ground from beneath him. This chapter will first examine the role played by classification practices in this debacle.

A recurring theme throughout this study has been the process by which maverick filmmakers spur changes in film regulation policy through work that pushes, and ultimately reconfigures, the boundaries of permissible cinematic content. Such results may be inadvertent or unintended, but often filmmakers operate with an immediate awareness of public tastes and standards, and through their work engage in historical dialogue with traditions of artistic provocation and aggravation. Chapter 6 attempted to approach *The Brown Bunny* with aesthetic and thematic reference to realist adult classics of the late 1960s like *The Graduate* (1967) and *Midnight Cowboy* (1969). It is perhaps not coincidental that evaluations of Gallo's film became ensconced in censorial language, given that these historical points of reference also influenced and were influenced by the cultural baggage of film classification.

In the case of *Welcome To New York* and its challenging content, the effects of market censorship are even more pronounced. Ferrara has long held a distinct reputation for refusing to shy away from graphic depictions of so-called deviant sexuality and criminal violence, but also for approaching such typically B-movie fodder with an emphasis on its moral philosophical implications, explored through an unflinching docudrama style heavily influenced by twentieth-century European art film aesthetics and the improvisational performance style of 1970s American filmmaker John Cassavetes. Ferrara's work constantly straddles the line between thoughtful exploration and lurid exploitation, and *Welcome to New York* is no exception. As is frequently the case in instances of market censorship, there is a certain temptation to assume that purely financial motives precipitated the removal of controversial material from the film.

Ferrara's original version, which appeared on the international festival circuit in 2014, contains the filmmaker's signature combination of sensationalist subject matter and probing, cerebral storytelling via gritty, realist treatment. It contains several prolonged, explicit sex scenes, most of which appear in the film's first act before their full narrative and thematic context, a sinister comingling of sex addiction and political corruption, has been established. The explicitness of these early sequences displays little regard for the standards of the R rating bracket, and can easily be misconstrued as excessive, given their complex relationship to the film's deeper preoccupations. As such, they pose a characteristic dilemma to a primary agent of market film censorship: the distributor. Some understanding of the complex mechanisms of US film distribution is necessary to fully illustrate the external pressures placed upon film content by classification and ratings.

Distributor as Censor

It would be an oversimplification to suggest that representatives of the voluntary ratings system of the American film industry exert any direct creative control over the content of films. MPAA classification categories merely lay out the criteria by which certain films are deemed suitable for certain audience segments, as grouped by age. The extent of classifiers' ability to influence film content is generally limited to the providing of notes and suggestions as to how filmmakers can re-edit their work to obtain a certain rating *should they so choose*. In the absence of governmental compulsion to tailor cinematic works to these criteria, filmmakers unwilling to self-censor risk no legal consequences for circumventing the MPAA ratings system. How then does an established artist like Ferrara, notorious for his unwillingness to compromise the content of his films (and unconcerned with their commercial viability), come to have his work gelded by a strict adherence to MPAA categorization standards?

One primary mechanism by which this process takes place involves the dictates and provisions of the feature film distribution deal. This contractual agreement between a distributor and, most often, a film's producer formalizes the conditions of a film's release and ultimately ends up determining the extent of its commercial reach. The notion of *distribution deal as mechanism of censorship* may seem exaggerated, due to the perception of the distribution process as one of voluntary negotiation. However, such an understanding underestimates the extent to which the requirements for curtailment contained in these deals are effectively imposed upon filmmakers, who do, after all, make films so that they can be seen by some audience.

In his exhaustive study of the feature film distribution deal, John W. Cones outlines numerous clauses typically written into producer-distributor agreements that bear significant influence upon the creative content of films. These

CENSORSHIP, DISTRIBUTION, AND CONTROL

clauses are commonly geared toward guaranteeing a film's profitability in certain markets by predetermining commercial considerations such as expected running time and approval of cast members. However, with respect to the inclusion of controversial material, three of these provisions are particularly relevant: editing rights, presence of "censorable" material, and minimum acceptable rating. The editing rights provision (or "final cut" clause) declares who has the right to make editing changes (i.e., who has the authority to produce the final cut of a film) (86). Censorable material refers to parts of a film's content that may be "considered objectionable" in a given jurisdiction (Cones notes how, by appearing in some distribution agreements as a producer warranty, this exceedingly vague definition may have a particularly alarming effect on first amendment rights of producers) (87). Lastly, distribution agreements impose a commitment regarding the film's MPAA classification, whereby the filmmakers guarantee that the film being produced will be qualified to receive a specific rating (88). If the producer delivers a product that fails to meet the conditions laid out in these provisions, the distributor may be absolved of his or her obligation to release the film. Thus, these provisions (considered on the basis of aggregate effect) imbue feature film distributors with a significant degree of creative authority, often one that trumps the creativity of the filmmaker.

By setting forth the desirability of certain types of film content, the control mechanisms of distribution agreements also determine, to a great extent, what films are made by the US film industry. The provisions of these agreements, some of which Scones characterizes as "unfair, unethical, anticompetitive, predatory and/or illegal," have aided distributors in maintaining their position of power over other segments of the film industry, "segments that might like to see other kinds of movies produced with substantially different content" (89). This holds true whether distributors are working in conglomeration with major studios (often themselves MPAA members) or, as in the case of *Welcome to New York*'s American distributor IFC Films, via independent distribution channels intended to offer alternative platforms for marketing and negotiation beyond the vertical integration of the Hollywood system.

Established in 2000 by AMC Networks Inc. (not to be confused with AMC Theatres), IFC Films comprises one third of the larger company IFC Entertainment, which also includes sister labels Sundance Selects (focussed on "prestige" films) and IFC Midnight (focussed on genre cinema). Since its formation, IFC Films has established itself as a leading distributor of independent cinema through a process of market branding that highlights how willing the company is to take bold risks by distributing titles too controversial or non-traditionally commercial for more mainstream companies. IFC's distribution of several NC-17-rated titles, such as the commercially successful *Blue is the Warmest Color* (2013; winner of the Palme d'Or at Cannes), seems to offer evidence that supports this carefully crafted public image. The repeatedly demonstrated willingness of IFC to release NC-17-rated films (and the financial rewards they have reaped by doing so), along with their apparent awareness of the marketing advantages of acquiring controversial titles, calls into serious question the company's insistence that their release of *Welcome to New York* adheres to the restrictive criteria of the R rating. Like Vincent Gallo's, Abel Ferrara's maverick "bad boy" reputation is a cornerstone of his (albeit limited) commercial appeal, and the centrality to IFC's marketing purposes of confrontational aesthetic risk-taking and signifying the film as an edgy alternative to the content of mainstream media platforms would seem to suggest that Ferrara's particular brand of provocative cinematic content should serve as an asset to the company (as opposed to an impediment).

Naturally, distributors must approach the content of the films they acquire on a case-by-case basis, factoring in variables such as the price they pay for acquisition or the channels through which they hope to distribute the film. Indeed, IFC publicly attributed its need for an edited version of *Welcome to New York* to "various economic reasons," declining to elaborate specifically on what these were (Weisberg). Radically cut back and restricted, the film could apparently make more money. What complicates this claim is the fact that when it sold the film to IFC, cut in apparent accordance with IFC's requirements, Wild Bunch went far beyond what would have been needed to obtain the desired R rating. The reduction of graphic physicality on display in the film's sex scenes, whether problematic in and of itself, is merely the tip of this censorial iceberg.

Based On True Events

Despite the written disclaimer that opens *Welcome to New York*, explicitly stating that the film is a work of artistic interpretation, its narrative corresponds quite closely to the official record of a highly publicized scandal involving Dominique Strauss-Kahn, then Managing Director of the International Monetary Fund and rumoured potential candidate for the presidency of France. Strauss-Kahn's fictional counterpart, Mr. Devereaux (Gérard Depardieu), arrives in New York City on a business trip and immediately engages in a series of sexual encounters with high-priced female escorts. In Ferrara's original 125-minute cut, these sequences are explicit and prolonged, but the various decadent excesses contained within them (e.g., Devereaux and his associates smear nude women with ice cream, before quickly ushering them out of their hotel room to make way for the arrival of another group) should not be read as Ferrara's own inventions. They instead represent the excesses of Strauss-Kahn's sexual proclivities and womanizing, rumoured at the time of the film's release but since confirmed throughout subsequent scandals involving massive "sex parties" and criminal "aggravated pimping" charges made against the politician in 2015 (Chrisafis, Samuel).

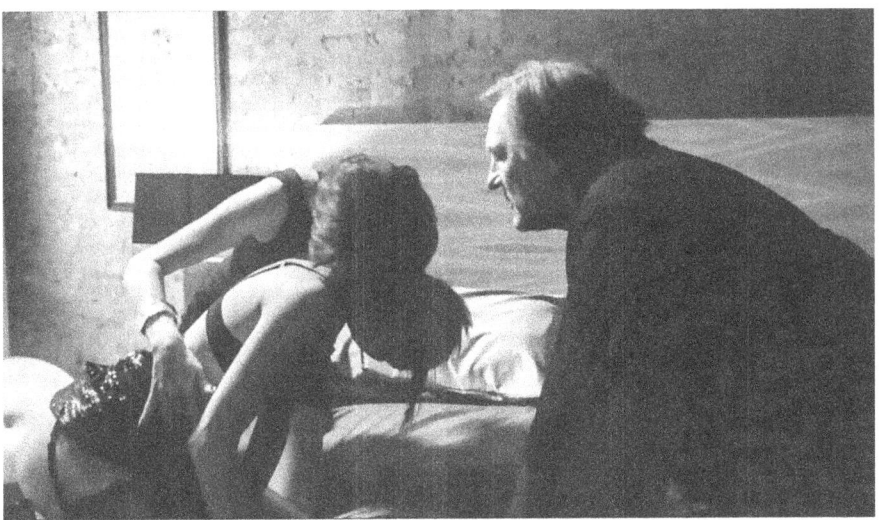

Figure 8.1　Gérard Depardieu (r.) in Abel Ferrara's *Welcome To New York* (Belladonna Productions, 2014).

The frankness and relentlessness of Ferrara's sexual content in the film's first act numbs the spectator to the images of nude bodies onscreen—effectively conjuring the mindset of Devereaux as sex-addict—while the objectification of female bodies on display establishes the key thematic context for the major dramatic incident that opens the second act.

When a member of a high-end hotel's housekeeping staff enters Devereaux's room, she finds him exiting the shower nude. After asking her, "Do you know who I am?" Devereaux proceeds to attack the terrified woman, pushing her to the floor and masturbating onto her face. Much of the scene plays out in hand-held shots, using stripped-down documentary-style photography to emphasize the spectatorial objectivity with which Ferrara seeks to present the event.

While Devereaux later boards a plane to France, the hotel maid reports the assault to NYPD detectives. The Port Authority Police remove Devereaux from the plane and, despite his claims of diplomatic immunity, detain him until NYPD detectives arrive.

Here the film slips into the realm of police procedural docudrama. Devereaux is methodically shown being arrested, booked for rape, taken to a holding cell, denied bail, stripped (exposing the once studly Depardieu's morbid obesity), and finally, humiliatingly, placed in lock-up with several other criminals. These scenes are surprisingly some of the film's most riveting, despite their intentionally flat stylistic presentation. In addition to the satisfaction viewers experience from seeing a rapist humiliated and stripped of power, Ferrara's

FILM REGULATION IN A CULTURAL CONTEXT

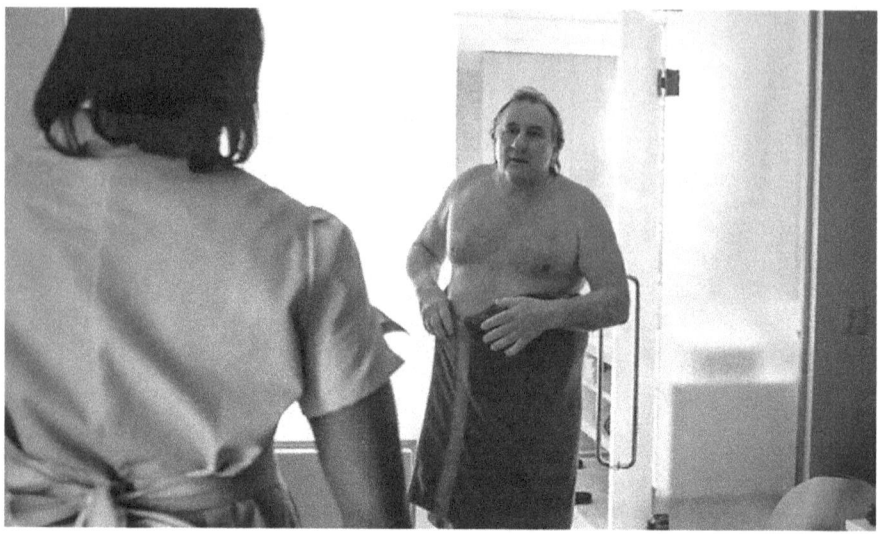

Figure 8.2   Devereaux exiting the shower in *Welcome To New York*.

casting of non-actors in the roles of police officials, and his rigorous attention to the minutiae of Devereaux's processing, bring the irony of the film's title into focus. The NYPD detectives, prosecutors, and jailers treat Devereaux as it seems they would any other criminal. A lifelong New Yorker himself, Ferrara communicates these moments with an unspoken sense of civic pride, honoring the seriousness and impartiality with which the New York Police Department treats sexual crimes.

The film's third act introduces Devereaux's wife Simone (Jacqueline Bisset), whose own extensive political resources (it is implied) eventually result in the charges against him being dropped. Like the real Strauss-Kahn, Devereaux admits to sexual activity with the housekeeper but insists to Simone that the encounter was consensual. Despite her own disgust with her husband's behavior, Simone is shown colluding with his lawyers to discredit the maid's testimony, a strategy that proved successful in the reality of Strauss-Kahn's acquittal (Eligon A1, Rashbaum A19). Devereaux ultimately goes free, and although it is suggested that both his marriage and his chance at presidential candidacy have been irreparably shattered, he remains thoroughly unrepentant. Like the protagonists of earlier Ferrara films including *The Driller Killer* (1979) and *Bad Lieutenant* (1992), Devereaux is at once the film's villain and its audience's sole point of entry into the narrative. It is important to note that the objectivity suggested by Ferrara's aesthetic style by no means extends to the morality of his characters. The depiction of Devereaux, and by extension Strauss-Kahn, is unambiguously damning, yet Ferrara never shies away from the ugliness of his characters. As Nicole Brenez has argued, an essential proposition underlying his work is that "modern cinema exists to come to terms with contemporary evil," adding that "Ferrara's enterprise renews for the twenty-first century what Roberto Rossellini accomplished for the twentieth" (5). While his work is sometimes misconstrued as wallowing in exploitative excess, his depictions of "evil" can be seen as being rooted in frightening but fundamental human truths.

A Change of Perspective

The R-rated version of *Welcome to New York*, distributed on DVD and Video-on-Demand in America by IFC Films, runs for 108 minutes. Notwithstanding that several of its sequences have been extended, more than seventeen minutes were presumably excised from the original director's cut. Much of the missing material is from the film's first act, with the opening "sex party" scenes now dramatically reduced in length and explicitness. At least one sequence—a flashback that appears late in the original cut, in which Devereaux attempts to rape a journalist (Shanyn Leigh)—has been removed completely (despite its modest presentation). Inspired by the accusation of a second alleged victim of Strauss-Kahn's who came forward after his New York arrest, this scene emphasized the point that the accusations made against him by the hotel maid, Nafissatou Diallo, known in the film simply as Maid (Pamela Afesi), were echoed by the testimonies of additional women who claimed similar experiences. Alterations such as this have resulted in speculation that, while some of the edits may have been made in response to the MPAA's criteria for R-rated classification, others seem to have been made in response to Strauss-Kahn's threats to sue the filmmakers for libel upon the film's initial screening out-of-competition at the 2014 Cannes Film Festival (Djurica). Perhaps the most damning piece of evidence bolstering this speculation is the altered placement of the sequence depicting Devereaux's sexual assault of the housekeeper.

In the R-rated version, the attack itself is presented in flashback, as the victim recounts her experience to NYPD detectives. Only the prelude to it—two people alone in a hotel room—is shown early on in proper chronological placement.

Co-chief of Wild Bunch Vincent Maraval, who oversaw the re-edit after Ferrara flatly refused to cooperate with IFC's demands, claims this was done in the interest of "suspense," stating:

> You see the beginning of the scene in the normal chronological order, and it repeats when she testifies to the cops [. . .] We suggested it, not to change the vision of Abel, but because we wanted to keep up suspense. We felt that to keep the full Abel version after [the first] half hour was not a good idea, so we proposed to [show] the end of that scene later and keep the suspense up longer. (Qtd. in Weisberg)

FILM REGULATION IN A CULTURAL CONTEXT

Figure 8.3 Pamela Afesi (r.) in *Welcome To New York*.

However, this change has the very significant effect of stripping the sequence of its original objectivity, but further, by moving to what Strauss-Kahn and his wife successfully labeled the housekeeper's wholly subjective "version" of the event, the edit works to discredit her by juxtaposing her claim against Devereaux's. Maraval seems to imply that the "suspense" he claims to have been cultivating with this change pertains merely to delaying the revelation of the grislier details of the attack. Yet, when presented both in flashback and simultaneously in contrast to Devereaux's own account of the attack, the "suspense" in Maraval's cut becomes that of a complicated web of he-said-she-said; in which what had at first been shown as the "truth" of the attack is now entirely obfuscated by a narrative of two competing stories, one of which has more social clout. As a result, what previously was presented as, to use Diane Wolfthal's phrasing, a "real rape" (i.e., an image of rape not designed merely as a means of exploring other issues) (5) instead becomes a naturalized plot device, a narrative technique simply used to move the plot forward. Despite the frequent allusions to the tradition of European art cinema present in Ferrara's work, his treatment of rape eschews its typical presentation in art cinema as a means of exploring issues related to ambiguity (Russell 2). As originally cut by Ferrara, little regarding Devereaux's attack was left to interpretation.

Rape has frequently been a subject in Ferrara's work, where it has unsurprisingly posed challenges to classification criteria. In the recutting of *Bad Lieutenant*, for example, the sequence depicting the rape of a nun, wherein two Latino teenagers use a crucifix to lacerate her vagina, was cut from forty-nine to fourteen seconds (Sandler, "Naked" 152). It should perhaps then be expected that rape and sexual assault would figure prominently in the *Welcome to New York* controversy. However, it must be noted that throughout his career Ferrara has been consistently and remarkably responsible with his treatment of the subject. Of his 1981 rape-revenge classic *Ms. 45*, feminist film critic Barbara Creed writes: "The film carefully avoids the sensational; the attacks on Thana are not filmed in order to encourage the audience to identify with the rapist, nor are her acts of vengeance filmed so as to invite the audience pleasure in scenes of blood and gore" (123). Ferrara goes so far as to make a cameo appearance as one of *Ms. 45*'s two rapists, acknowledging the connection between the director and the "voyeuristic, sexual predator" that is, according to Creed and Laura Mulvey, "always at the center of film violence towards women" (124). For Maraval to tamper with *Welcome to New York*'s treatment of rape in such an irresponsible way, regardless of motivation, could have been seen by Ferrara as a particularly egregious affront to his artistic autonomy.

Because it is a sensitive topic, Ferrara knows that sexual assault requires the utmost care when depicted cinematically. It has routinely been a preoccupation of censors since appearing alongside prostitution and lustful kissing in the Production Code list of topics filmmakers should "be careful" when addressing (Semonche 109). The Code stated that, non-categorically, "Rape must never be shown by explicit method" (Doherty, "Censor" Appendix), a proclamation so encompassing in its reach that Ferrara's interest in stripping his presentation of issues related to ambiguity would have been impossible to achieve in the Production Code era. Yet the inclusion of the clause regarding rape in the Code, part of a broader goal of ensuring that Hollywood art would be "morally good, lifting men to higher levels," reduces the morality of its visual representation to black-and-white terms. The reality is often more complex.

Discussing the representation of rape in fiction, Jane Mills writes that "we have to analyze the most ancient stories of western tradition to discover how female and male sexuality has been constructed around naturalized representations of rape that posit women as innately vulnerable and dumb" (153). The logic of Mills's statement, one could argue, is equally applicable to enforced omissions from such representations. Along with what has been shown throughout the history of cinema regarding representations of rape, we must also analyze what has *not* been shown—or more specifically—what *has not been allowed* to be shown. In the case of *Welcome to New York*, the ambiguity of the R-rated version implicates the victim in the exoneration of her attacker by censoring Ferrara's moral vision of the crime.

For all the reasons cited above, it is unsurprising that Ferrara was indignant about the gelding of *Welcome to New York* by Wild Bunch, as well as about the complicity of IFC as its distributor. Maraval's tampering with Ferrara's artistic vision goes far beyond the typical effects of routine market censorship practices, and the changes to the film's content do not simply weaken the impact of its message (as any imposed adherence to ratings criteria so often does); they thoroughly undermine it. They force the filmmaker to say that maybe Devereaux did rape the housekeeper, and maybe he did not. For Ferrara, the situation was anything but ambiguous in that way.

As American filmmaker James Ivory once stated, power struggles over "final cut" are often complex: "One can certainly sympathize with the distributor without advocating hasty trimming, and many disciplined directors have coolly cut excess footage without regrets once they've seen how their films played" (6). However, this is entirely different from the Maraval and Ferrara situation and:

> that of the filmmaker whose work is taken away from him and drastically altered: when the story line has changed so that the purpose and point of view of director and writer are made unclear; when material is removed that is needed to reveal the characters, while other material already discarded by the director is introduced to provoke easy laughs or prurient interest in which the style and texture of the piece would have been debased. (6)

It remains unclear whether the distribution deal explicitly protected Ferrara's right to a final cut, as no journalist has gained access to the contract. Unless his contract protected that right, so basic to any kind of personal expression in films, Ferrara is likely to lose this battle. Commenting on the scandal, Ferrara was quoted as stating:

> I've made five films with Vincent, and we've never had a problem. IFC, for years, has put out my films—never had a problem. Then this happens. I've got final cut . . . I haven't had to deal with that bullshit since 1985, or '91—some time so long ago I can barely remember it. IFC has nothing to do with me. This film, the way we went at it, we went at it, okay? We just did a film about this event the way we did it. I'm an artist: I react to the fuckin' world. When something comes out of me, it's a work of art . . . I have one right, and it's my right of expression. (Qtd. in Abrams)

Despite IFC and Wild Bunch's insistence that any action was within their contractual rights, Ferrara's view of this debacle as an assault on his right to free expression is not without merit. Whether the result of financial incentives, legal intimidation or genuine ignorance, the increased ambiguity of Devereaux's guilt in IFC's version is political: it trivializes rape and perverts Ferrara's original vision for the project.

As what actually took place in the hotel room is not a matter of record, interference with its presentation is not necessarily a question of factual inaccuracy, but rather a meddling with Ferrara's ultimately polemical interpretation of Devereaux (and by extension Strauss-Kahn) as rich and incredibly powerful men who see the world around them (as well as its living breathing inhabitants) as property to be acquired (text messages showed Strauss-Kahn would often refer to the prostitutes at his sex parties as "equipment" [Eligon A1]). Like the other filmmakers profiled in this study, Ferrara's resistance to generic categorization (in this case, categories of exploration vs. exploitation) makes him a prime target for classification troubles, an effect further compounded by his brash outspokenness as a critic of some of capitalism's more pernicious excesses. It is especially concerning when art that vilifies capitalistic excess is censored by political and corporate powers, and even more so when this takes place under the guise of simply "doing business." The subordination of art to commercial considerations has become such a matter of routine in contemporary culture that powerful artistic statements can be filtered out of public discourse with hardly an eye batted. If the censorship of *Welcome to New York* has any positive outcome, it will perhaps be in its drawing of public attention to the way in which economic forces, including film ratings, distribution agreements, and the broader corporatization of artistic media can disguise moral and political censorship as mere products of consumer choices and inevitable outcomes of entrenched market structures. "Economic forces" here means, of course, not only producers, distributors, exhibitors, and fans all over the world, but also a man who was running the International Monetary Fund—indeed, a force to be reckoned with.

In shifting the presentation of the housekeeper's rape from the omniscient perspective of Ferrara's camera to a subjective flashback experienced by Devereaux's victim, Maraval perpetuates several troubling tendencies that permeate the discourses surrounding sexual violence both on and offscreen. First, the treatment reinforces the censorial impulse dating back to the Production Code that rape should only be hinted at, and never shown. Secondly, the alteration disempowers the victim, who in Ferrara's original film is a traumatized but strong woman, and in Maraval's version, a potentially conniving one (echoing the assertions of Strauss-Kahn's lawyers in reality). Lastly, the *Welcome to New York* case suggests a certain class differentiation in which the controversy that surrounded the film in some ways mirrored the one it sought to explore. Through his greater control of economic resources, Maraval (like Strauss-Kahn) was able to exorcise considerable power over public knowledge of the event, rendering the perspective offered by the significantly less powerful Ferrara (like Diallo) utterly disposable. In a final irony, Ferrara's original cut remains available only online via illegal file-sharing and torrent sites. Thus, to witness *Welcome to New York*'s damning treatment of criminality as it was intended, one must become a criminal and steal it.

The censorship of *Welcome to New York* is an extreme example of market disciplines placing external constraints upon film content, thereby shaping and altering the moral implications of the representations contained therein. However, the peculiarities of this case: its powerful real-life subject; tricky sexual politics; outspokenly anti-establishment director, merely point toward market and self-censorship processes that operate much more broadly in many diverse industry and cultural contexts. Steven Goldman writes of the current state of Hollywood film markets, and the economic forces that comprise the institutional structures and practices of American film production:

> In looking back at the course of recent events, it seems clear that the greatest detriment to creative expression in the US film industry remains that which is self-generated. The decision to create inoffensive films designed to reach the widest possible audiences, the exclusion of minority voices, even the classification of the films themselves, is a decision taken from within the film industry. Writers and Directors working in the studio system, while still producing some of the most challenging films to be seen anywhere, publicly lament the current and continued state of affairs. (140)

Welcome to New York may provide a particularly flagrant example of the ways in which market and moral censorship overlap to varying degrees, but it is by no means an isolated case. As Goldman astutely observes, the financial structure of film markets and the resulting emphasis of producers and distributors on the "bottom-line," the profit margins associated with wider potential audiences, necessitates and internally rewards the removal of socially and politically unpopular sentiments from mainstream films. This is troubling when considered alongside the fact that cinema and other cultural products are often thought of to be, to an extent, reflections of the changing social and political cultures that produce them. When market censors appoint themselves as mediators of public morals, genuine artistic vision, along with its capacity to move social and political dialogue forward, is reduced to an obstacle for corporate powers to overcome.

AFTERWORD

While the case studies examined in the preceding chapters have varied widely in the details of their respective national contexts, aesthetic issues, censorial challenges, market accessibility, political sensitivities, and critical appreciation, some overall significant cultural and historical patterns can be gleaned from examining them together. To do so is, naturally, to risk wading into the territory of top-down critical analysis, in which theories have been offered and examples have been selectively cherry-picked to support pre-determined theses. It is not my aim or intention to extrapolate an overly generalized monolithic definition of the complex relationships between cinematic innovation and social control from these few select examples, as doing so would risk engaging in a dramatic oversimplification of the various intersections between discourses of sex, violence, censorship, free expression, artistic experimentation, commercial distribution, and economic systems identified and engaged within them. However, in the interest of synthesizing a set of complicated processes for the purposes of shedding light on the cultural functions and histories of post-millennial cinematic transgression and the moral, legal, ethical, economic, and aesthetic questions that surround it, some measure of consolidation is perhaps useful.

If there is one concept that can potentially clarify the focus of the cross-national, trans-historical, multi-system comparison that this study comprises, it is perhaps most succinctly symbolized in the umbrella term *classification*. Throughout the preceding chapters, this notion has been employed, interrogated, and analyzed in several different ways. Yet its expansive reach as a concept is characterized chiefly by a remarkably consistent symbolic meaning and implication.

It is perhaps no surprise that classification has come to replace censorship as an essential tool in the lexicon of both critical and governmental discourses. Its versatility in this study alone suggests its importance as a cipher of cultural meaning. Classification can be many things in many different contexts. It is the mandated goal of contemporary review boards, whether governmental or industry initiated. It is the process by which "art" comes to be accredited as such. It is the primary toolkit of the cinema critic, commercial or academic. It is a conceit by which films are successfully marketed. It is a means of social control through labeling of deviance of subject matter, of approach, of cinematic gesture. It is, at once, the impulse to erect borders and how those borders might be successfully permeated. It is, in my feeling, the core of the social and historical processes of which the controversies examined in this study become representative products.

While the preceding chapters have drawn together sociological theories of labeling, critical theories of cinematic genres, historical theories of censorship, and economic theories of market systematization, the aim has been constant: to illuminate the centrality of classification that underlies them. The layered and, at times, flaring tension between transgressive post-millennial cinematic art and the censorial conservatism, official or unofficial, that has dogged this art's existence is characterized, more than anything else, by the collapsing of old and the formulation of new classification criteria. Social problems; artistic innovations; morality; all are issues so complex, so messy in their conceptions, executions, and implications, that categorization comes to be heavily relied upon in various social and cultural contexts to simplify their nature and allow for the formulation of necessary proscriptions.

Politically, the tension between censors and artists is too often categorized in simplistic Left and Right terms. Artists are thought to champion and embody the liberal cause of free speech, while censors fight to uphold the conservative character of traditional moral values. These case studies have hopefully demonstrated that the reality is often more complex. Yet if we step back from the political baggage of these terms, and focus on their broader, more abstract meaning, a clear analytical framework presents itself. To be "liberal," it can perhaps be said, is to hold a belief that borders, in their many forms, ought to be more porous. The reverse is true for "conservatives," who desire to see borders as clearly defined and closed. This notion characterizes nearly every dimension of contemporary political debate, particularly as regards the most contentious and sensitive of political issues such as immigration or sexual identity. In the case of film censorship, contemporary understandings of the importance of free expression and socially challenging art had, by the turn of the millennium, all but eradicated the overt, a priori, regulative cinematic state censorship that affixed itself to the medium since its early days. However, the films and filmmakers examined in this study nevertheless pushed the analytical systems of classification, that aide many institutions and audiences in their attempts to make sense of the contemporary cultural world, further than they ever previously had been.

As these case studies reveal, it is, time and again, the collapsing of categorical distinctions that single out certain artworks as targets for social disciplining. The transgressions of the filmmakers discussed here are, in some imprecise sense, found within their affronts to cultural sensitivities and tastes. More fundamentally, however, the boundaries that their films are engaged in transgressing are only superficially those of mere right and wrong (or Right and Left). The respective dilemmas that *Fat Girl* (2001), *Ken Park* (2002), *Irréversible* (2002), *The Brown Bunny* (2003), *Wolf Creek* (2005), and *Welcome to New York* (2014) posed to the primary agents of film regulation (state, market, or otherwise) were inextricably bound to the films' resistance to generic classification and their combining of disparate artistic traditions. While the "new cinematic extremism" (the very identification of which represents its own process of cultural classification) has been identified with respect to a far greater number of films and filmmakers, the examples selected for in-depth examination in this study are clear indicators of the social and political disturbance caused by the intersection of two such radically separate and opposed notions as "art" and "exploitation." Regulative systems of cultural control had, for many decades, employed entirely separate criteria for approaching each, justified by the perception of their respective aims and audiences as diametrically opposite. In blurring the lines between these categories in ways more unequivocal than any filmmaker had before, these films play a critical role in understanding complex issues of film censorship in the contemporary media landscape.

Beyond its ubiquity as a tool for understanding the social world, and beyond its effectiveness as a substitute for terms more suggestive of classical regulative censorship, classification carries an additional, more insidious implication. What these case studies collectively point to is the degree to which classification labels can be profoundly detrimental to the things they are instituted to identify. Classifiers, like censors before them, exist to patrol the boundaries between categories that they themselves have defined. The social systems in place for approaching art, pornography, or "trash" are different and distinct from one another, and the role of the classifier is to ensure that cultural products are viewed through the appropriate lens. When these labels are applied with imprecision and uncertainty, a certain kind of cultural chaos ensues. If art is mislabeled as pornography, as was the case with *Fat Girl* or *Ken Park*, bold aesthetic strategies are suffocated by stringent (at other times necessary) regulation. If trash is mislabeled as art, as some critics claimed was the case with *Irréversible* and *The Brown Bunny*, the fear arises that art's redemptive qualities have been reduced to delivering the cheapest of base thrills. If art is mislabelled as trash, as happened with *Welcome to New York*, its meaning can be perverted without respect or regard for its creator's intentions. In all of these cases, it is evident how various systems of classification become the primary determiners of art's cultural definition.

Looking forward, one cannot help but feel a certain sense of ambivalence about the future of free expression with regard to cinema. Since the turn of the millennium, the power of regulative state censorship over cinema has waned further, due in no small part to the boundary-pushing aesthetic strategies of filmmakers like Breillat and Noé. Classification and ratings will no doubt remain a popular process of regulation as long as children are perceived as vulnerable to "psychologically damaging" (once "morally corrupting") material. Yet this alone is not necessarily cause for despair. Whatever the validity of various cultural claims regarding the potential for media to negatively impact the behavior of young viewers, the notion of restricting certain images to those with the capacity for responsibly consenting to see them is one with few fervent opponents. Because they are younger, children have not developed a full armature of expression. Thus, they cannot themselves credibly claim that they are not vulnerable to disturbance from filmed images. The protection of children—precious in the eyes of would-be censors as symbols of innocence and uncorrupted moral virtue—has become the last remaining rationale for censorship, but one persuasive enough to suggest that classification is unlikely to disappear anytime soon.

The victories of Breillat and Noé lay chiefly within the increased discretion and aesthetic sensitivity afforded to classifiers during this process. However, as portions of this study have hopefully illustrated, classification is one of many market disciplines that restrict the cultural dissemination of certain ideas and perspectives. Others, most pressingly the corporatization of new media technologies, are only growing stronger and more pervasive, unlike conventional regulative censorship strategies. While the Internet once promised a free and unregulated flow of cultural content between artists and audiences, corporations such as Google and Netflix have seized control of online distribution in the years since its introduction. Within this media milieu unpopular artistic sentiments, such as those voiced by Gallo and Ferrara, can be successfully stifled.

While a "free" market for cultural products is ultimately preferable to a state controlled one (i.e., no one is jailed for resisting Netflix's policies), we must remain mindful of the systems and structures that mediate our engagement with the cultural world. The replacement of the term "censorship" by "classification" and the reoriented goals of previously censorial governmental institutions should not blind us to the power of pressures routinely exerted upon cinematic content. Perhaps one reassuring outcome of the shift from censorship to classification, if this study is any indication, is the public notice with which modern censorship, now renamed classification, so often proceeds. The prior restraint that once allowed government censors to operate in shadows has been loosened, and while the Internet is vulnerable to the exclusionary processes and oligopolistic patterns of corporatization that perpetuate and naturalize market censorship, its communications reach, as John Semonche points out, has also aided in publicizing censorship controversies, bringing them to the attention of concerned individuals and groups ready to do battle (230). With regulative film censorship no longer the threat to free expression it once was, it falls upon us, the spectators, to retain a firm grasp of the complex issues that surround the cultural system by which we can access, evaluate, and appreciate art, if we harbor any wish for it to remain exciting, rejuvenating, and significantly representative of the contemporary world.

WORKS CITED AND CONSULTED

ABC Staff. "Wolf Creek Ban Puzzles Director." *ABC News Online* (December 15, 2005). <http://abc.net.au/news/2005-12-15/wolf-creek-ban-puzzles-director/762116>. Accessed March 15, 2020.

Abrams, Simon. "Abel Ferrara is Angry about *Welcome to New York*." *The Dissolve* (March 25, 2015). <http://thedissolve.com/features/interview/970-abel-ferrara-is-angry-about-welcome-to-new-york/>. Accessed February 12, 2017.

Adorno, Theodor. *Aesthetic Theory*. Minneapolis, MN: University of Minnesota Press, 1998.

Altman, Rick. *Film/Genre*. London: British Film Institute, 1999.

[AP Archive]. *CANNES D8 RYDER* [Video File] (May 21, 2003). <http://aparchive.com/metadata/youtube/81eff847c2f372c6b9d2920e350ba75f>. Accessed July 11, 2015.

Arnold, Gary. "Fat Girl Tips Scales of Lewdness." *The Washington Times* (November 16, 2001), 9.

Atkinson, Paul. "Time, Memory and Movement in Gaspar Noé's *Irréversible*." *Millennial Cinema*. Eds. Amresh Sinha and Terence McSweeney. London: Wallflower Press, 2011, 17–36.

Baillie, Andrea. "Controversial Movie Featuring Teen Nudity Banned in Ontario." *The Kingston Whig-Standard* (November 14, 2001), 30.

Balio, Tino. *The Foreign Film Renaissance on American Screens, 1946–1973*. Madison, WI: University of Wisconsin Press, 2010.

Barber, Sian. *Censoring the 1970s: The BBFC and the Decade that Taste Forgot*. Newcastle-upon-Tyne: Cambridge Scholars Publishing, 2011.

Barker, Martin. "Typically French: Mediating Screened Rape to British Audiences." *Rape in Art Cinema*. Ed. Dominique Russell., New York, NY: Continuum, 2010, 145–58.

WORKS CITED AND CONSULTED

———. "Watching Rape, Enjoying Watching Rape . . .: How Does a Study of Audience Challenge Film Studies Approaches?" *The New Extremism in Cinema*. Eds. Tanya Horeck and Tina Kendall. Edinburgh: Edinburgh University Press, 2011, 105–16.
Barker, Martin, Jane Arthurs, and Ramaswami Harindranath. *The Crash Controversy*. London: Wallflower Press, 2001.
Balanzategui, Jessica. "The Babadook and the Haunted Space between High and Low Genres in the Australian Horror Tradition." *Studies in Australasian Cinema* 11.1 (2017): 18–23.
Best, Joel. *Threatened Children: Rhetoric and Concern about Child-Victims*. Chicago, IL: University of Chicago Press, 1990.
Beugnet, Martine. *Cinema and Sensation: French Film and the Art of Transgression*. Carbondale, IL: Southern Illinois University Press, 2007.
Black, Gregory D. *Hollywood Censored: Morality Codes, Catholics, and the Movies*. Cambridge: Cambridge University Press, 1994.
Blackwood, Gemma. "*Wolf Creek*: an UnAustralian Story?" *Continuum: Journal of Media and Cultural Studies* 21.4 (2007): 489–97.
[Bogani, Alessio]. *FEAR ON FILM: Landis, Carpenter, Cronenberg!* [Video File] (July 20, 2014). <http://youtube.com/watch?v=F9VfvUVrlgs>. Accessed July 11, 2015.
Bordwell, David. *Making Meaning*. Cambridge, MA: Harvard University Press, 1991.
Brenez, Nicole. *Abel Ferrara*. Urbana, IL: University of Illinois Press, 2007.
Busch, Anita. "B Grade For 'Turtles': What CinemaScores Mean and Why Exit Polling Matters." *Deadline* (August 9, 2014). <http://deadline.com/2014/08/b-grade-for-turtles-what-cinemascores-mean-and-why-exit-polling-matters-816538>. Accessed June 13, 2021.
[ceasestoexist]. *VG HS 2004* [Video File] (October 24, 2012). <http://youtube.com/watch?v=EYgllrSDl5I>. Accessed Jul 11, 2015.
Chai, Paul. "'Wolf Pack Sets Pace." *Variety* (May 2, 2004), A4.
Chrisafis, Angelique. "Dominique Strauss-Kahn Acquitted in Pimping Trial." *The Guardian* (June 12, 2015). <http://theguardian.com/world/2015/jun/12/dominique-strauss-kahn-acquitted-in-pimping-trial>. Accessed March 13, 2017.
Cohen, Stanley. *Folk Devils and Moral Panics*. London: Routledge, 1972.
Cones, John W. *The Feature Film Distribution Deal*. Carbondale, IL: Southern Illinois University Press, 1997.
Conrad, Peter, and Joseph W. Schneider. *Deviance and Medicalization: From Badness to Sickness*. St. Louis, MO: C. V. Mosby Company, 1980.
Coulthard, Lisa. "Uncanny Horrors: Male Rape in Bruno Dumont's *Twentynine Palms*." *Rape in Art Cinema*. Ed. Dominique Russell. New York, NY: Continuum, 2011, 171–84.
Creed, Barbara. *The Monstrous-feminine: Film, Feminism, Psychoanalysis*. London: Routledge, 1993.
Critcher, Chas. *Moral Panics and the Media*. New York, NY: Open University Press, 2003.
Cronenberg, David. "David Cronenberg: [Ontario Edition]." *Toronto Star* (November 23, 2001), F03.
Cronin, Theresa. "Media Effects and the Subjectification of Film Regulation." *The Velvet Light Trap* 63 (2009): 3–21.

Davidson, Sean. "Meet the New Censor Law, Same as the Old Law?" *Playback: Canada's Broadcast and Production Journal* (August 15, 2005), 2, 9.
Day, Matt. "Exclusive Interview with Larry Clark." *The Digital FX* (December 17, 2003). <http://thedigitalfix.com/film/exclusive-interview-with-larry-clark/>. Accessed November 10, 2020.
De Valck, Marijke. *Film Festivals: From European Geopolitics to Global Cinephilia*. Amsterdam: Amsterdam University Press, 2007.
De Young, Mary. *The Day Care Ritual Abuse Moral Panic*. Jefferson, NC: McFarland, 2004.
Dean, Malcolm. *Censored! Only in Canada: The History of Film Censorship—The Scandal Off the Screen*. Toronto: Virgo Press, 1981.
Dewe Matthews, Tom. *Censored*. London: Chatto & Windus, 1994.
DiGiacomo, Frank. "Vincent Gallo's Bunny Trop." *Observer* (June 9, 2003). <http://observer.com/2003/06/vincent-gallos-bunny-trop>. Accessed October 10, 2016.
Djurica, Marko. "France's Strauss-Kahn to Sue Over Cannes Sex Addict Film." *Reuters* (May 19, 2014). <http://reuters.com/article/us-filmfestival-cannes-dsk-idUSBREA4I07B20140519>. Accessed January 11, 2017.
Doherty, Thomas. *Pre-Code Hollywood: Sex, Immorality and Insurrection in American Cinema, 1930–1934*. New York, NY: Columbia University Press, 1999.
——. *Hollywood Censor: Joseph I. Breen and the Production Code Administration*. New York, NY: Columbia University Press, 2009.
Durgnat, Raymond. *Sexual Alienation in the Cinema*. Worthing: Littlehampton Book Services, 1974.
Duval, Robin. "The Last Days of the Board." *Behind the Scenes at the BBFC: Film Classification from the Silver Screen to the Digital Age*. Ed. Edward Lamberti. London: Palgrave Macmillan, 2012, 146–61.
Ebert, Roger. "*Elephant*." *RogerEbert.com* (November 7, 2003). <http://rogerebert.com/reviews/elephant-2003≥. Accessed November 12, 2016.
——. "Gallo's 'Bunny' Hops to the Top of the 'All-Time Worst' List.'" *RogerEbert.com* (May 22, 2003). <http://rogerebert.com/festivals-and-awards/gallos-bunny-hops-to-the-top-of-all-time-worst-list>. Accessed November 12, 2016.
——. "*Mystic River*." *RogerEbert.com* (October 8, 2003). <http://rogerebert.com/reviews/mystic-river-2003.> Accessed November 12, 2016.
——. "*A Slough of Despair*." *RogerEbert.com* (December 22, 2005). <http://rogerebert.com/reviews/wolf-creek-2005>. Accessed April 5, 2021.
——. "Straw Dogs." *Chicago Sun-Times* (December 27, 1971). <http://rogerebert.com/reviews/straw-dogs-1971>. Accessed April 2, 2017.
Egan, Kate. *Trash or Treasure?: Censorship and the Changing Meanings of the Video Nasties*. Manchester: Manchester University Press, 2007.
Eligon, John. "Strauss-Kahn is Released as Case Teeters." *New York Times* (July 2, 2011), A1.
Felperin, Leslie. "Irréversible." *Sight and Sound* 13.3 (2003), 46–8.
Flowers, Lisa. "'Off-Halloween' Recommendations: Bruno Dumont's 'Twentynine Palms'." *Luna Luna Magazine* (December 6, 2016). <http://www.lunalunamagazine.com /blog/off-halloween-recommendations-bruno-dumonts-twentynine-palms>. Accessed April 26, 2020.

Foucault, Michel. "The Confession of the Flesh." *Power/Knowledge*. Ed. Colin Gordon. Brighton: Harvester Press, 1980, 194–228.

Fox, David J. "Blockbuster Video Rates NC-17 Films Unsuitable for All." *Los Angeles Times* (January 14, 1991), 59.

Fuchs, Cynthia J. "'All the Animals Come Out at Night': Vietnam meets Noir in *Taxi Driver*." *Inventing Vietnam: The War in Film and Television*. Ed. Michael A. Anderegg. Philadelphia, PA: Temple University Press, 1991, 33–55.

——."*The Brown Bunny*." *Popmatters* (September 17, 2003). <http://popmatters.com/review/brown-bunny/>. Accessed January 11, 2017.

Gerstel, Judy. "Breillat Plays Sex for Laughs; Fat Girl Takes a Shot at Ontario Censors." *Toronto Star* (September 13, 2002), C04.

Gibbons, Fiachra. "Contrite Gallo Apologises for Pretension." *The Guardian* (May 24, 2003). <http://theguardian.com/theguardian/2010/jun/01/archive-contrite-gallo-apologises-2003>. Accessed December 18, 2016.

Gibbons, Fiachra, and Stuart Jeffries. "Cannes Audience Left Open-mouthed." *The Guardian* (May 14, 2001), 6.

Goldman, Steven. "Dear Mickey Mouse." *Film and Censorship: The Index Reader*. Ed. Ruth Petrie. London: Cassell, 1997, 137–42.

Graham-Dixon, Charles. "How 'Torture Porn' Captured the Violent Atmosphere of a Post-9/11 World." *Vice* (September 18, 2018). <http://vice.com/en/article/xwpddd/how-torture-porn-captured-the-violent-atmosphere-of-a-post-911-world>. Accessed April 5, 2021.

Grønstad, Asbjørn. *Screening the Unwatchable: Spaces of Negation in Post-Millennial Art Cinema*. New York, NY: Palgrave Macmillan, 2012.

Gunning, Tom. "Flickers: On Cinema's Power for Evil." *BAD: Infamy, Darkness, Evil, and Slime on Screen*. Ed. Murray Pomerance. Albany, NY: SUNY Press, 2004, 21–38.

Gusfield, Joseph. *The Culture of Public Problems: Drinking-Driving and the Symbolic Order*. Chicago, IL: University of Chicago Press, 1981.

Hagman, Hampus. "'Every Cannes Needs its Scandal': Between Art and Exploitation in Contemporary French Film." *Film International* 5.5 (2007): 32–41.

Hall, Sarah. "Off-screen Violence gets Maverick Director's Film Pulled from Festival." *The Guardian* (November 11, 2002). <http://theguardian.com/uk/2002/nov/11/filmnews.londonfilmfestival2002>. Accessed June 10, 2017.

Heller-Nicholas, Alexandra. *Rape-Revenge Films: A Critical Study*. Jefferson, NC: McFarland, 2011.

——. "Dreaming of a Red Christmas: Craig Anderson on Australian Horror." *Metro Magazine: Media & Education Magazine* 190 (2016), 54–9.

Herzberg, Bob. *The FBI and the Movies: A History of the Bureau on Screen and Behind the Scenes in Hollywood*. Jefferson, NC: McFarland, 2007.

Hicklin, Daniel. "Censorship, Reception, and the Films of Gaspar Noé." *The New Extremism in Cinema*. Eds. Tanya Horeck and Tina Kendall. Edinburgh: Edinburgh University Press, 2011, 117–29.

Hoberman, James. "Roads to Perdition." *The Village Voice* (January 3, 2003). <http://villagevoice.com/2003/06/03/roads-to-perdition/>. Accessed October 10, 2016.

Horeck, Tanya. "Shame and the Sisters: Catharine Breillat's *À ma soeur!* (*Fat Girl*)." *Rape in Art Cinema*. Ed. Dominique Russell. New York, NY: Continuum, 2010, 195–210.

Horeck, Tanya, and Tina Kendall, eds. "Introduction." *The New Extremism in Cinema*. Edinburgh: Edinburgh University Press, 2011, 1–17.
Howell, Peter. "New Tolerance Level Put to the Test." *Toronto Star* (March 14, 2003), B01.
Hunter, I. Q. "A Clockwork Orange: Exploitation and the Art Film." *British Science Fiction Film and Television: Critical Essays*. Eds. Tobias Hochscherf, James Leggott, and Donald E. Palumbo. Jefferson, NC: McFarland, 2011, 96–103.
Hunter, Stephen. "'*Irréversible*': Move Over, Dante; Gaspar Noé's Unforgettable Trip to Heaven." *Washington Post* (April 11, 2003), C04.
Hutsul, Christopher. "Board Upholds Ban on Acclaimed Movie." *Toronto Star* (November 21, 2001), A02.
Ivory, James. "Hollywood Versus Hollywood." *Film and Censorship: The Index Reader*. Ed. Ruth Petrie. London: Cassell, 1997, 151–4.
James, Nick, and Mark Kermode. "Horror Movie." *Sight & Sound* 13.2 (February 2003), 21–2.
Jamie, Cameron, and Bruce Hainley. "Kids in America." *Frieze* (January 1998). <http://harmony-korine.com/paper/int/hk/america.html>. Accessed June 19, 2019.
Jansen, Sue Curry. *The Knot that Binds Power and Knowledge*. London: Oxford University Press, 1991.
——. "Ambiguities and Imperatives of Market Censorship: The Brief History of a Critical Concept." *Westminster Papers in Communication and Culture* 7: 2 (2010), 12–30.
Jeffries, Stuart. "I Am the Opposite of Ashamed." *The Guardian* (January 24, 2005). <http://theguardian.com/film/2005/jan/24/1>. Accessed June 10, 2017.
Jenkins, Phillip. *Using Murder: The Social Construction of Serial Homicide*. New Brunswick, NJ: Transaction, 1994.
Kael, Pauline. "Stanley Strangelove." *The New Yorker* (January 1, 1972), 50–3.
Kakmi, Dmetri. "The Hideous Blank at Wolf Creek." *Metro Magazine* 148, 72–7.
Kampmark, Binoy. "A Wowseristic Affair: History and Politics behind the Banning of *Ken Park*, *Baise-Moi* and other Like Depravities." *Continuum: Journal of Media and Cultural Studies* 20.3 (2006), 345–61.
Keane, John. *The Media and Democracy*. Cambridge: Polity Press, 1991.
Kerner, Aaron Michael, and Jonathan L. Knapp. *Extreme Cinema: Affective Strategies in Transnational Media*. Edinburgh: Edinburgh University Press, 2016.
Keslassy, Elsa. "Conservative Group, Filmmakers at Odds over Movie Ratings in France." *Yahoo! Entertainment* (March 25, 2016). <http://yahoo.com/entertainment/conservative-group-filmmakers-odds-over-movie-ratings-france-170059162.html>. Accessed September 9, 2019.
——. "France's Right Wing Declares War on Sex." *Variety* 33.8 (2016), 52–3.
Korine, Harmony. "Film; Work Index." *Icon Thoughtsyle* (1997). <http://harmony-korine.com/paper/text/past/filmography.html>. Accessed January 11, 2017.
Kuhn, Annette. *Cinema, Censorship, and Sexuality*. New York, NY: Routledge, 1988.
Lacey, Brad. "Classification: The Art of Banning a Film." *Metro Magazine: Media & Education Magazine* 148 (2006), 54–9.

Lawrence, Christopher. "Las Vegan's Polling Company Keeps Tabs on Hollywood." *Las Vegas Review Journal* (August 30, 2016). <http://reviewjournal.com/entertainment/las-vegans-polling-company-keeps-tabs-on-hollywood>. Accessed January 3, 2018.

Lee, Jason. "Are You Kidding?: Reassessing Morality, Sexuality and Desire in *Kids* (1995)." *Film International* 85 (2018), 16–26.

Léger, Marc James. "SAD BUNNY: Vincent Gallo and The Melancholia of Gender." *Canadian Journal of Film Studies* 16.2 (2007), 82–98.

Leigh, Danny. "No More Public Exposure: Vincent Gallo Puts his Films Away." *The Guardian* (August 5, 2011). <http://theguardian.com/film/filmblog/2011/aug/05/vincent-gallo-promises-written-water>. Accessed December 29, 2016.

Leotta, Alfio. "'This isn't a Movie . . . it's a Tourism ad for Australia': The Dundee Campaign and the Semiotics of Audiovisual Tourism Promotion," *Tourist Studies* 20.2 (2020), 203–21.

Lewis, Jon. *Hollywood v. Hard-Core: How the Struggle Over Censorship Created the Modern Film Industry.* New York, NY: NYU Press, 2002.

Lim, Dennis. "Turn on, Tune in to a Trippy Afterlife." *The New York Times* (September 19, 2010), A19.

Loseke, Donileen R. *Thinking about Social Problems: An Introduction to Constructionist Perspectives.* New York, NY: Aldine De Gruyter, 1999.

Lowenstein, Adam. *Shocking Representation: Historical Trauma, National Cinema, and the Modern Horror Film.* New York, NY: Columbia University Press, 2005.

Lowney, K. S. "Claims Making, Culture, and the Media in the Social Construction Process." *The Handbook of Constructionist Research.* Eds. J. A. Holstein and J. F. Gubrium. New York, NY: Guilford Press, 2007, 331–53.

Machen, Peter. "For Real." *PeterMachen.com.* <http://petermachen.com/larry-clark.html>. Accessed March 24, 2019.

MacKenzie, Scott. "*Baise-Moi*, Feminist Cinemas, and the Censorship Controversy." *Screen* 43.3 (2002): 315–24.

Mank, Gregory William. *The Very Witching Time of Night: Dark Alleys of Classic Horror Cinema.* Jefferson, NC: McFarland, 2014.

Martin, Michael. "The Nerve Interview: Larry Clark." *Nerve* (September 6, 2006). <http://harmony-korine.com/paper/int/lc/nerve.html>. Accessed January 10, 2016.

Maslin, Janet. "CRITIC'S NOTEBOOK; A Ratings To-Do Over a Raw Tale of City Teen-Agers." *The New York Times* (May 23, 1995), C13.

Mazdon, Lucy. "Transnational 'French Cinema: The Cannes Film Festival'." *Modern & Contemporary France* 15.1 (2007): 9–20.

McCarthy, Todd. "Review: 'The Brown Bunny'." *Variety* (May 21, 2003). <http://variety.com/2003/film/markets-festivals/the-brown-bunny-2-1200541509/>. Accessed January 10, 2016.

McGregor, Alexander. *The Catholic Church and Hollywood: Censorship and Morality in 1930s Cinema.* London: I. B. Tauris, 2013.

McKay, John. "Ontario Film Review Board Approves Previously Banned French Film *Fat Girl*." *Canadian Press Newswire* (January 29, 2003).

McKenzie, Sarah. "Classification and Censorship." *Screen Education* 37 (2004), 52–5.

McLennan, Neil. "Springtime for Sickos: Moviegoers are Flocking to Twisted Torture Flicks. Get Ready for More Gore." *Western Standard* (January 20, 2006), 48.

Metz, Christian. *The Imaginary Signifier: Psychoanalysis and the Cinema*. Bloomington, IN: Indiana University Press, 1982.

Mills, Jane. "Screening Rape." *Film and Censorship: The Index Reader*. Ed. Ruth Petrie. London: Cassell, 1997, 151–4.

Moore, Paul S. *Now Playing: Early Moviegoing and the Regulation of Fun*. Albany, NY: State University of New York Press, 2008.

Mulvey, Laura. *Visual and Other Pleasures*. Bloomington, IN: Indiana University Press, 1989.

Murray, Rebecca. "Interview: Vincent Gallo on the Controversial 'The Brown Bunny, 2016'." *Thoughtco.com* (October 2, 2016). <http://thoughtco.com/vincent-gallo-discusses-the-brown-bunny-2430406>. Accessed January 10, 2016.

Mutlu, Dilek Kaya. "Film Censorship During the Golden Era of Turkish Cinema." *Silencing Cinema: Film Censorship Around the World*. Eds. Daniel Biltereyst and Roel Vande Winkel. New York: Palgrave Macmillan, 2013, 131–48.

Neale, Stephen. *Genre and Hollywood*. London: Routledge, 2005.

Nicodemo, Timothy. "Cinematography and Sensorial Assault in Gaspar Noé's *Irréversible*." *Cinephile* 8.2 (2012): 30–8.

Ontario Film Review Board. *Annual Report 2002/2003* Report From The Chair, 4, 2003.

Ontario.ca. *Film Classification Act, 2005: Ontario Regulation 452/05*. <http://ontario.ca/laws/regulation/050452>. Accessed September 20, 2015.

Osborn, Guy, and Alex Sinclair. "The 'Poacher Turned Game-Keeper': James Ferman and the Increasing Intervention of the Law." *Behind the Scenes at the BBFC: Film Classification from the Silver Screen to the Digital Age*. Ed. Edward Lamberti. London: Palgrave Macmillan, 2012, 93–109.

Overy, Richard. *The Inter-War Crisis 1919–1939*. London: Longman, 2007.

Palmer, Tim. *Brutal Intimacy: Analyzing Contemporary French Cinema*. Middletown, CT: Wesleyan, 2011.

Petley, Julien. *Film and Video Censorship in Modern Britain*. Edinburgh: Edinburgh University Press, 2011.

———. "'Are We Insane?' The 'Video Nasty' Moral Panic." *Moral Panics in the Contemporary World*. Eds. Julian Petley, Chris Critcher, Jason Hughes, and Amanda Rohloff. London: Bloomsbury, 2013, 73–98.

Phelps, Guy. "Britain: Out of Fear and Ignorance." *Film and Censorship: The Index Reader*. Ed. Ruth Petrie. London: Cassell, 1997, 61–70.

Pomerance, Murray. *The Horse Who Drank the Sky: Film Experience Beyond Narrative and Theory*. New Brunswick, NJ: Rutgers University Press, 2008.

———. *Michelangelo Red Antonioni Blue: Eight Reflections on Cinema*. Berkeley, CA: University of California Press, 2011.

Posner, Michael. "Chief of Censor Board Quits for Personal Reasons." *The Globe and Mail* (November 2, 2002), R2.

Priggé, Steven. *Movie Moguls Speak*. Jefferson, NC: McFarland, 2004.

Prince, Stephen. "The Aesthetics of Slow Motion Violence in the Films of Sam Peckinpah." *Screening Violence*. Ed. Stephen Prince. New Brunswick, NJ: Rutgers University Press, 2000, 175–204.

———. *Classical Film Violence: Designing and Regulating Brutality in Hollywood Cinema, 1930–1968*. New Brunswick, NJ: Rutgers University Press, 2003.

Quandt, James. "Flesh and Blood: Sex and Violence in Recent French Cinema." *The New Extremism in Cinema*. Eds. Tanya Horeck and Tina Kendall. Edinburgh: Edinburgh University Press, 2011, 18–28.

Rafter, Nicole. *Shots in the Mirror: Crime Films and Society*. Oxford: Oxford University Press, 2006.

Rashbaum, William K. "Strauss-Kahn Won't Plead Guilty to Any Charges, His Lawyers Say." *The New York Times* (July 7, 2011), A19.

Readman, Mark. *Teaching Film Censorship and Controversy*. London: British Film Institute, 2005.

Reinarman, Craig. "The Social Construction of Drug Scares." *Deviance: The Interactionist Perspective. Sixth ed.* Eds. Earl Rubington and Martin S. Weinberg. Boston, MA: Allyn and Bacon, 1996, 77–86.

Robertson, James C. *The Hidden Cinema: British Film Censorship in Action, 1913–1971*. London: Routledge, 1993.

Robinson, Janet S. "Re-imagining Censorship as "Reel" Mutilation: Why Not Release a G-rated Version of David Cronenberg's *Crash*?" *The Dark Side of Love: From Euro-horror to American Cinema*. Eds. Karen A. Ritzenhoff and Karen Randall. New York, NY: Palgrave Macmillan, 2012, 19–31.

RottenTomatoes. "*Wolf Creek*." *RottenTomatoes.com*. <http://rottentomatoes.com/m/wolf_creek>. Accessed February 23, 2018.

Russell, Dominique, ed. "Introduction: Why Rape?" *Rape in Art Cinema*. New York, NY: Continuum, 2010, 1–14.

Ryan, Mark David. "Australian Cinema's Dark Sun: The Boom in Australian Horror Film Production." *Studies in Australasian Cinema* 4.1 (2010), 23–41.

Ryan, Mark David, and Ben Goldsmith. "Returning to Australian Horror Film and Ozploitation Cinema Debate: Introduction." *Studies in Australasian Cinema* 11.1 (2017): 2–4.

Samuel, Henry. "Dominique Strauss-Kahn Acquitted of Pimping Charges." *The Telegraph* (June 12, 2015). <http://telegraph.co.uk/news/worldnews/dominique-strauss-kahn/11670268/Dominique-Strauss-Kahn-acquitted-of-pimping-charges.html.> Accessed February 16, 2017.

Sandler, Kevin. "David Cronenberg. *Crash*." *Censorship: A World Encyclopedia*. Ed. Derek Jones. Ann Arbor, MI: University of Michigan Press, 2001, 600–2.

———. *The Naked Truth: Why Hollywood Doesn't Make X-Rated Movies*. New Brunswick, NJ: Rutgers University Press, 2007.

SBS Movies. "Arthouse Shocker 'Baise-moi', Banned in Australia, Screens on World Movies Tonight." *SBS MOVIES*, September 23, 2016. http://sbs.com.au/movies/article/2016/09/22/arthouse-shocker-baise-moi-banned-australia-screens-world-movies-tonight>. Accessed December 13, 2021.

Schatz, Thomas. *Hollywood Genre: Formulas, Filmmaking, and the Studio System*. New York, NY: Random House, 1981.

Schwarzbaum, Lisa. "Critic's Choice." *EntertainmentWeekly.com*, June 6, 2003. <http://ew.com/article/2003/06/06/critics-choice-2/>. Accessed December 18, 2016.

Scott, John, and Dean Biron. "*Wolf Creek*, Rurality and the Australian Gothic." *Continuum: Journal of Media and Cultural Studies* 24.2 (2010): 307–22.

Semonche, John E. *Censoring Sex: A Historical Journey Through American Media*. Lanham, MD: Rowman & Littlefield, 2007.

Shiel, Mark. "American Cinema 1970–1975." Eds. Linda Ruth Williams and Michael Hammond. *Contemporary American Cinema*. Berkshire: Open University Press, 2006, 124–57.

Siegel, Carol. *Sex Radical Cinema*. Bloomington, IN: Indiana University Press, 2015.

Simkin, Stevie. *Straw Dogs*. Basingstoke: Palgrave Macmillan, 2011.

——. "Wake of Flood: Key Issues in UK Censorship 1970–5." *Behind the Scenes at the BBFC: Film Classification from the Silver Screen to the Digital Age*. Ed. Edward Lamberti. London: Palgrave Macmillan, 2012, 72–93.

Slotkin, Richard. *Gunfighter Nation: The Myth of the Frontier in Twentieth Century America*. Norman, OK: University of Oklahoma Press, 1992.

Smith, Nigel M. "Gaspar Noé Talks *Irréversible*." *Indiewire* (July 12, 2011). <http://indiewire.com/2011/07/from-the-iw-vaults-gaspar-noe-talks-irreversible-53317/>. Accessed November 22, 2016.

Smith, Sarah. *Children, Cinema and Censorship: from Dracula to the Dead End Kids*. London: I. B. Tauris, 2005.

Sobchack, Vivian C. "The Violent Dance: A Personal Memoir of Death at the Movies." *Screening Violence*. Ed. Stephen Prince. New Brunswick, NJ: Rutgers University Press, 2000, 110–24.Spector, Malcolm, and John I. Kitsuse. *Constructing Social Problems*. London: Transaction, 1987.

Staiger, Janet. *Bad Women. Regulating Sexuality in Early American Cinema*. Minneapolis, MN: University of Minnesota Press, 1995.

——. *Interpreting Films: Studies in the Historical Reception of America*. Princeton, NJ: Princeton University Press, 2000.

Sterritt, David. *Guiltless Pleasures: A David Sterritt Film Reader*. Jackson, MS: University Press of Mississippi, 2005.

Stone, Jay. "*Fat Girl* Furore Proves Film Board's Irrelevance." *Ottawa Citizen* (February 10, 2003), B1.

[Takano, Hikari]. *Vincent Gallo Interview* [Audio File] (February 2004). <http://hikaritakano.co./index.php/audio-interviews/vincent-gallo>. Accessed August 28, 2016.

Thompson, Kenneth. *Moral Panics*. London: Routledge, 1998.

[TIFF Live]. *Special Event: Onstage Conversation with SLAVOJ ŽIŽEK | TIFF 2016* [Video File] (May 24, 2016). <http://youtube.com/watch?v=F9VfvUVrlgs.> Accessed June 20, 2016.

Tyner, James A. *Space, Place, and Violence: Violence and the Embodied Geographies of Race, Sex and Gender*. London: Routledge, 2011.

Vaizey, Marina. "Art Language." *The State of Language*. Eds. Christopher Ricks and Leonard Michaels. Berkeley, CA: University of California Press, 1989.

Variety Staff. "Review: 'Straw Dogs'." *Variety* (December 31, 1970). <http://variety.com/1970/film/reviews/straw-dogs-2-1200422432/>. Accessed March 13, 2017.

Veronneau, Pierre. "When Cinema Faces Social Values: One-hundred Years of Film Censorship in Canada." *Silencing Cinema: Film Censorship Around the World*. Eds. Daniel Biltereyst and Roel Vande Winkel. New York, NY: Palgrave Macmillan, 2013, 49–62.

Victor, Jeffrey S. *Satanic Panic: The Creation of a Contemporary Legend*. Chicago, IL: Open Court, 1993.

Wajda, Andrzej. "Two Types of Censorship." *Film and Censorship: The Index Reader*. Ed. Ruth Petrie. London: Cassell, 1997, 107–10.

Weintraub, Bernard. "Critics Assail Ratings Board Over 'Eyes Wide Shut'." *The New York Times* (July 28, 1999). <http://nytimes.com/library/film/072899eyes-movie.html>. Accessed January 3, 2017.

Weisberg, Sam. "The (Sort of) Truth Behind the Two Versions of Abel Ferrara's 'Welcome to New York'." *Screen Comment* (March 27 2015). <http://screencomment.com/2015/03/abel-ferrara-welcome-to-newyork/#sthash.8jKfA6tI.dpbs>. Accessed March 18, 2017.

West, Alexandra. *Films of The New French Extremity: Visceral Horror and National Identity*. Jefferson, NC: McFarland, 2016.

Whyte, Murray. "Censors Lift Ontario Ban on *Fat Girl*." *Toronto Star* (January 30, 2003), A29.

Williams, Linda. *Screening Sex*. Durham, NC: Duke University Press, 2008.

——. "Generic Pleasures." *Pornography: Film and Culture*. Ed. Peter Lehman. New Brunswick, NJ: Rutgers University Press, 2006, 60–86.

Williams, Linda Ruth. *"Taxi Driver."* *Contemporary American Cinema*. Eds. Linda Ruth Williams and Michael Hammond. Berkshire: Open University Press, 2006, 157–60.

Williams, Linda Ruth, and Michael Hammond. "The Nineties and Beyond: Introduction." *Contemporary American Cinema*. Berkshire: Open University Press, 2006, 325–33.

Wittern-Keller, Laura. *Freedom of the Screen: Legal Challenges to State Film Censorship, 1915–1981*. Lexington, KY: University Press of Kentucky, 2008.

Wolfthal, Diane. *Images of Rape: The "Heroic" Tradition and its Alternatives*. Cambridge: Cambridge University Press, 1999.

Wood, Robin. "The American Nightmare: Horror in the 70s." *Hollywood from Vietnam to Reagan*. Ed. Robin Wood. New York, NY: Columbia University Press, 1986, 70–80.

Yang, Fang, Bruce Vanden Bergh, and Joonghwa Lee. "Do Violent Movies Scare Away Potential Visitors?" *International Journal of Advertising* 36.2 (2017), 314–35.

Xiao, Zhiwei. "Prohibition, Politics and Nation Building: A History of Film Censorship in China." *Silencing Cinema: Film Censorship Around the World*. Eds. Daniel Biltereyst and Roel Vande Winkel. New York, NY: Palgrave Macmillan, 2013, 109–30.

INDEX

Adorno, Theodor, 100
Altman, Rick, 56, 141, 153
apparatus, 2
audiences
   audience-based research, 77, 112, 149
   CinemaScore ratings, 148–9, 150, 158
   classification and the hypothetical audience, 142, 149
   copycat reactions to onscreen violence, 34, 38, 40, 48, 143, 146
   engagement, 149, 150
   experiences of watching *Irréversible*, 102–3, 104, 107
   genre conventions, 56, 141–2, 154
   mass commercial audiences for *Wolf Creek*, 146, 148
   responses to depictions of sexual violence, 15, 48, 77, 112, 150
   role in censorial discourses, 6
   role of spectatorship in *Fat Girl*, 70–2
   spectatorial complicity in NFE films, 45, 50
   spectatorship theory, 149–50
   text-spectator relationship, 14–16
Australia

Australian Gothic, 147–8
ban of *Salò* (Pasolini), 32
early film censorship, 22
film classification system, 81
see also Office of Film and Literature Classification (OFLC); *Wolf Creek* (McLean)

Bad Lieutenant (Ferrara), 35, 37, 38, 172
Baise-moi (Despentes & Trinh Thi)
   non-classification in Australia, 52, 81–2, 85, 94
   sexual violence in, 49–52, 65, 66, 78
Barker, Martin, 77, 112, 150
Becker, Howard, x
Beugnet, Martine, 53–4, 72
Blockbuster Films, 37
bodies
   gender and nude scenes, 132
   in New French Extremity films, 44–5
   slow motion corporeal damage, 45–6
Boorman, John, 57, 147
Breen, Joseph I., 23

INDEX

Breillat, Catherine
  international standing, 65–6
  Romance, 64, 66
  see also *Fat Girl*
British Board of Classification (BBFC)
  censorship of *Fat Girl*, 74
  censorship of horror films, 140
  classification and release of *Crash*, 38–9, 40–3, 78
  formation of, 21, 22
  as an institutional protector of artistic freedoms, 3, 39–40, 41
  mandatory review process, 98–9
  non-distribution of *Ken Park*, 86, 94–5
  pressures from the national press, 33, 38–40
  release of *Irréversible*, 86, 99–100, 111–12, 120
  release of *Straw Dogs*, 27–30, 111–12
  remit to censor depictions of sexual violence, 99
  shift from censorship to classification, 1, 90–6, 112, 120
  use of experts for decision-making, 111
  Video Recordings Act (VRA), 32, 38
  X certificate, 24, 39
Brown Bunny, The (Gallo)
  acute critical censure, 8, 122, 123, 124, 130–1, 132–3, 134, 136, 167
  at the Cannes film festival, 121–2, 134–5, 138
  Gallo's alleged apology for, 134
  and Gallo's offscreen persona, 134–7, 170
  genre transgression, 123–4, 137–8
  minimalist narrative, 124–6, 127–30, 131, 133
  pornographic aesthetics of, 122, 123, 128–9, 131–3, 135–6, 137
  post-classification censorship, 8, 9
  use of landscape, 125, 126
Buñuel, Luis, 100, 101, 103

Canada
  history of film censorship, 21–2, 78
  Ontario Theatres Act, 66–7, 68, 72, 75
  ratings system, 42–3
  see also Ontario Film Review Board (OFRB)
Cannes film festival
  The Brown Bunny's premiere, 8, 121, 123, 124, 130, 131, 133–4
  controversy and spectacle at, 133–4, 136, 138–9
  of the international film festival circuit, 133–4, 136
  Irréversible at, 103
  Mystic River at, 133, 136
  Trouble Every Day at, 53
Castell, Ron, 37
Castle, William, 103
censorship
  claim-making, 5, 118–19
  concept, x–xi, 1
  constituent censorships, 6–7
  contemporary, x, 1–2
  cultural context, 9–10
  within cultural regulation processes, x–xi, 3, 32
  by distributors, 121, 168–70
  early film censorship, 21–4
  within film criticism, 118–19, 120, 121
  government institutions, 1, 8
  harm framings for, 5–6, 32–3, 76–7
  labelling processes, x, xii, 181–2
  liberalization of, 1–2, 3, 8
  market processes of, 8, 35–8, 121, 138, 164–7, 170, 177
  political-artistic tensions, xi, 180–1
  post-classification censorship, 8
  the Production Code (USA), 22–4, 25, 36, 142, 175
  protection of minors, 83, 92, 98, 99, 183
  scholarship on, 2–3
  shift to classification, 1, 3, 39–40, 65, 81–2, 90–6, 112, 120–1, 180, 182–3

195

China, 9
claim-making
 audience responses, 6
 in censorship practices, 5, 118–19
 critics as cultural claims makers, 118–19
 "harmful" materials and, 5–6, 32–3, 76–7
 moral-panic literature, 6
 rhetorical strategies, 4–7
Clark, Larry
 filmmaking, 84–5
 Kids, 73, 83–4, 85, 86, 93
 see also *Ken Park* (Clark & Lachman)
classification
 censorship's shift to, 1, 3, 39–40, 65, 81–2, 90–6, 120–1, 180, 182–3
 concept, 179–81
 the hypothetical audience and, 142, 149
 legal dimensions of, 42–3, 63
 see also British Board of Classification (BBFC); Office of Film and Literature Classification (OFLC); Ontario Film Review Board (OFRB); regulation
Classification and Rating Administration (CARA), 36, 165
Clockwork Orange, A (Kubrick), 27, 31, 46, 117
Code and Rating Administration, 25
Cohen, Stanley, 32
Commonwealth Classification Act, 81, 82, 86, 92
Cones, John W., 168–9
Conrad, Peter, 118
Crash (Cronenberg), 38, 39, 40–3, 78
Creed, Barbara, 175
critics
 censorship functions, 118–19, 120, 121
 critical censure of *The Brown Bunny*, 8, 122, 123, 124, 130–1, 132–3, 134, 136, 167
 as cultural claims makers, 118–19
 market censorship practices, 54–5, 124

online film reviews and, 138
 professional performances of personal taste, 119–20
 reviews of *Ken Park*, 84
 reviews of *Trouble Every Day*, 45, 52–5, 123, 131
 reviews of *Wolf Creek*, 146–7, 150, 160
 as social commentators and gatekeepers, 117–18, 120
Cronenberg, David
 on the artistic merits of *Fat Girl* (Breillat), 75
 on the Canadian ratings system, 42–3
 Crash, 38, 39, 40–3, 78
 status as a commercial auteur, 41
Cronin, Theresa, 6, 143

Dalí, Salvador, 100, 101, 103
Deliverance (Boorman), 57, 147
Denis, Claire
 genre blending, 141
 within New French Extremity, 44
 see also *Trouble Every Day*
Department of Public Prosecution (DPP), 33, 34
Despentes, Virginie, 49–52, 78
Devils, The (Russell), 117
distributors
 censorship role, 121, 168–70
 classification processes and, 164
 corporatization of, 164–5
 distribution deals, 168–9
 "problematic" artworks and, 164
 of *Welcome to New York*, 121, 166, 176
Doherty, Thomas, 21, 23, 26
Driller Killer (Ferrara), 33–5, 37, 38, 172
Dumont, Bruno, *Twentynine Palms*, 44, 45, 55–8, 127, 141, 146–7, 151

Eastwood, Clint, 133, 136
Ebert, Roger
 professional stature, 138
 review of Eastwood's *Mystic River*, 133

review of Gus Van Sant's *Elephant*, 133
review of *The Brown Bunny*, 124, 130–1, 132–3, 134, 137
review of *Wolf Creek*, 147, 150, 160
Eyes Wide Shut (Kubrick), 37–8

Fat Girl (Breillat)
 artistic merits, 3–4, 75, 79
 audience responses to depictions of sexual violence, 77
 censorship controversies, x, 3–4, 6, 8
 critical reception, 64
 depictions of rape, 66, 74–5
 exploration of sexual rites of passage, 66, 69–71, 73–4
 genre transgression, 69–70, 72–3
 impact on classification policies, 117
 OFRB's non-classification of, 63, 64, 76, 78, 79
 and the OFRB's policy revisions, 64–5, 78–9
 the Ontario Theatres Act and, 66, 67, 68, 72, 75
 role of spectatorship, 70–2
Federal Bureau of Investigation (FBI), 39
Felperin, Leslie, 111
Ferman, James, 41
Ferrara, Abel
 Bad Lieutenant, 35, 37, 38, 172, 174–5
 Driller Killer, 33–5, 37, 38, 172
 as a maverick auteur, 35, 166, 167, 170
 Ms. 45, 102, 175
 treatment of rape, 174–5
 see also *Welcome to New York* (Ferrara)
Foucault, Michel, 2
Fuchs, Cynthia, 46, 135

Gallo, Vincent
 Buffalo 66, 133
 Promises Written in Water, 122
 self-censorship, 122–3, 139
 see also *Brown Bunny, The* (Gallo)

genre
 in advertising and promotional materials, 154
 and audience expectations, 56, 141–2, 154
 based-on-true-events genre, 155
 genre frameworks, 55–6, 141–2, 153
 rape-revenge genre, 102, 108–9
 serial crime films, 156
 see also horror genre
genre transgression
 of *The Brown Bunny*, 123–4, 137–8
 of *Fat Girl*, 69–70, 72–3
 genre transgression of *Twentynine Palms*, 45, 55–8, 127, 141, 146–7
 in New French Extremity films, 51, 53–5, 68, 72–3, 141, 181
 scholarship on, ix–x
 sex and violence in, 14–16, 25
 of *Trouble Every Day*, 53–5
Goldman, Steven, 178
Graduate, The (Nicols), 26, 27, 137–8, 167
Great Britain (GB)
 early film censorship, 21, 22
 media campaign against *Crash* in the UK, 38, 40–1, 78
 media role in video regulation, 33, 38
 see also British Board of Classification (BBFC)
Grønstad, Asbjørn, 15, 68, 76, 125
Gunning, Tom, 22
Gusfield, Joseph, 5–6

Hagman, Hampus, 54
Hays, Will, 22–3
Heller-Nicholas, Alexandra, 109, 157
Henslen, James M., 39
Hitchcock, Alfred, 25, 26, 57, 151, 159
Hollywood
 boundary-pushing content, 25–6
 CinemaScore, 148–9, 150, 158, 162–3
 Code and Rating Administration, 25–7
 early film censorship, 22
 early motion picture morality, 21
 films under the First Amendment, 22

Hollywood (cont.)
  the Production Code, 22–4, 25, 36, 175
  self-regulation in the ratings era, 36
  trash cinema, 26–7
Horeck, Tanya, 71, 74
horror genre
  audience categories for, 142–3
  censorship of, 140, 149
  classification of, 142–3
  Driller Killer, 33–5, 37, 38, 172
  high-impact violence in, 140
  Hostel, 143, 144, 145, 146, 147, 153, 155
  low-budget films, 143, 144
  New French Extremity's use of, 140–1, 146
  problematic audiences for, 143, 146
  Saw, 143, 144–5, 146, 155, 156
  scholarship on, ix–x
  sexual violence in, 140, 143
  social function, 144, 145, 154
  torture porn, 143–5, 155, 159
  tourism horror, 145–6, 147
  Trouble Every Day, 53–4, 140–1, 146
  Twentynine Palms, x, 55, 58, 141, 146–7, 151
  video nasty panic, 32–4, 37
  see also *Wolf Creek* (McLean)
Howell, Peter, 118, 120
Hunt, Alan, 32–3, 77–8
Hunter, I. Q., 27

I Stand Alone (Noé), 45–9, 50, 105
IFC Films, 166, 169–70, 173, 175–6
Irréversible (Noé)
  as an apocalyptic narrative, 108
  artistic intent of extreme violence, 3–4, 100, 112, 113–14
  audience experiences, 102–3, 104, 107
  BBFC release of, 86, 99–100, 111–12, 120
  censorship controversies, 3–4, 6, 8
  dynamic camerawork, 103–5
  within the horror genre, x
  impact on classification policies, 117
  rape scene, 99, 106–7, 111

  reverse chronology of its plotline, 102, 108–10
  role of spectatorship, 102–3, 104, 107
  shocking violence of, 99, 102, 103, 105–6

Jansen, Sue Curry, 2, 3, 6, 8, 35–7, 39, 54–5, 120, 138
Jenkins, Phillip, 39

Kael, Pauline, 31, 46, 47, 101, 103, 112–13
Keane, John, 164–5
Ken Park (Clark & Lachman)
  artistic merits, 3–4, 92
  censorship controversies, 3–4, 6, 8
  critical reception, 84
  dysfunctional adult characters, 87–9, 96
  harm of the broader narrative message, 83, 86, 90–6
  impact on classification policies, 117
  lack of global distribution, 85–6, 94
  narrative, 86–90
  non-classification of in Australia, 82–3, 85, 86, 94, 95–6
  raiding of the Sydney protest screening, 82, 83, 96–7
  treatment of sexuality and depictions of minors, 85, 86, 87, 88, 89, 90–2, 95
Kermode, Mark, ix, 34–5, 109
Kids (Clark), 12, 83–4, 85, 86, 93
Korine, Harmony
  Gummo, 93–4
  Kids, 83, 84, 85, 92, 93
Kubrick, Stanley
  A Clockwork Orange, 27, 31, 46, 117
  Eyes Wide Shut, 37–8
Kuhn, Annette, 2, 3, 24, 32

Lachman, Edward; see also *Ken Park* (Clark & Lachman)
law
  legal dimensions of the classification system, 42–3, 63

legal enforcement of proscriptive regulation, 82, 83, 98
protest screening of *Ken Park*, 82, 83, 96–7
Legion of Decency, 9, 23

McAlpine, Hamish, 86, 94
McCarthy, Todd, 130
McLean, Greg see *Wolf Creek* (McLean)
Maraval, Vincent, 166, 173–4, 175–6
Marceau, Jean-Paul, 53, 123
market forces
  corporatization of distribution channels, 164–5
  and the distribution of "problematic" artworks, 164
  of film criticism, 54–5, 124
  of the international film festival circuit, 138–9
  market censorship of *Welcome to New York*, 121, 166–7, 170, 176–7
  market censorship practices, 8, 35–8, 121, 138, 164–7, 170, 177
Matthews, Tom Dewe, 132
media
  British media campaign against *Crash*, 38, 40–1, 78
  influence over video regulation, 33, 38–9
Midnight Cowboy (Schlesinger), 26, 27, 137–8, 167
Moody, Bill, 78
morality
  of the American Catholic Church, 9, 22, 23–4, 38
  censorship of the moral vision in *Welcome to New York*, 172–3, 175–8
  critics as social commentators and gatekeepers, 117–18, 120
  market processes of censorship and, 35–8, 176–7
  moral assessments of violence, 30, 31, 45–6, 47, 48

moral panic, 6, 32–4, 37
  of the Production Code, 22–4, 25, 36
Motion Picture Association of America (MPAA)
  NC-17 rating, 35, 36, 37–8, 84, 93–4, 165, 169–70
  ratings system, 26, 31, 35, 36, 42, 43, 98, 120–1, 165, 168, 169
Murphy, Stephen, 27–8

Neale, Steve, 141, 154
Nelson, Adie, 39
New Cinematic Extremism, 14, 44, 58–9
New French Extremity (NFE)
  artistic risk-taking, 103, 112, 114, 117–18
  Baise-moi, 45, 49–52, 65, 66
  as a cinéma du corps, 44–5
  genre transgression, 51, 53, 68, 72–3, 141, 181
  horror genre conventions in, 140–1, 146
  I Stand Alone, 45–9, 50, 105
  labelling processes, 58–9, 181–2
  scholarship, ix
  spectatorial complicity, 45, 50
  term, 44, 55, 141, 146
  Trouble Every Day, x, 45, 52–5, 123, 131, 140–1, 146
  Twentynine Palms, 45, 55–8, 127, 141, 146–7, 151
Nicodemo, Timothy, 104
Nicols, Mike, 26, 27, 137–8, 167
Noé, Gaspar
  Enter the Void, 106
  filmmaking, 45
  genre blending, 141
  I Stand Alone, 45–9, 50, 105
  impact of *Straw Dogs*, 101–2, 106, 111
  Love, 132
  see also *Irréversible* (Noé)

Office of Film and Literature Classification (OFLC)
  censorship of horror films, 140
  Commonwealth Classification Act, 81, 82, 86, 92
  mandatory review process, 98–9
  non-classification of *Baise-moi*, 52, 81–2, 85
  non-classification of *Ken Park*, 82–3, 85, 86, 94, 95–6
  shift to classification, 1, 81–2
Ontario Censorship Board, 21–2
Ontario Film Review Board (OFRB)
  approval of *Irréversible*, 99–100
  censorship role, 65
  classification of *Baise-moi*, 50–1, 65, 66, 78
  evaluation criteria for depictions of sexual activity, 67–8
  Film Classification Act, 51, 64, 65, 67–8, 79–80, 118
  legal dimensions of film regulation, 63
  mandatory review process, 42–3, 98–9
  non-classification of *Fat Girl*, 63, 64, 76, 78, 79
  reforms to, 64–5, 78–9, 99, 118
  regulation of "harmful" materials, 64, 65, 73, 76, 77, 79
  shift to classification, 1, 65

Palmer, Tim, 44–5, 104
Pasolini, Pier Paolo, 32
Peckinpah, Sam
  Straw Dogs (Peckinpah), 27–30, 31, 101–2, 106, 117
  Wild Bunch, The (Peckinpah), 25, 29, 45
Phelps, Guy, 8
Pomeranz, Margaret, 82
pornography
  the Ontario Theatres Act and, 66–7, 68, 79
  pornographic aesthetics of *The Brown Bunny*, 122, 123, 128–9, 131–3, 135–6, 137
  torture porn, 143–5, 155, 159
Prince, Stephen, 29, 30

Psycho (Hitchcock), 25, 26, 57, 151, 159

Quandt, James, 44, 55, 141, 146

rape *see* sexual violence
ratings
  CinemaScore, 148–9, 150, 162–3
  Code and Rating Administration, 25–7
  MPAA system, 26, 31, 35, 165, 168, 169
  NC-17 rating, 35, 36, 37–8, 84, 93–4, 165, 169–70
  unrated films, 25, 35, 42, 121
  X rating, 24, 27–8, 37
Ray, Nicholas, 24, 96
Rebel Without a Cause (Ray), 24, 96
regulation, definition, 8
Robinson, Janet, 51
Russell, Ken, 117

Salò, or The 120 Days of Sodom (Pasolini), 32
Schlesinger, John, 26, 27, 137–8, 167
Schlöndorff, Volker, 67
Schneider, Joseph W., 118
Schwarzbaum, Lisa, 124, 131, 138
Scorsese, Martin
  The Departed, 101
  Taxi Driver, 25, 29, 30, 34, 47–9
serial murder, 39, 156
sexual violence
  audience responses to, 15, 48, 77, 112, 150
  in *Baise-moi*, 49–52, 65, 66, 78
  challenges of interpretation, 111–12
  cinematic representations, 16–17, 175–6
  in the horror genre, 140, 143
  rape scene from *Bad Lieutenant*, 35, 174–5
  rape scene from *Baise-moi*, 50–2
  rape scene from *Fat Girl*, 66, 74–5
  rape scene from *Irréversible*, 99, 106–7, 111

rape scene from *Straw Dogs*, 27–8, 29–30, 101–2, 106
rape scene from *Welcome to New York*, 171, 174, 175
rape-revenge genre, 102, 108–9, 175
torture porn, 143–5, 155, 159
in *Wolf Creek* (McLean), 147, 159
sexuality
in *The Brown Bunny*, 122, 123, 128–9, 131
in *Crash*, 41–2
onscreen depictions of sexual penetration, 50
sexual behaviour under the Production code, 24, 175
sexual coming of age in *Fat Girl* (Breillat), 66, 69–71, 73–4
sexual content of *Welcome to New York*, 166, 168, 170–1, 173, 174
sexuality and depictions of minors in *Ken Park*, 85, 86, 87, 88, 89, 90–2, 95
in transgressive films, 14–16, 25
see also pornography
Sobchack, Vivian, 29–30, 101, 103, 113
spectatorship theory, 149–50
Staiger, Janet, 112, 137
Sterritt, David, 108
Strauss-Kahn, Dominique, 166, 167, 170, 172, 173; see also *Welcome to New York* (Ferrara)
Straw Dogs (Peckinpah)
BBFC certification of, 27–30, 117–18
impact on classification policies, 117
impact on Gaspar Noé, 101–2, 106, 111
violence of, 108

Taxi Driver (Scorsese), 25, 29, 30, 34, 47–9
Texas Chain Saw Massacre, The, 144, 147, 151, 155, 159
Tin Drum, The (Schlöndorff), 67
Trinh Thi, Coralie, 49–52, 78
Trouble Every Day (Denis)
critical reception, 45, 52–5, 123, 131
cultural impact of, x

genre transgression, 53–5
within the horror genre, x, 52–4, 140–1, 146
Twentynine Palms (Dumont), x, 44, 55–8, 127, 141, 146–7, 151

Un chien andalou, 100, 101, 103
United States of America (USA)
Catholic Church's moral influence, 9, 22, 23–4, 38
early film censorship, 22
post-9/11 cultural milieu, 144–5
the Production Code, 22–4, 142
see also Hollywood

Vaizey, Marina, 58
Valenti, Jack, 31
video nasty panic, 32–4, 37
Video Recordings Act (VRA), 32, 38
violence
artistic intent of *Irréversible*'s extreme violence, 3–4, 100, 112, 113–14
artistic shock tactics, 100–1
in *Baise-moi*, 49–50
in *A Clockwork Orange*, 46, 117
in commercial genre film, 101
content of Hollywood films, 25–6
copycat reactions to onscreen violence, 34, 38, 40, 48, 143, 146
depictions of under the CARA system, 25
desensitization to, 46, 48, 112–13
high-impact violence in the horror genre, 140
I Stand Alone, 45–9, 50, 105
inclusion in art, 100
in *Irréversible*, 99, 102, 103, 105–6
moral assessments of, 30, 31, 45–6, 47, 48
of *Psycho* (Hitchcock), 26, 57
responsible vs exploitative depictions of, 28–9, 31
stylization of, 45–6
in transgressive films, 14–16
viewer confrontation of, 30–1, 101, 103
see also sexual violence
Von Trier, Lars, 50, 132

Wajda, Andrzej, 8
Walker, Alexander, 117–18, 120
Warren, Robert, 51, 65, 72, 77, 78
Welcome to New York (Ferrara)
    censorship of Ferrara's moral vision, 172–3, 175–8
    distributors, 166, 176
    market censorship of, 121, 166–7, 170, 176–7
    narrative, 166, 170–3
    original version, 166, 168, 170–3, 176
    the rape scene, 171, 174, 175
    the R-rated cut, 8, 166, 170, 173–8
    sexual content, 166, 168, 170–1, 173, 174
    temporal reordering, 166–7, 173–4
Wild Bunch Films, 8, 166, 170, 173, 175–6
Wild Bunch, The (Peckinpah), 29, 45
Williams, Linda Ruth, 47, 72, 137
Winterbottom, Michael, 132
Wolf Creek (McLean)
    allusions to aliens, 153, 155, 157–8

    audience genre-based preconceptions of, 146, 148, 151–2
    Australian setting, 147, 151, 152, 157
    CinemaScore rating, 148–9, 150, 151–2, 158, 162–3
    as a cinematic hand grenade, 151, 156
    commercial success, 146, 148–9, 150
    critical reception, 146–7, 150, 160
    within the horror genre, 146–7, 153–4, 157
    marketing and promotion of, 148, 152–7, 163
    narrative, 147, 152–3, 157–60
    post-classification censorship, 8, 9
    problematic audiences for, 143, 146
    quasi-documentary aesthetic, 153, 155
    sexual violence in, 147, 159
    sub-genre conceit, 147–8, 151, 153, 156–62
    temporary banning in Northern Australia, 147, 162
    as tourism horror, 146, 147
Wood, Robin, ix, 154

EU representative:
Easy Access System Europe
Mustamäe tee 50, 10621 Tallinn, Estonia
Gpsr.requests@easproject.com

www.ingramcontent.com/pod-product-compliance
Lightning Source LLC
Chambersburg PA
CBHW071415160426
43195CB00013B/1700